THE LIBRARY
ST. MARY'S COLLEGE OF MARYLAND
ST. MARY'S CITY, MARYLAND 20686

D1559016

THE WORKING CLASS IN EUROPEAN HISTORY

Editorial Advisers:
Standish Meacham
Joan Scott
Reginald Zelnik

BOOKS IN THE SERIES

ENGLISH
LAUNDRESSES

ENGLISH
LAUNDRESSES

A Social History,
1850–1930

Patricia E. Malcolmson

UNIVERSITY OF ILLINOIS PRESS
Urbana and Chicago

© 1986 by the Board of Trustees of the University of Illinois
Manufactured in the United States of America
C   5   4   3   2   1

This book is printed on acid-free paper.

Library of Congress Cataloging in Publication Data
Malcolmson, Patricia E., 1944–
    English laundresses.

    (The Working class in European history)
    Bibliography: p.
    Includes index.
    1. Laundresses—England—Social conditions.
2. Laundresses—England—History.   3. Laundry
workers—England—History.   I. Title.   II. Series.
HD6073.L32G75   1986   305.4'3648'0942   85-24599
ISBN 0-252-01293-3

For Stuart and Bob

She mustn't think, but must work on, washing the bedclothes until she could wash no longer. Wash Wash, all the week long; it was only by working till one o'clock in the morning that she sometimes managed to get the Sabbath free of washing. . . . a strange weakness came over her. She thought of the endless work that awaited her in the cellar, the great copper on the fire, the heaps of soiled linen in the corner, the steam rising from the wash-tub, and she felt she had not enough strength to get through another week of such work.

George Moore, *Esther Waters,* 1894

Contents

Preface

Out of the steam comes mother's face—pinkish-purple, sweating, her black hair putting forth lank wisps that hang over her forehead and cling to the nape of her neck. The hairpins in her hair rust in the damp and steam.

"Christ!" she gasps, and wipes the sweat from her face, and for a few moments rests her hands on the side of the washtub—hands unnaturally crinkled and bleached from the stinging soda water.

"Wash, wash, wash; it's like washing your guts away."[1]

Such was one daughter's best remembered vision of her mother—a vision far removed from that of "the angel of the house." No soft-handed, sweet-natured, decorous creature she; rather, she was rough-tongued, often hard drinking, quick to lash out with hand and tongue, a woman to whom life dealt poverty, unremitting toil, ulcerated legs, too many children, an invalid husband, and no cause for hope. Her work—and that of her sister laundry workers—was arduous, agonizing, and largely unremarked upon by her contemporaries. A substantially unskilled, ill-paid, poorly organized, highly seasonal, and often physically isolated occupation, laundry work remains remarkably elusive. The English laundress is the subject of this book. Its focus is on her work, her health, her life-style, her family, her attitudes and habits, and the changes that occurred to all of these over a period of roughly one hundred years.

This study is also designed to be more than a reconstruction of the experiences of the English laundress. It is intended to be a case study through which a number of themes in economic, social, labor, and women's history can be explored. Laundresses and their labor provide an avenue for exploring the relationship between home and workplace; for dissecting the complexities of the household economies of the poor; for analyzing the growth of the service sector of the economy; for examining the transformation of an industry from handwork to industrial processes; and for elucidating the connection between consumer tastes and habits and working conditions. The campaign to bring the industry within the compass of government regulation can deepen our understanding of the way public policy was formulated, of the pressures that could expedite or delay the passage of social policy, and of the factors that might limit or enhance the effectiveness of those measures. In addition, laundresses can provide a microcosm of some of the issues played out around women's employment by feminists, trade union organizers, and other reformers.

The laundry industry was an important part of the nineteenth-century shift in the economy toward services.[2] Like department stores, chain stores, restaurants and other service industries, the laundry trade was labor intensive. It employed more than 200,000 people at the turn of the century, according to the conservative reckoning of the census. The majority of its jobs were unskilled or readily learned, especially so after mechanization. They were usually filled by women and frequently performed in a part-time or episodic fashion. Another mark of the industry's status as a service trade was its sensitivity to small fluctuations in fashion, taste, or economic well-being. Laundry work, therefore, can serve as a useful case study of the technological and market changes associated with the rise of the service sector and can contribute to our understanding of the character of service employment. Recent studies have examined domestic service, but household workers who did not live with their employers or who performed traditional domestic tasks in a factory or workshop environment have not yet been the subject of much scholarly scrutiny.

The English laundry worker is usually portrayed as a disheveled woman, rough in habits, uneducated, poor, often the sole or primary support of her family; and her work is seen as one of the lowest occupations open to women. As wage work derived directly from household tasks, laundry work could be viewed as simple, uncomplicated traditional labor; and as such it has aroused scant interest among historians primarily concerned with a rapidly industrializing society.[3] Moreover, the timing of mechanization and factory organization within the laundry trade does not fit into the conventional periodization of much labor history. As E. J. Hobsbawm has said, "The great age of British technical and organizational revolution in industry was, on the whole, over by 1850."[4] The laundry trade was a latecomer to this process of change since, by and large, the development of mechanized laundries was not possible until the 1860s, and the extensive creation of steam laundries was a development of the period from the 1890s to the First World War.[5] In addition, it is clear that industrialization never completely eradicated the work of the autonomous washerwoman who eked out a living in her own home or that of her employer. The persistence of hand work, often performed in isolation, which made the trade hard to regulate, has also made it difficult to examine. Finally, laundry work was essentially segregated work: the percentage of women and girls in the trade ranged from 99 percent in 1861 to 93.1 percent in 1911.[6] Studying the late and incomplete transformation of the laundry industry from home to workshop to factory, from hand to machine production, and from small to large scale ownership can add a new perspective to economic history and perhaps stimulate a rethinking of the role of service industries in the process of industrialization.

The women who toiled as laundry workers, whether at the village stream or at the controls of a power-driven ironing machine, can provide another vantage point from which to examine the family life and neighborhood economies of the English poor. Laundresses' work was unusual in that it could be carried on over a lifetime, was dominated by married or widowed women, and could be adapted to domestic responsibilities more readily than most other occupations. Since the requisite skills were widespread and the basic equipment was readily acquired, it was a trade often turned to in adversity; indeed, contributing to the purchase of an item of laundry equipment, such as a mangle, was one of the neighborly strategies employed to help a widow to support herself and her children. Much of this labor went unrecorded because it was seasonal, episodic, or part-time. As a result, the labor force participation of married women has been understated, certainly with respect to laundry work, and probably for other domestic employments as well, such as charring or office cleaning. Because this paid work has escaped most historians' attention, the intricacies of the household economies of a great many Victorian and Edwardian households have not been fully appreciated.[7] I hope that this study can help to restore some of the detail.

The laundry trade, because it was so often performed by married women, and because its regulation was the subject of protracted and occasionally bitter debate, can be used to examine both the active disputes in this period over whether married women, particularly those with children, should take up paid employment, and the related controversy over the appropriateness of enacting protective legislation to regulate women's hours and conditions of work. Advocates of protective labor law, many of them feminists, argued that the most disadvantaged women in the workplace needed the protection of the law to preserve their health, their morals, and their ability to bear and rear children. Eugenics was for some the primary justification for special legislation. "No selfish employer," comments one historian of the parallel movement in the United States, "could be allowed to undermine the strength of the race by threatening the health of future mothers or tempting the morality of future homemakers."[8] For some reformers state intervention was justified by the apparent impossibility of gaining similar results through collective action—unionization among women was notoriously difficult to initiate and sustain—while by others the regulation of hours and working conditions for wage-earning women was viewed as an opening wedge for obtaining protection for all unorganized workers. Many feminists, however, opposed any measures that asserted women's weakness or that implicitly valued a woman's domestic role over her role as an independent wage-earner. Laundry workers were at the center of this controversy. Since their trade industrialized late, it was only considered for regulation at roughly the same time the feminist and suffrage movement was at its most active and the eugenics lobby was at its height. Add to this the dominance of married women in the trade and all the elements are there to make laundresses a valuable focal point for understanding one of the central debates of the women's movement.

Acknowledgments

Although clearly the product of much solitary labor, every book is also a cooperative endeavor. It is the result not only of an author's effort and invention but is also very much the product of the generosity of others—social, scholarly, material, and professional. I owe my greatest debt to Robert Malcolmson, who, as colleague, companion, critic, and friend, has given unstintingly of all of these. Without his support, the task of writing social history, especially while employed in an unrelated field, would have been insurmountable. Friends and historians Donald Akenson, Bryan Palmer, and Richard Price helped this book into existence by reading and commenting on parts of the text and, most important, by offering me their moral support. The late Jim Dyos passed on to me something of his fascination for the urban environment in general and

London in particular; his enthusiasm nourished my historical interests while his pedagogical skill honed them. Anna Davin, Eunice Lipton, and Sallie Purkis wrote to me and openly shared ideas and information. To all of them I extend my thanks.

I would like as well to express my appreciation to the small army of archivists, curators, and librarians who have guided me through their respective collections. Particularly valuable assistance was rendered by: Melvyn Barnes (Westminster Central Library), J. A. Chaldecott (Science Museum Library, Kensington), J. Coburn (Greater London Record Office), Brian Curle (Kensington Central Library), R. J. Ensing (Kensington Central Library), Naomi Evetts (Liverpool Record Office), Michael Farrar (Cambridgeshire County Record Office), M. Ginsburg (Victoria and Albert Museum), M. Gooding (Central Library, Borough of Ealing), G. G. Hand (York Central Library), Felix Hull (Kent County Record Office), R. Jakes (Cambridge Central Library), David Mander (Museum of Local History, Walthamstow), Phil Philo (Gunnersbury Park Museum), P. K. Pratt (Chelsea Library), Neil Rankin (Central Library, Leamington Spa), T. Rix (Fulham Library), R. G. Roberts (Hull Central Library), E. Watkins (Brighton Area Library), J. Watson (Local History Library, Greenwich), Charles A. Wilson (Wilson's Laundry, Brighton), and R. Wilson (Cambridge and County Folk Museum).

I would like to acknowledge the assistance of the Social Sciences and Humanities Research Council of Canada and the School of Graduate Studies and Research, Queen's University at Kingston, for grants which helped to defray the costs of my research. In addition, I would like to express my appreciation to the editors of *Victorian Studies* and the Trustees of Indiana University for permission to reprint portions of an article I published in that journal in 1981.

Finally, my thanks are due to the University of Illinois Press and particularly to Richard Wentworth, the press's director and editor, and to Lewis Bateman, editor of this volume, both of whom smoothed the passage of this work from manuscript to book.

ENGLISH
LAUNDRESSES

Introduction

Laundering is an ancient craft. Its precise origins, like those of other domestic trades, is impossible to establish. Representatives of laundry associations sometimes endeavor to create a pedigree for their industry by citing evidence of laundering by prehistoric men and women, of Egyptian laundries in operation nearly 4,000 years ago, or of commercial laundering establishments in ancient Rome. The trade's lineage is further confirmed through allusions to the laundering references made by authors ranging from Homer to Chaucer to Shakespeare.[1] (Unflattering references, such as those to be found in Zola's *L'Assommoir* [1887], are tactfully omitted.) This scattered evidence confirms that laundry work is indeed an occupation which, whether performed by householders and their servants or by commercial washerwomen and launderers, extends back many centuries. At the same time, the data show that, as an enterprise involving hot water, soap, a copper, and heated iron implements for smoothing fabric, its history is more recent.

In many parts of Great Britain, particularly Ireland and Scotland, trampling clothes underfoot was, until well into the nineteenth century, the preferred method of washing. It was a method also favored by launderers in ancient Pompeii, nineteenth-century Japan and Britanny, and elsewhere.[2] This was the simplest of all laundering methods since it required only a source of water, usually the nearest stream, and human energy. A tub or vat to hold the water facilitated the process, but a shallow stream and a smooth rock or stream bottom would suffice. A second method of washing linen, closely allied to trampling, was the more widespread practice of pounding or beetling. Beetling simply entailed the use of a wooden bat or beetle to pound the wash clean against the rocks by the edge of a stream or against a special washing block located in the bank of a stream, beside a well, or (later) a standpipe. As with trampling, the process required no soap or other cleansing material; the pounding alone served to dislodge soil while the sun acted as a bleaching agent. Bats, beetles, or battledores could take several different forms. They could be at least as long as a cricket bat and of similar form or they could be shovel-shaped and short handled. Occasionally, these bats might be ornately carved or sometimes painted. (Ornate bats or beetles were most common in Wales where, like carved spoons, they were intended as gifts or love tokens.)[3] In remote areas of the British Isles, this laundering technique was employed into the late nineteenth century and, in rare instances, as late as the First World War.[4] The washing bat, though a basic tool, was very flexible since it could be used not only to pound soil from clothing but could also serve as a primitive mangle to squeeze water from linen wrapped around it and to smooth out creases.

Another major washing technique, and one that was somewhat more sophisticated, involved the addition of a cleansing agent, usually with bleaching properties, to the wash water. Urine, dung, and lye were the most commonly used solutions. All three were fairly effective cleansing agents when combined with cold water. Perhaps the best known of these methods is the lye-wash or "buckwash." This method was common in wood-burning regions, since lye is an alkaline solution obtained by pouring water through wood ashes. Oak ashes, according to one source, were thought to produce the strongest solution but lye from apple tree ashes was considered to give the whitest wash. Household inventories, particularly in the seventeenth and eighteenth centuries, almost always mention a lye dropper (a wooden box with holes in the bottom that was filled with ashes and fitted over the washtub), a bucking or lye tub, and the sale or purchase of ashes.[5] The term "buckwash" came to denote a wash of coarse or heavy items as opposed to the laundering of more delicate items to which soap and hot water might be applied. Sometimes the term "bucking" was used to distinguish the lye wash carried out by a household from the work of professional launderers or whitsters.[6]

Results similar to those of the lye solution could be obtained with dung. In the region around Boston, Lincolnshire in the 1690s, the local people in doing their laundering were said to "gather up Hogs-dung and steep it in Water, and having well stirred it, strain it, and so use it to wash Cloaths, which, when bleached in the Summer, will become white and sweet. . . ."[7]

This method of laundering could be found throughout the British Isles but declined in use by the early nineteenth century. Indeed, the value of dung for other purposes meant that this was a much less widespread technique than either bucking or washing with urine. Stale urine, a natural source of cleansing ammonia, was in contrast a very commonly used cleansing medium. Called variously "lant," "old waish," "wash," or "weetin," urine was collected for washing in town and country alike and continued to be used well into the nineteenth century. One author suggests that the foul smell of which the Whitechapel medical officer of health complained when the poor washed their clothing was probably not due to the filth of the linen but was instead attributable to the stale urine solution in which it was being laundered.[8]

A number of variants on these long-established washing methods could be described. However, the essential point here is simply to note that before the nineteenth century and continuing well into it, a number of alternative laundering methods were in use in addition to the "traditional" method of washing linen in hot soapy water. The hot, soapy trade pursued by Victorian and Edwardian laundry workers may have constituted the predominant approach to laundering, but it was not the only one.

Images of the Laundress

The labor of the laundress was as sweated as any but the conditions of her work were the focus of much less popular attention than those of the more refined dressmaker, the attractive shop assistant, or the faintly exotic plight of the Cradley Heath chainmaker. Victorian women of all backgrounds could understand something of the seamstress's toil; the anguish of the elegant shop assistant was easy for more fortunate women to empathize with; and the "unwomanly" work of the chainmaker was an attractive object of middle-class social concern. The laundress and her work, in contrast, were too commonplace, too rough, and too undramatic to attract much interest or public attention. As long as laundry work remained a small-scale, technologically unsophisticated trade, often performed by isolated women in their own or their employers' homes, contemporaries were little concerned to investigate, document, or regulate it. The trade was seen as a strictly private domestic arrangement between householder and "outdoor servant" or small laundry owner.

The relatively infrequent artistic depictions of laundry work in England usually show servants or householders rather than full-time laundry workers. In addition, these images tend to focus on the decorous ironing of finery—*A Servant Ironing* by Henry Robert Morland (c. 1767) is one example—instead of the most arduous aspects of the work. The attractive young servant in Morland's genre painting is smoothing a small article of finery with a box iron. She is seated to perform her task (a highly unusual posture for work that required considerable elbow grease) and to all appearances is engaged in pleasant, untaxing work. The painting titillates the viewer with a portrait of a woman only partially clothed; the ironer is wearing a low-cut bodice and stays to which she has not yet pinned her gown, and on the chair behind her is the shawl, which she would usually (one presumes) wear modestly around her shoulders. In the infrequent instances when washing was portrayed, it was often as satire: cartoon-like images depicted the disruption washing caused to the domestic environment or showed washerwomen as slatternly gossips. Other drawings were more provocative. In an 1810 print by Isaac Cruikshank, *Scotch Washing,* laundresses are shown out of doors cleansing the laundry by trampling it underfoot in washtubs. Again, the depiction is a highly sexualized one. The laundresses have lifted their skirts, exposing most of their legs, to trample the clothes; their arms are also bare and bodices low-cut. In the background, one of the women is shown wielding a beetle (an instrument used to beat garments) to chase off a voyeur. In an earlier (1792) print on the same subject, bearing the same title, Cruikshank shows a laundress with a particularly lewd expression trampling clothes bare-legged to the evident enjoyment of the kilted Scot seated on the ground in front of her. There is no suggestion of the unpleasantness of laundering outdoors, bare-legged, all year round in the inclement Scottish climate.

Most artistic renderings of laundry work were intended less to reveal the realities of the work than to expose the bare limbs and bosom of the worker, and frequently, to display the frilly feminine undergarments that were part of the laundress's work. Analyzing portrayals of the laundress in nineteenth-century French art where the laundress was a much more popular artistic subject than in England, one author has concluded: "More often than not, real toil was altogether eschewed in the paintings. Among the images of ironers a depiction of hard work is rarely found; virtually all of the ironers directly or indirectly flirt with the spectator."[9] The viewer is invited to appreciate the allure of the subject's décolletage, not the skill of her work. Laundry work was hot work; it provided the artist with the excuse to portray the worker semiclothed. English representations, though much less numerous, similarly portray the laundress not as a worker, but as a sex object or as an object of ridicule.

The Scale and Distribution of
Laundry Employment

Workers in the laundry trade, although they were almost certainly under-reported in the census, were remarkably numerous. In 1861, the 167,607 people employed as laundry workers ranked eleventh in a table of principal occupations in England and Wales.[10] The numbers employed in the trade rose over the rest of the century, reaching a high of 205,015 in 1901. In terms of sheer numbers, the second half of the nineteenth century was the heyday of the laundry trade. Until about 1881, the expansion of the trade roughly kept up with the increase in the population and the growth in size, wealth, and aspirations of the Victorian middle class. A great many Victorian families with more pretensions than money had inadequate space, staff, and facilities to do much washing at home, and even such a careful housekeeper as Eliza Warren, whose *How I Managed My House on Two Hundred Pounds a Year* was the domestic bible of many middle-class women, budgeted ten pounds a year "for washing."[11] Analyzing middle-class expenditure, J. A. Banks has shown that the smaller the family income, the greater the proportion spent on food, and that when there was a rise in income, it was immediately followed by a disproportionately large increase in expenditure on washing and mangling.[12] The wearing of frequently washed and perfectly pressed linen, along with servants, carriages, and public schools, had become part of the paraphernalia of gentility that were essential for those aspiring to upward social mobility. The growth in size and numbers of both public and private institutions, such as the London County Council, hospitals, hotels, and restaurants, further increased the demand for laundry services. At the lower end of the social scale, cramped urban dwellings—often tiny single rooms in the case of the growing numbers of single women working and living on their own—made washing at home very difficult and consequently increased the work of professional laundresses. Launderers in the early twentieth century responded to this need by the creation of the Bobwash: the laundry provided a bag into which as many washables as possible could be crammed, and washed and dried them for a shilling.[13]

Concentrations of laundry workers were found in three main locations: the metropolis; large ports; and in communities with large numbers of temporary residents such as spa, seaside, and university towns. In 1891 London laundry workers represented 28.2 percent of all those enumerated in the trade and close to half (45.8 percent) of the men and boys working in laundries.[14] While the census recorded 51,018 female laundry workers in London in 1891, a canvass conducted the same year by the Women's Trade Union League uncovered some 67,506 "bona fide laundresses" in the metropolis.[15] This substantial variation is perhaps some measure of the extent of census underreportage of the occupation. The essentially episodic nature of so much laundry work, performed by women in response to a variety of domestic crises and catastrophes, makes the calculation of precise figures virtually impossible. The demand for laundry work was particularly heavy in London, and stemmed from the high concentration in the metropolis of wealthy households, lodgers, and large institutions such as government offices, hotels, and shipping lines. The large number of small-scale workshops and the widespread practice of giving outwork set the tone for much women's employment in Victorian and Edwardian London: laundry work is a major example of the traditionalism of metropolitan women's employments, reinforced by the structural circumstances of the London economy. Small workshop laundries, often called hand laundries, even though many used some small machinery, predominated throughout central London. As late as 1901, 72.8 percent of the laundries on the factory inspectorate's register for the London district were hand laundries.[16] In those parts of West London serving the luxury trade, workshop laundries honeycombed many streets. In Kensington for instance 75.8 percent of the 260 laundries inspected by the local authority in 1908 were workshops.[17]

The years from the 1890s to the First World War witnessed major structural changes in much of the laundry trade toward large steam laundries; yet throughout the Victorian period small workshop laundries, as well as unrecorded numbers of individuals laboring in their homes, continued to ply their trade. By the early twentieth century, the majority of laundries, even many very small concerns, would have used some mechanized equipment. As one observer noted, "Now it is no uncommon thing to find a row of houses in separate occupation, the back yard of each of which is roofed in and packed with laundry machinery, all driven by an engine installed at the end of the row."[18] At the same time, a steadily growing number of large factory laundries had been established in the developing suburbs of London. An early example of such an establishment, set up at Rushey Green near Lewisham in 1869, specialized in contract work: the firm was responsible for all the laundry work of the London Stock Exchange along with that of many city institutions, firms, and restaurants; it added to its contracts the laundering needs of the growing catering firm of J. Lyons and

Company in 1900.[19] Fulham, Hammersmith, and particularly Acton in the western suburbs became centers where, by the end of the century, there were concentrations of large and small factory laundries so prominent that the term "Soapsuds Island" became their identifying sobriquet displacing the earlier prominence of the hand laundry communities in the inner western suburbs. The Sunlight Laundry, Fulham, with its sixteen receiving offices and 12,000 square feet of laundering space, is representative of the scale of factory laundries.[20] The combination in London of large numbers of workshop laundries, substantial (but hard to measure) numbers of individuals and families engaged in the trade, and growing numbers of mechanically sophisticated factory laundries, accounts for the emphasis that must be placed on the metropolis in any study of the Victorian laundry trade.

Laundry work was also prominent in certain kinds of provincial towns. Port towns, for instance, usually generated a significant volume of laundry work. In the middle years of the nineteenth century, the great port towns grew both in volume of shipping and general population: Liverpool was the country's major Atlantic port, and five ports—Dundee, Newcastle-upon-Tyne, Hull, Plymouth, and Portsmouth—grew to cities of more than 100,000 inhabitants. A large shipping industry generated much employment for laundry workers as well as sailors, dockers, and provisioners. According to one estimate early in the twentieth century, Liverpool provided work for nearly 600 laundries of all sizes, employing many thousands of hands, while in 1901 nearly 3,500 Glasgow women were employed in laundry work.[21] The shipping industry, the hotels, and restaurants that catered to railway and liner travelers produced large amounts of laundry—laundry that needed to be processed with dispatch, a requirement that exacerbated the long hours already so common in the trade. Newcastle, Liverpool, Glasgow, and other port laundries worked very long hours in response to large volumes of ships' laundry, even when workplaces were otherwise well run. Investigating conditions in the trade, Mary Paterson, a factory inspector, learned that most employees with three or four years experience had become familiar with overnight work, and one woman reported having worked for forty-two hours at a stretch.[22] The final areas in which laundry work was a major source of employment were the spa and resort towns and the university towns. By the second half of the century, cheap railway travel and holidays with pay—bank clerks for instance were usually allowed a week to a fortnight's holiday per year according to length of service with a firm[23]—permitted members of the lower middle class and even a few members of the working class to make annual trips to seaside and resort towns where their presence produced employment for laundry workers as well as other service-sector workers. The upper middle class had already set the fashion by their regular trips to fashionable spas and watering places, and in these communities, service jobs of all sorts had long dominated the local economies. In Bath, for instance, 40 percent of those employed women in the middle of the nineteenth century who were not domestic servants (by far the most common occupation) were washerwomen.[24] The university towns also generated large if seasonal amounts of laundry: enough in fact to occupy nearly the entire female labor force of the village of Headington Quarry near Oxford and an estimated 600 women in Cambridge at the turn of the century. Gloucester, a town of similar size, employed only half that number.[25] In all these communities, the problem of seasonality that plagued the trade everywhere was writ large and was highlighted by the relative absence of alternative employment, particularly for those women whose age and/or domestic commitments ruled out domestic service.

These, then, are some of the structural circumstances, in broad outline, of the laundry trade and its importance in the Victorian economy. It is to those who worked in the trade, and the manner in which work fitted into the overall circumstances of their lives, that we will now turn our attention.

CHAPTER 1

—•—

Hand Laundry Work and the Family Economy

Economic Strategies

Washing and ironing other peoples' dirty linen could be a life's work (sometimes even a skilled craft); it could also be a temporary income source in times of adversity. Either way it was very much a married woman's trade. According to one historian, "It seems to have been taken for granted that laundry work was the prerogative of married women."[1] The occupational tables of the 1901 census, distinguishing marital status for the first time, show 55.9 percent of laundresses to have been either married or widowed. Laundry work was one of only two women's occupations (the other being charring) in which the unmarried were in a minority. Of these married and widowed laundry workers, 46 percent were classified as homeworkers—that is, they were employed either in their own homes or in the smallest workshops and often took work home—as compared with only 26 percent of the single women in the trade.[2] Unfortunately, since the married and widowed were grouped together, it is impossible to calculate the proportion of married women at this date. In the nineteenth century, married women clearly dominated. An examination of the 1861 census enumerators' books for three London communities in which laundry work was by far the most important female occupation—the Potteries and Jennings Buildings in Kensington, and Kensal New Town, a detached portion of Chelsea—reveals that between 51.1 percent and 61.4 percent of all laundresses were married women.[3] Edward Cadbury, M. Cecile Matheson, and

George Shann, in their study of women's work in Birmingham, found 63 percent of all laundresses to be married, a larger percentage than in any other trade.[4] Even these high figures underestimate the numbers of married women in the trade. Many women were employed only part-time or episodically, with the result that their employment went unreported in the census; and pride—that of the women or their spouses—kept others from admitting to the census enumerator that their labor was necessary for the family's survival.

Laundry work, for a number of reasons, was particularly attractive to married women as an occupation which could be dovetailed with the irregular work of men. First of all, the peaks in the availability of laundry work often coincided with troughs in the male employment cycle. In London, laundry work fluctuated with the "season;" West End laundries took on extra labor at the beginning of the "season," with a major peak of employment in June, a trough in August, and another minor peak in October or November, coinciding with the opening of Parliament.[5] The early summer peak matched the period of layoffs in the gas industry while the winter peak paralleled the beginning of severe underemployment in the building trades. For example, in Battersea—as in much of North Kensington—the gasworks and building industry formed the dominant foci of male employment. The existence of complementary laundry employment for women made dovetailing a successful strategy for the family economic unit. Gas workers' spouses did laundry work in the summer while builders' wives worked as laundresses in the winter.[6] Similarly, women in the university towns relied on laundry work to support their families during the periods when their laborer, brickmaker, painter, and coal heaver husbands were out of work.[7] Raphael Samuel observed that in Headington Quarry "laundry work was far from being a mere supplement to the man's earnings; in winter time it often had to serve in their stead." The availability of laundry work for the Oxford colleges sometimes undermined a man's efforts to provide for his family: "Nearly all the women in Quarry used to take in laundry work 'cos half their husbands didn't take any money home. . . . They used to sup that in beer while they was at work. . . . Women had to do laundry work to keep the family going."[8]

In certain areas, then, this juxtaposition of seasonal employments formed an established part of the local economy. Most working-class women could expect to work for wages at some time during their married lives, but on the whole they worked regularly only when pressured to by necessity; thus, areas where laundry workers predominated were marked by poverty. Charles Booth, describing one such community, noted: "Here we find poverty as deep and dark as anywhere in London."[9] The supply of laundresses' labor depended less on the demand for it than upon the demand for the labor of their husbands. A laundry proprietor told the Royal Commission on Labour that nearly all his laundresses were married who worked when their husbands (mostly builders' laborers) were unemployed, and a laundress confirmed that washers were nearly always married women who "had often been servants obliged to work after marriage, with no trade to turn to. Their husbands were often labourers, and frequently out of work."[10] Albert Paul (born 1903), the ninth of ten children, records in his reminiscences that since his building laborer father was out of work for at least three months out of every twelve, "mother went out to work in a laundry and also took in washing to get a few more shillings to buy us children food and clothing."[11] In one Brighton household, it was as much the husband's lack of competence in his chosen trade as general economic conditions which dictated the need for his wife's labor, as A. E. Coppard recalled: "This tailor had once been a good soldier but had served his time, and because he was not a good tailor his wife Kate, a fine upstanding creature whose face was also pitted with smallpox, had to go out ironing in a laundry, a task known professionally as 'getting up' the linen."[12]

Many employers were astute enough to take advantage of the structural weaknesses of the casual labor market. The Poor Law Commission learned from one employer the extent of his business's dependence on married women's need for work:

> It is the men going idle that keeps our factory going . . . The great majority of ironers are married women. I like to get them because married women for the greater part of the year must work. The chief tradesmen here are bricklayers, plasterers, and joiners, especially the first. They only work for part of the year and are idle for the rest. When the husbands are busy, the wives are less keen to work. When the men are thrown out of work, the wives are eager to work.[13]

Throughout the Victorian period washers in full-time work earned two shillings to two shillings and six pence per day while ironers, who were generally pieceworkers, earned from three shillings to three shillings and six pence, all usually with an allowance of beer. Washerwomen going into private homes to assist with the family's washing might expect to receive as recompense for their heavy labor a shilling or a shilling and six pence a day, plus their meals. Since these itinerant washerwomen often had young children to support, they were also often given bread, cheese, food scraps and occasionally cast-off clothing.[14] In all types of laundry work, individual earnings could vary widely, and where work was paid by the piece, a premium was placed on youth, strength, quickness, and dexterity. In one London laundry in the 1890s, nearly half of the workers earned less than twelve shillings a week, while as late as 1907 average London wages were thirteen shillings and six pence, and for hand laundries throughout the country twelve shillings and six pence.[15] It was only after 1919, with growing union strength buttressed by Trade Board minimum wage rates, that the situation improved. Even these wages could not be sustained throughout the year in a seasonal trade: employers were reluctant to lose their best hands to other laundries and frequently divided the work among their most proficient employees (usually fancy-work ironers) during those periods when work was scarce. One laundry proprietor reported that he gave his best hands work in August, September, and sometimes October in order to keep them even though he would have preferred to shut down during these months.[16]

Labor at the washtub, mangle, or ironing board sustained life in many working-class families. Its prominence was intimately related to the irregularity and casual character of so much of the work done by the husbands of these women. Observing "the preponderance of the rural accent" in Notting Dale, a community where laundry work was the dominant women's trade, George R. Sims noted that this was one of many enclaves in London that served as a stopping off point for "thousands of honest country folk who crowd up year after year to the great city that they believe to be paved with gold." He convincingly described a scenario in which "the husband fails to find the work he expected to be ready to his hand in busy London. The little savings are soon gone; the man and his wife are driven to the common lodging-house or, if there are children with them, to the furnished room. The wife perhaps goes to the laundry work. The husband's enforced idleness often ends in his becoming a confirmed loafer, contented to live off what his wife can earn."[17] Clementina Black, in her examination of married women's work, found that the spouses of laundresses were underemployed rather than what would now be called "work-shy." In a sample of sixty-two London laundresses she found that only two had husbands who were deliberately poor providers but that "very few husbands had regular employment."[18]

The occupational pattern for men in the Kensington communities dominated by female laundry work had several common features. The vast majority of male workers were unskilled or at best employed in jobs that could be learned in a few days. Laboring was by far the most common employment, and the construction trade was the one broad occupational area that engaged large numbers of laborers, semiskilled workers, and a few artisans. Opportunities for factory employment were few, the Kensal Green Gas Works being the only industrial enterprise of any size in the region. Most important, nearly all men's jobs were either seasonal or irregular; the building trades, most gas work, brickmaking, and market gardening were all seasonal, and laboring, the most important occupation, was highly irregular. Luck, the weather, the state of the economy, the distance to a possible job, and the age and general health of the individual laborer all combined to produce great insecurity of employment. Most casual and seasonal workers had an uncertain life, and the casual earnings of the men virtually necessitated the supplementary earnings of the women. In 1908, a report by the Charity Organization Society Committee on Unskilled Labor remarked:

> Where one irregular or casual trade established itself, an attraction exists for other seasonal or casual labour trades to come into the district to take advantage of cheap labour. Moreover, women's trades will tend to spring up, whereby the irregular earnings of the men may be supplemented by the irregular earnings of the women. The result is the formation of a large market for casual labour. The opportunities for finding casual work are increased. At the same time, the chief stimulus to decasualization of any given industry is removed—namely, the difficulty of obtaining a fluctuating supply of labour of sufficient quality.[19]

Areas in which laundry work was prominent reinforce these conclusions. The West London communities in which laundresses were most heavily concentrated were characterized by close proximity to substantial upper middle-class residential areas; these areas generated employment for women in laundry work, charring, and to some extent needlework and prostitution; and there was a marked lack of factories and other outlets for male employment. As the metropolis grew westward, there had been plentiful employment for men as navvies, builders' laborers, and artisans, but as the march of bricks and mortar extended outward and the new suburban villas became occupied, male employment opportunities contracted while those for females increased.

Not only did a functional complementarity exist between laundry work and many forms of male employment; laundering was also attractive because it could be meshed with other cash-producing activities. A few jobs regularly produced opportunities for added income from laundry work: Cambridge bedmakers often added to their wages by taking home the laundry of those men whose rooms they cleaned; women who took in lodgers commonly added to their rent money by doing lodgers' laundry; and charwomen and day domestics, either in private homes or boarding houses, could supplement their earnings by laundering.[20] In port towns, doing ships' laundry was often combined with cleaning ships' interiors.[21] The unevenness of the work throughout the week in a small laundry, or for a woman doing laundry on her own, meant that some women added street selling, sewing, or charring to their work as laundresses. "Why I has to go out a charin' some days, as the things haven't come in," reported one laundress.[22]

Since laundry work itself was seasonal, laundry workers, especially those with minimal support from spouses, had to work out additional strategies to augment the family income. One of the most popular options was harvesting, which provided something of a family country "holiday" and meshed nicely with the low point in the laundry worker's year. London laundry workers and their families joined hundreds of other working-class families who made the annual migration to the hop fields of Kent or for fruit picking.[23] One London laundress, who was her family's main support—her husband was consumptive—reported that the family's autumn migration to the hop field "quite set her up" for the winter.[24] In Cambridge out-of-work laundresses went fruit-picking and then followed their "pickings" into the large jam factory in the neighborhood.[25] A few laundresses were even inconsiderate enough to take their pea-picking vacation before the busy laundry season was over, to the great disgust of at least one employer.[26] In the lower-class end of the trade, where summer seasonality was not so great, women laundry workers and dyers went into the india-rubber factories in winter.[27]

It was even possible to dovetail laundry work with laundry work. According to Evelyn March-Phillips in 1894, "In London, and large towns, regular laundry workers are, to some extent, migratory, and move in batches to the nearest seaside resorts for the holiday season. The secretary of a trade society tells me that she receives letters in the autumn from laundry proprietors in Ramsgate, Margate, and Folkstone asking for lists of workers."[28] Some laundresses moved between resort towns during the summer (Bournemouth, Bath, and Cheltenham) and university towns during term time. For laundresses permanently resident in resort towns, winter was a time of great distress.[29] For women whose financial circum-

stances were strained, employment in a large laundry might be supplemented with labor at a small cottage laundry or by doing washing in her
own home. One hard-worked Brighton woman with a large family and a
consumptive husband augmented her laundry earnings with the extra
pence she could garner by washing her neighbors' clothes in the evenings.[30]
Complaining of the consequences of incomplete regulation of the trade at
the turn of the century, one launderer noted that "it is well known that
women who have put in a good day's work at a laundry working under the
Factory Act frequently proceed to the so-called cottage laundry when regulation closing time has arrived, and slave away as long as they can stand on
their feet. . . ."[31]

Laundry work, especially when performed as home work, could be fitted
into a woman's domestic routine and turned to in times of distress, such as
when a spouse was injured or unexpectedly lost his job. Income from
laundry work could also supplement a man's income when the latter was
inadequate for the needs of a large family.[32] Taking in washing or going out
to do it was one of the major strategies (others included charring and
sewing) employed by working-class wives in order to put a bit aside for an
expected birth.[33] Because it was a service in demand year round and in all
communities, laundry work was usually available for those desperate
enough to accept the lowest wages and longest hours. One such woman
described how she worked after her husband had gone out to work at
night: "Many times till 4 o'clock in the morning in bitter cold I have been
washing, and have just been able to get two hours' sleep before the child
woke up, which he did about 6 o'clock."[34] For most laundry workers the
normal working week was four to four-and-a-half days, which afforded a
degree of flexibility for women with household responsibilities. The division of the labor of laundry work into the tasks of washing, rinsing, drying,
starching, and ironing meant that, especially in smaller establishments,
washers were slack on Mondays and Saturdays, and ironers on Mondays
and Tuesdays.[35] This four-day week, according to one employer, "was popular with these married workers who did their own washing on Monday,
and on Saturday made their purchases and put their homes shipshape."[36]
Moreover, in some establishments married women were allowed to begin
work an hour later than their unmarried colleagues, and in areas like
Acton, which was dominated by laundries, older children or baby-sitters
brought infants to the laundries to be nursed during the midday meal
break.[37] Finally, the possibility of doing the work in one's own home or in a
neighborhood laundry offered obvious attractions for relatively immobile
married or widowed women.

Laundry Labor and Family Welfare

Laundry work, in contrast to many other employments, was an occupation that was easy to enter and could be pursued by a woman throughout her working life. Women in Kensal New Town, Charles Booth observed, started to work in laundries when they were about fifteen years of age and continued into their seventies.[38] More than half of the laundresses here were married women, and of the single women, some 47 percent were under the age of twenty, many of them presumably daughters doing their bit to contribute to the precarious family economy. Mrs. Ballard, a Leamington Spa laundress, when advertising her services, noted that she "has spent 40 years of her life in connection with the business, 23 of which she has carried on a laundry for herself with a gratifying amount of success establishing in the process a good connection among the gentry and trades-men." In some areas, such as the hamlet of Golgotha on the outskirts of Lancaster, washerwomen "plied their trade for several successive genera-tions" to meet the laundering needs of what one laundress called "all the big bugs."[39]

Few skills and no expensive tools were required of the woman who went out to work in a laundry or to do laundry in a private home. A few ironers underwent a three month "apprenticeship" and young girls were taken on as "learners," but most adult women either had the necessary skills or could learn them very quickly on the job.[40] More extensive training was reserved primarily for middle-class women destined for managerial posi-tions in large factory laundries and was uncommon before the twentieth century. (Training for work in factory laundries will be examined in chap-ter 5.) It was easy, then, for women trained in other trades to resort to the laundry in times of economic adversity; one woman who testified before the Royal Commission on Labour said she turned to laundry work after her husband became ill and family poverty necessitated the sale of her sewing machine, thereby ending her home work as a tailoress.[41] So easy was the trade to enter and so widespread the skills required, that laundry work was the obvious choice for many widowed women, particularly those with young children to support. "In those days," writes George Woodcock of the 1870s, "there were no pensions for widows or orphans, and to avoid the dreaded workhouse she [Woodcock's widowed great-grandmother] made a kind of living by taking in washing."[42] In a similar vein, A. E. Coppard remembered:

On the death of my father we plunged into acute poverty, and my poor
mother had to alternate between working at the laundry and a job as auxil-

iary kitchen maid at the Lion Mansion Hotel where she was entitled, allowed, or somehow managed, to bring home the kitchen scraps to feed her children on, the four of us. . . . This fortune lasted only for the summer season, after which, no longer required there, Mother would take to the laundry again; thus for some years, eked out with Parish Relief, we subsisted and survived.[43]

Turning to laundry work for a living was so commonplace that in 1894 a writer in the *Pall Mall Gazette* was able to observe that "widows and washing, misery and mangles seem, somehow, indissolubly connected."[44]

To set up in business in the laundry trade was relatively easy from a financial point of view. Most working-class women measured their resources in shillings or at most a few pounds, and it was possible to become a home laundry worker with a small expenditure. For example, the purchase of an old wooden mangle for one pound, the last of her meager funds, enabled a Cambridge woman to support herself and her four children at the end of the nineteenth century by mangling her neighbors' already washed clothes in exchange for a few pennies and odd bits of food and cast-off clothing.[45] Similarly, an elderly widow, named Lil Kistler, who had "no asset in the world but her mangle," managed to eke out a living by renting the use of the mangle to her neighbors at a halfpenny a load.[46] By the later years of the century, after large numbers of local authorities had taken advantage of the provisions of the Baths and Washhouses Act, it became possible for very poor women to earn a few pence by doing others' washing at the local washhouses.[47] In fact, the practice of earning a living at laundry work with the aid of the public washhouse became sufficiently prevalent that it was sometimes attacked by professional launderers as a "scandal" and an "Abuse of Public Washhouses."[48]

Laundry work could be made to support a family because it was often based on the labor of many family members. In Kensal New Town in 1871, laundrymen, nearly 7 percent of the male heads of household, represented the closest the village had to an entrepreneurial class: they ran small cottage businesses based on the work of their wives and children, and employed in addition one or two neighborhood women as washers, manglers, and ironers, with the youngest employed to pick up and deliver the wash. Quite often a washerwoman's husband would help her with the heavier parts of the work. One dock laborer reported that "the party my wife works for has a mangle, and I go sometimes to help; for if she has 6d. of washing to do at home then I go to turn the mangle for an hour instead of her—she's not strong enough."[49] An old watercress seller told Mayhew that when he was at home he assisted his laundress wife by turning the mangle for her.[50] According to the testimony of his son, one Yorkshire miner assisted his wife in ironing "because it was a way of getting a few coppers." He also tolerated a state of affairs which dictated that drying laundry shared the space before the fire when he washed away the day's coal dust.[51] Other husbands helped out as dollymen, punching or pounding clothing with a wooden instrument known as a dolly, and along with other male relatives might assist with the fetching and carrying of wash, water, or coals. A husband who had a pony and cart or hand truck was invaluable since such transport would allow a laundress to take on a greater quantity of washing. Men, especially in London, might be employed for part of the year in larger laundries as carmen, dollymen, and manglers. In Headington Quarry, laundry delivery was undertaken by the older boys:

> Me and our Flimp—Flimpy, that was my uncle—used to drive old Peter to take this washing back every Friday . . . all round Oxford, up Banbury Road, up Woodstock Road, all them houses . . . Granny Webb worked for . . . we used generally to take it at night time . . . if it was summer we'd start about four, then . . . take our time. . . . We used to deliver round Oxford . . . on a Friday. Allus took the washin' back on a Friday, yes and I think it was Cudd'sdon College on a Thursday. . . . It was white clean washing—Oh there was two big hampers like this, look, much as we could lift up in this old cart.[52]

Male assistance could also be part of the ritual of courting a laundress: one young man "walking out" with a young laundress regularly spent the whole of his Saturday afternoon hauling water for her use on Monday.[53]

By far the greatest asset a woman forced to support herself and her family by laundry work could have was the labor of her children. Children, especially daughters (or occasionally other female relatives), were a crucial resource for "those will be best off who have the most of them."[54] With the help of their daughters, many widows and wives whose husbands provided no support were able to sustain themselves entirely by laundry work—but usually only at the cost of extremely long hours. Many mother-and-daughter teams worked until midnight or even all through the night during the busy season.[55] Older children labored at the washtub, mangle, and ironing board while younger children sorted and packaged bundles, carried in dried clothes for ironing, and helped to carry the laundry to their mothers' customers and to collect work for the following day. For the latter task, sugar boxes mounted on pram wheels or an old barrow proved an ideal vehicle.[56] For less fortunate youngsters other strategems had to be found, Peter Arnold reported that as a child "my sisters and I used to go out on a Monday morning to fetch washing from different houses. We used to have tied round us, two or three different bundles at a time. It had to be tied on because we weren't very big, otherwise we should have had to make several journeys. . . . We took it back in a big basket."[57] As children grew older and stronger, they were pressed into service fetching water from the pump to fill the washing copper, cleaning and stoking the coke-fired ironing stove or the fire beneath the copper as well as assisting with flat work ironing.[58] One author, who investigated child labor in England commented: "Particularly severe is the lot of the children of small laundresses who are often employed both in homework and in ironing, in a steam laden atmosphere, for two or three nights weekly till 10 o'clock, and all day Saturday."[59] The report of the interdepartmental committee on the employment of school children concluded that "some of the worst cases of overworking of little girls of which we have heard occurred in the small laundries, which are exempt from the Factory Act."[60]

Being "mother's helper" was frequently the focal point of the life of the laundress's child. The daughter of a mangler recalled how

we helped mother in her efforts to get us a living. It was hard work. At first we couldn't reach the handle at the top of its stroke and we used a scarf to help us pull the handle round. But as we grew taller we were able to turn the wheel without it. . . . We would work on the mangling as soon as we came home from school. Emily and I would work on with mother until we were very tired and then we would rest . . . later Mother would then wake us up and make our tea, and my sister and I would undress and dress ourselves again to wake ourselves up. . . . Then once more the mangling started. We worked on and on as long as we could so as to have as many clothes as possible ready for delivering to the customers next morning before we went to school.[61]

Of the mangle which dominated their lives she later reflected: "It wasn't only the clothes you pressed—You mangled out our young lives."[62] One young woman, whose father purchased a box mangle for her mother in the 1880s as a means of supplementing the family's meager resources, attributed the fact that she was a cripple by the age of thirteen to the hard work involved in operating the machine at a tender age.[63] The reminiscences of another, stolidly stoical woman depict an equally hard childhood: "My mother kep' 'leven of us, we *had* to work—I've been up at laundry work at four o'clock a Saturday morning and I haven't finished till six o'clock at night, and hard work never hurt me. I'm sixty-six nearly, so it didn't hurt me did it?"[64] Laundry work was back-breaking work, but without it many women might have had to taste (in John Burns's colorful phrase) "the crumb of charity or the loaf of lust."[65] "The brutal overwork in domestic laundries to which washerwomen are subjected" was well known to the Member for Battersea, for Burns's mother had been a washerwoman and his sisters ironers and as a youth he had delivered bundles of linen for them.[66] Charles Dickens, in *Bleak House,* described a thirteen-year-old orphan girl, "Charley," who, after her father's death, supported herself, her brothers, and her sisters through laundry work. Her real life counterpart, Annie Smith, testified before a Marylebone coroner's inquest in 1896 that "she kept not only her father and mother, but had supported till death the illegitimate child of a deceased sister. All this she managed to accomplish by constant labour at the washtub, and evidently had no idea she was doing anything out of the ordinary."[67]

Occasionally a small laundry could be relatively lucrative; a woman and her daughters might be comfortable enough to be able to afford the luxury of keeping the Sabbath (the Sabbath-breaking habits of many laundresses made them prime targets for the reprimands of city missionaries), or to employ other women.[68] Sometimes the business went so well that a laundry could become the workplace of choice for employees who had had other occupations. For example, one middle-aged Irish street seller told Henry Mayhew that she was leaving street trading for laundry work, at which she had long worked part-time, because, with her proficiency as an ironer and the opportunity to work in her aunt's laundry, she could do much better than on the street.[69] In a few fortunate cases, the hard work of a woman and her daughter could turn into a very successful venture. In 1850, Lucy Mills, assisted by her daughter, began to launder the linen for a few local families in the underground kitchen of her cottage in Black Rock, Brighton. From a small business for which water was carried on a yoke from the mains at the end of the street and washing collected and delivered by hand cart, the business has grown to a large family-run firm with five receiving shops and a staff of 180, with which her daughter was still connected in 1980 when she was ninety-six years of age. Few laundries, however, were ever as successful as this one.[70]

Laundry work involved many hardships for the laundress and her family, and when performed in the home it permeated everyday family life: "Imagine what it is like in wet or wintry weather to have the narrow passage filled with a double line of wet clothes, and the one living room completely blocked up with them."[71] Work in a mid-nineteenth-century Brighton laundry began when "every Monday morning the carpet in the front sitting room was taken up, the furniture moved into a corner of the room so that the space left could be used as an ironing room for the rest of the week [washing was done in the basement kitchen].[72] The weekly rhythms of the work molded everyday family life, and the process of the work assaulted the senses. The week began with the obnoxious, stale smell of many families' dirty laundry—the piles of clothes providing temporary messy playhouses for the youngest children. There soon followed the smell of soap, bleach, bluing, and starch mingled with steam, puddles of soapy water interspersed with unsteady islands of loose bricks or old mats, and the high temperatures—often reaching ninety degrees Fahrenheit and converting the family kitchen into a Turkish bath. Dripping clothes democratically dampened the heads and shoulders of all. Later in the week the heated atmosphere shifted to the parlor-ironing room where the coke or gas stove used to heat the irons maintained the temperature and added noxious fumes, fumes confined indoors by the closed windows that guarded against the laundress's enemy—the so-called London smuts. The thonk of the heavy wooden box mangle, the hiss of irons, the thwack of the dolly, the slosh of washing, the quiet swish of linen on washboards and of scrubbing brushes on heavy fabrics, the splash of seeming oceans of water, mingled with muttered curses—these were the lullabies of the laundrywoman's child.

The Hand-Laundering Process

A fuller description of the way clothes were washed and "got up" can give the reader a more complete appreciation of the disruption laundering could cause in a household, particularly when the home was a small urban dwelling. In such homes, some semblance of normal family life was restored only on Sundays when all signs of industry were cleared away for a few hours. The principal focus here is upon the laundress working in her own home, but it should be remembered that in all but the grandest houses there was little space—beyond perhaps a lean-to washhouse in the garden—set aside exclusively for washing, and even where there was ample outdoor drying space, a wet washday produced an all-pervasive domestic gloom. Even if washing could be done outside the family's living space— either in a washhouse or in the open—the rest of the laundering processes (mangling, starching, ironing, folding, airing) usually took place in the house. Doing the wash, therefore, was almost everywhere an activity that caused a major dislocation of domestic life. Indeed, so arduous and disruptive was laundering that well into the nineteenth century it was still carried out in some private homes at relatively infrequent intervals. At the Norfolk Parsonage of the Reverend James Woodforde in 1799, it was the household custom to wash every five weeks.[73] A monthly wash was still fairly common in the 1830s and 1840s, particularly in rural areas and small towns, although even less frequent laundering was recommended by some. In 1838, the *Workman's Guide* advocated: "It is the best economy to wash by the year, or by the quarter, in places where it can be done, and by the score or dozen in preference to by the piece."[74] If its very unpleasantness initially dictated well-spaced washdays, the ownership of sufficient linen to be able to follow this practice soon became a status symbol. In her well-known chronicle of English rural life, *Lark Rise to Candleford*, Flora Thompson recorded that Miss Lane, the postmistress of Candleford Green in the 1890s, "still kept to the old middle class custom of one huge washing every six weeks. In her girlhood it would have been thought poor looking to have had a weekly or fortnightly washday. The better off a family was, the more changes of linen its members were supposed to possess, and the less frequent the washday."[75]

As towns and cities grew in the nineteenth century, doing the laundry at home became even more inconvenient for most families. Closely packed urban dwellings, tiny or nonexistent gardens, and polluted air both increased the volume of laundry to be done and made drying the linen outside impractical. Given these constraints, it comes as no surprise to find Mrs. Beeton, in 1861, noting that, while in country places washing at home was virtually universal, in urban areas, which by this date housed more than half of the English population, "the family linen is chiefly done by professional laundresses and companies."[76] (The "family wash" Beeton generalizes about belonged, of course, to relatively affluent families.) When the family wash disappeared into commercial laundries, the outward signs of washday were no longer available for nosy neighbors to scrutinize and thus the custom of infrequent washes also vanished. Unfortunately for laundry workers, the demise of this custom was not accompanied by any alteration in the long hallowed ritual of beginning the wash on Monday or Tuesday so that the freshly prepared linen could be ready to use or wear by week's end. When washes were infrequent this pattern made some sense. The volume of laundry to be done in a large and relatively affluent household was so great that a concentrated and orderly pattern of working was necessary to ensure that the task was completed before the week was over and to guarantee that some time was left over for other activities.

Laundering usually consumed four days (more if the weather was unusually foul)—very long days at that. Early in the nineteenth century, Mrs. Wollaston, the wife of a Clapham merchant and banker, required her housemaid on washing Mondays "to get up with the laundrymaid to wash at 1 a.m."; after an interval to perform her usual tasks between 5:00 a.m. or 6:00 a.m. and 10:30 a.m. or 11:00 a.m., she "returns to the washing till 9 p.m."[77] Similar hours were worked not only by other servants but by professional washerwomen who arrived at their employers' homes at dawn. John Thomas Smith recorded in 1839 that laundresses "may be seen in winter time, shivering at the doors, at three or four o'clock in the morning, and are seldom dismissed before ten at night."[78] At the end of the nineteenth century and well into the twentieth, these itinerant laundrywomen worked punishingly long hours at their arduous work, though eleven or twelve hour days were more common than the eighteen to nineteen hours cited by Smith.[79] In less affluent households the rigid weekly pattern was dictated less by the volume of wash to be got through than by the need to share a copper or other equipment and, particularly where washing was done outdoors at a common location, by the welcome distraction companionship and conversation brought to hard work.

Whatever the reasons, the folklore adage to launder early in the week persisted even where the work had been transferred from the home to a commercial establishment. Traditionally, throughout the United Kingdom, to wash on Monday was to be virtuous but

> Who washes on Friday
> Is half a slut;
> Who that wash on Saturday
> Is a slut to the bone.[80]

The weekly washing cycle seemed to be a sacrosanct part of English life. For the professional laundry worker, her customers' traditionalism meant not virtue, but only brutal overwork. Individual washerwomen and large commercial launderers both found that, as late as 1893, "even an offer of cheaper rates have not induced the public to depart from ancient custom."[81] Because of this consumer conservatism the pattern of the laundry worker's labor was fairly consistent across the nation with the exception of concerns specializing in hotel, restaurant, railway, and shipping work—and these were usually large mechanized factory laundries or institutional laundries.

Almost everywhere, then, hand laundry work followed an unvarying routine: the early part of the week was occupied with the collection, sorting, marking, soaking, washing, mangling, blueing, and starching of laundry, while the later part of the week was devoted to ironing, airing, folding, packing, and, finally, delivery of the snowy linen. The laundry "got up" by most hand laundresses consisted primarily of cotton and linen along with some flannel items. Delicate articles such as silks were usually laundered at home by householders and their servants, although a few specialized hand laundries catering to an elite clientele would undertake the laundering of these special care items. (Dealing with spots and stains on nonwashable clothing, unpicking complex clothing for laundering and reassembling it later, and cleaning very fragile laundry still left plenty of work for the middle-class woman and her servants.)[82]

Laundry work involved two broad processes: cleaning and ironing. In a small hand laundry, the employees, in common with the laundress working on her own, required competence in the details of both processes (though an individual woman might be "known" for one part of the work), but in larger establishments a rough specialization of the work into washing and ironing took place. The itinerant washerwoman was a specialist of sorts although she was hired as much for her brute strength as for her expertise. According to one estimate, a simplified laundry process involving a single washing, one period of boiling and one rinse, used about four hundred pounds (fifty gallons) of water, which had to be moved about in tubs or boilers weighing forty or fifty pounds apiece.[83] Washerwomen were hired by families across a wide social spectrum to provide relief from the most back-breaking aspects of laundry labor. So unpleasant was the task before piped and heated water and domestic appliances eased the burden that paying someone else to do the laundry was a top priority of many households when funds permitted a lightening of the domestic burden. Even when piped water was available or willing males were on hand to carry the needed water, washing entailed a great deal of lifting and carrying, as well as (where wringers or mangles were unavailable) the extraordinarily heavy job of wringing out sodden linen. Kate Mary Edwards, a mill hand's spouse from Lotting Fen, Huntingdonshire observed: "You had to be as strong as a man to lift the great wooden wash tubs, allus left full o' suds, to keep em binged [soaked], even without the weight o' the wet clothes; and then you had to lift the great iron pot, full of water, on and off the pot hook over a hot turf fire, and drag the wet washing in a clothes basket to the line down the garden, and put it in and out again, perhaps four or fives times if it were a wet day."[84]

Even when householders were too poor to spare themselves all this arduous labor, they were often able to avail themselves of the services of another specialist, the mangler. This laundry worker gained her specialization, not through skill or long training, but by owning a mangle, the most substantial piece of laundry equipment in use before the mechanization of the industry. This apparatus, designed for pressing linen flat between two rollers, was frequently used instead of ironing for large flat items and, in many poor households, for all laundered items. When a woman was widowed, the neighbors might take up a collection to buy her a mangle (any insurance money remaining after funeral expenses could also be used for this purpose) so that she could support herself and her children. The front window of many a small cottage displayed a card announcing: "Mangling Done Here—1 1/2 d. a dozen." Neighbors would bring their clean laundry for smoothing, leaving in payment a penny or two and whatever scraps of food or used clothing could be spared for a less fortunate neighbor. Most often mangling was used to augment a family's meager resources and was turned to by women too old or too much burdened with young children to be employable elsewhere. Professional laundresses might also purchase mangles (usually "on time"); with these they eased the burden of the work they did for their middle-class clientele and also mangled the neighborhood laundry for small sums. One woman recalled that when she was a child, "I used to have to take my mother's washing to an old woman named Alice Woodward, to be mangled. She used to mangle all her neighbours' washing for a penny a basketful. She'd take each article out o' the basket and fold it careful on to the board under the roller, and then load the top o' the mangle up with bricks. Then the old mangle 'ould rumble away as the roller turned over the clothes and the bricks fell down again."[85]

The other laundry specialist was, naturally, the ironer. Ironers—that is, workers who were not expected to take part in the washing of linen—normally were employed only in larger laundries and worked a different weekly pattern from the washerwomen. Instead of beginning work at dawn early in the week, ironers commonly started work on Tuesday afternoon or Wednesday morning and continued their toil until late on Saturday night or into the early hours of Sunday. Variations in the day of the week when work commenced depended on the size of the laundry, the geographical distribution of its clientele, and the method and efficiency with which the week's washing was collected. Small laundries with a neighborhood clientele would be able to collect, sort, and mark the week's work early enough on Monday that washing could begin the same day, while in larger hand laundries both washers and ironers would be slack on Mondays and ironing would not get underway until Wednesday. Women working on their own either obtained work as washerwomen or "took in" washing; the latter employment normally included ironing while the former rarely did. To be employed independently as an ironer was exceptional. An exception occurred in poor neighborhoods where not all families possessed the implements, in particular polishing irons, to lend the desired finish to men's best shirts. In many working-class households the possession of one set of correctly laundered "proper" clothes was seen as a mark of respectability. To ensure that they were correctly turned out for Sundays and special events, families who could not afford the luxury of having someone else do the entire wash might pay a neighbor to wash, iron, and starch a special item or two. In the fens at the end of the nineteenth century, "women who had a 'polishing iron' for doing starched things with, made themselves a copper or two a week by doing things for their neighbours. They would wash and starch and iron and polish a collar and front for a ha'penny."[86]

With only minor variations, the laundering process followed the same pattern almost everywhere. First, the soiled wash was sorted so that specific items could be handled in the most appropriate manner. Colored items (only a small proportion of the weekly Victorian wash) were set aside from whites; linen and cotton were separated from flannels, wool, silk or other fabrics; and coarse materials such as work clothes, sack aprons, or rough linen, once called the buckwash, were isolated for separate treatment. The itinerant laundress would arrive at her employer's home early on washday to find that whites and heavily soiled clothing had been soaked overnight to loosen the dirt. When laundry was done outside the owner's home, overnight soaking was rare, but the most heavily soiled items might be soaked while work proceeded with the rest of the wash. White linens and cottons, the major part of the wash and in some households the only items regularly sent out to be laundered professionally, were cleaned according to a strict schedule. Since noncolored cottons and linens were always boiled, it was important that the most stubborn stains and dirt be dislodged to avoid having them permanently set in the fabric. For this reason soaking and/or scrubbing always preceded boiling. These operations were carried out in wooden tubs (galvanized metal tubs appeared only at the end of the nineteenth century), and cleansing was aided by a variety of chemical solutions.

Throughout the nineteenth century most washing, particularly as performed by commercial laundry workers, was carried on with the cleansing aid of soap, even though the excise tax on soap was not removed until 1853.[87] The soap commonly used was the yellow or mottled brown household variety. Shaved off a large block or cut into small pieces, it was dissolved in boiling water to form a jelly that would disperse readily in the wash water. In its solid form, soap would be rubbed directly on stains. Other cleansing substances especially prepared for the removal of the offending substance were also used to remove marks from clothing. Tar, a particular hazard to wearers of long skirts, could be removed by rubbing with lard prior to washing, while rust marks, a common problem before the invention of zippers and stainless steel pins and fastenings, could be lifted by applying acid, such as the oxalic acid present in stewed rhubarb. It is not our purpose here to document the range of innovative techniques devised to remove stubborn stains. However, it is worth noting that the value of petroleum products for cleaning was known well in advance of the official invention of "soapless soaps." Kerosene, paraffin, or a small quantity of petrol served as early forms of detergent.[88] These substances were found to be an excellent solvent for grease when combined with sufficient soap and hot water. Soda, ammonia, or the old standby, lye, might also be added to the wash water. Then as now soaps were vigorously advertised. In the 1880s, one new laundry product was lauded in the following fashion:

Crosfield's Perfection Soap is offered as the outcome of long and most expensive scientific experiments; for cleaning floors, paint, kitchen, and other rough household work, it cannot be excelled. Its greatest victory will be obtained in the laundry, where it will indeed prove itself a "wonder worker." Its great lathering and dirt-extracting properties will lighten the toil of the user, make clothes cleaner and whiter, and save its cost to the purchaser for no soda or dry soap need be used with this wonderful washing soap. Against disease and infection it is all powerful, being a pure disinfectant, and, as a *skin soap*, it is *invaluable*.[89]

Then as now users were astute enough to read such claims as hyperbole. Even if these commercial products did not work wonders and did not entirely eliminate the need for elbow grease, they were a great improvement over lye, "lant," and water alone. They also saved the effort of making one's own soap.

Few nineteenth century laundresses outside of rural areas would have made their own soap. One exception was the laundry community of Notting Dale in North Kensington, London, where the nature of the local economy facilitated soapmaking. In this poor neighborhood, pig keeping and laundry work were along with brickmaking the principal occupations. The proximity of affluent "West End" households made it easy for the pig keepers to feed their animals and, at the same time, provided a source of fat for soapmaking. In 1860, the wife of a local pig keeper explained how the system worked: "We most of us keep a horse, or a donkey and cart, and we go round early in the morning to the gentlefolks' houses and collects the *refuges* from the kitchens. When we comes home, we sorts it out; the best of it we eats ourselves or gives it to a neighbour, the fat is boiled down, and the rest we gives to the pigs. . . ."[90] The fat thus acquired could be combined with wood ashes, available in part from the brickmaking process, to make soap. In 1869 there were sixty-nine fat-boiling coppers on six short streets of Notting Dale. But the stench caused by the process resulted in strenuous efforts to eliminate the practice when surrounding streets came to be inhabited by wealthy residents. By the turn of the century, only one boiling copper remained, and most laundresses were purchasing bar soap by the hundredweight.[91]

Whether made at home or purchased from commercial manufacturers, the one thing that soap requires to perform effectively is hot water. In nineteenth century hand laundries, water for washing was usually heated in a copper, a vessel with a capacity of twenty gallons or more, which was set in brickwork and heated by a fire set underneath it. In establishments which were poorer or where washing was an occupation only resorted to in times of adversity, water was simply heated in the largest available receptacle. When laundry was done at home, washdays were days for cold dinners, not only because the wash engaged the energies of all the household's women but also because, in many instances, all the family cooking vessels had been pressed into service. Ownership of a copper was a decided boon, as one woman recounted: "When we begun to have a proper brick copper to heat the water, it was easier, and there'd allus be a nice lot o' hot suds to scrub your doorway with when the washing was done."[92] The capacity of the copper made it easier for commercial laundresses to handle a large volume of washing, and the contained fire beneath the copper was considered a particularly efficient method of heating water (it required fewer coals than an open fire and might be fueled in part by combustible waste). Once heated, water was ladled into washing tubs, into which the laundry was transferred after soaking. In the hot soapy water, clothes were beaten or agitated with a dolly and scrubbed or, more properly, kneaded and squeezed to release the soil without damaging the fabric.

The washing dolly, or peggy, was a wooden implement used for pounding or rotating heavily soiled linen in the wash water. In its most common form, the dolly was a four- or five-legged stool attached to an upright handle about three feet long with a crossbar handle at the top. Other similar washing aids included the laundry punch, a tool in which the dolly's stool-like foot was replaced by a block of wood indented at intervals to catch the clothes, and the "possing stick," which ended in a perforated copper cone. The latter piece of equipment operated on the suction principle and looked very much like a modern plumber's plunger. These implements could be used on their own or fitted with a lid and used with a matched wooden tub, an apparatus that could be mistaken for a churn. Whatever its form or name, and both were subject to regional variation, the dolly was generally operated as a Cumberland author once described it: "The dolly is plunged into the mass and worked by the dollier with both arms, with a curious lateral motion to right and left alternately, care being taken not to let the feet touch the bottom of the tub."[93] wIn an earlier time, rough woolen and fustian garments were subjected Dollying was arduous work, a part of the washing cycle in which male help was especially to this vigorous treatment; most cotton fabrics, however, could not withstand such handling, and by the second half of the nineteenth century the use of dollies seems to have been restricted to the heaviest and most unwieldy items, such as blankets, sheets, and quilts. Sheets made of twill or unbleached calico, for example, were among the linen that might be beaten with a dolly. Kate Mary Edwards recalled the difficulty of laundering this sturdy linen: "Sheets were homemade, of unbleached calico for strength and wear. When this stuff was new, it was so thick with 'dress' as to be like thin cardboard. When you washed them, you just cou'n't get no lather on the water, however much soap you used, for the first few washes, and of course they were a mucky yellowish colour. . . . They were rough and coarse and so heavy to handle when wet."[94]

Once kneaded, squeezed, scrubbed, or dollied, the laundry was wrung out, rinsed in clear water, wrung out once more, and lifted into the copper, or other suitable receptable, for boiling. The wash was then simmered for about half an hour in hot soapy water to which soap, borax, or some other whitening agent might be added.[95] (In private households, boiling might continue for hours, but understandably this was a luxury that the commercial laundry or the laundress working in her own home could not afford.) Without a copper, boiling could be a stressful experience: soot and ash might blacken the newly whitened laundry or the cauldron could boil over, filling the room with ash and steam. Linen, after it had been boiled, was rinsed at least twice to remove all traces of soap or soda that might yellow the fabric. A solution of blueing was usually added to the final rinse water. Care had to be taken with the use of blue; if too much was used, the linen would look gray; and if the solution was not mixed well enough, the laundry might be streaked. Selected items, in particular men's shirts, were also dipped in a hot-water starch solution. Then, at last, the linen was wrung out again ready for drying. Between soaking and hanging to dry, the wet laundry was lifted between containers and wrung out, on average, no less than six times. Delicate and colored fabrics were washed separately, usually without prior soaking and were rarely boiled. Since such items constituted only a small proportion of the average laundress's work, their handling will not be examined in detail here.

Washing was tiring work, carried out, as a rule, under dreadful conditions. One young woman described her experiences working in small laundries established by the owners in their own ill-adapted homes. Employees worked in literally sweated circumstances:

> I was at one place in Liverpool where, although I worked from 76 to 82 hours a-week, the most I ever got was eleven shillings. . . . I am glad to say that place is shut up. . . . Another place I worked in was a terrible hole. They had knocked two cellars into one, and down there we had eight tubs with a woman at each, the boilers, and four wringing machines. There was one window at the front and a coal grid behind which supplied what ventilation there was. The floor was always an inch or two deep in water, and the place was always full of steam. The heat was awful, and I have seen the time when we had to strip to the waist to do our work.
>
> The system adopted was for so many scores of clothes, big and little, to be given to us in the morning, and when these were all washed we got paid a lump sum, which was divided amongst us, the weak or indifferent, or shirking washer got just as much as the best. The only way we kept up at all was by drinking beer, and I am sorry to say we drank a lot when the weather was hot.[96]

Even in conditions as bad as these, the work was eased somewhat by the use of wringers. Box mangles, the large wooden structures in which linen was smoothed by being wrapped around rollers and pressed beneath a wooden box filled with several hundredweight of stones, first gained popularity in the eighteenth century, and their use became widespread in the nineteenth as technical improvements made them easier to operate. However, it was the compact mangle, a product of the burgeoning iron industry, which significantly lightened the burden of laundry work. Free-standing or designed to be attached to the side of a laundry tub, the combined wringer-mangle could be used to wring out wet linen and to smooth clean dried laundry. A flexible and compact tool, the wringer-mangle sold in huge numbers in the second half of the nineteenth century and could usually be found in all but the most transient laundries.[97]

After washing, the laundry was hung to dry. Ideally, drying was done outdoors where the natural bleaching action of oxygen in the presence of moisture and light helped to whiten the wash. In the countryside, this was (weather permitting) usually possible, while in urban areas laundries could be found clustered in outlying regions upwind of the worst of industrial air pollution. The London laundry center of Acton grew up on the city's western periphery where drying grounds were plentiful and the air relatively clear. All too often foul weather, lack of space, and smoke-laden air necessitated indoor drying. In a small laundry or household, wet laundry was draped over clothes horses, or hung from lines, wherever space permitted. Wet laundry clearly meant a most unpleasant working environment, but where home and workplace were one, it was much worse. Flora Thompson recalled: "No-one who has not experienced it can imagine the misery of living with a firmament of drying clothes on lines overhead."[98] Once dry, laundry had to be smoothed or ironed. Flat household linens were mangled both to smooth them and impart the gloss that was considered desirable in table linens. To achieve this effect, mangling cloths, made of plain brown Holland material, were wrapped around the laundry before it was passed through the rollers of the mangle.[99] Mangling was heavy work but, as we have seen, straightforward enough to be done by children.

Ironing was another matter: it required considerably more skill than the washing processes. Ironing with a red-hot flat iron, the basic ironing implement, required a sure touch. An ironer needed to have the ability to gauge the correct temperature for pressing a particular fabric, the skill to avoid scorching the garment, the attentiveness to avoid soiling the clothes with soot or starch residue, and the strength to polish garments to the required gloss. Flatirons came in many sizes and designs, from tiny irons to finish intricate garments to large weighty goose irons meant for the heaviest fabrics. What they all had in common was the need to be constantly reheated, which inevitably made ironing hot and steamy labor. Flatirons were heated by being propped upright against the fire on a metal stand suspended from the firebars, or by being placed face down upon a stove. In the late nineteenth century, many laundresses installed specially constructed iron stoves, which heated irons without making them dirty. Box irons, hollow irons heated by pieces of hot metal placed inside them, remained cleaner and somewhat cooler than flat irons and were thus sometimes preferred to them. A range of crimping and finishing irons, which were also heated by slugs of hot metal, were used to finish the bands, frills, and ruffles of complex Victorian clothing. While they were less likely to scorch or mark, these internally heated implements also demanded considerable skill; manipulating slugs of red-hot metal required dexterity as well as the judgment to determine when the metal had been heated for just the right period of time, since overheated metal expanded too much to fit inside the iron. To make the best use of this array of ironing equipment, special boards were considered desirable. For instance, a bosom-board was thought by some to be essential for the ironing of shirts. It was to be "made of seasoned wood, a foot wide, one foot and a half long, and one inch thick. This should be covered with two or three thicknesses of flannel, drawn tight and well tacked in place. Cover again with an outside slip of white cotton fitted to the board, and put a clean slip every week."[100]

The poor woman eking out a living in her own home would probably not own such a board; indeed, she generally had to work without the aid of the full variety of irons, boards, and other equipment that were advised by manuals of household management written for the middle-class housewife. Ironing would most often be performed on a tabletop covered with a blanket or cloth, and the number of irons would be limited. One former servant who took in washing after her marriage, and who had a reputation for high quality work, was able to do her laundering in cramped quarters with a modicum of equipment, and her working conditions were not very different from thousands of other laundresses: "She used to wash for the big houses and all this linen was brought to her cottage in a wheelbarrow. How she used to manage all this washing in her cottage without the use of anything, I don't know. She had an old brick copper. She said she'd stand up till two in the morning ironing with a box iron. Sixpence an hour she was paid. Her husband was away in the army and she washed."[101] With these humble tools and a few "tricks of the trade," such as the use of a little paraffin or candle wax to improve the gloss on collars, cuffs, and shirt fronts, the laundress and ironer turned out piles of snowy and well "got up" linen week after week.

Laundresses as Parents

One of the most pressing problems facing the laundress—a problem that was exacerbated by her long and irregular hours—was the care of her children. Her options were few and often expensive. One study of working mothers established that half left their infants in the care of relatives,

another 30 percent employed neighbors as baby-sitters, while only 14 percent placed their children in day nurseries—establishments that were few
in number and often with hours useless for women whose work often
extended far into the night.[102] In a few of the areas dominated by laundry
work, a handful of suitable nurseries were established. One of the earliest
infant day nurseries to be established was that set up in Kensal New Town
around 1873 "for the benefit of working women compelled to leave their
homes and go out washing and charing" and supported by both subscrip-
tions and parents' payments. Utilized by local laundresses, this establishment was affectionately known as "the Screech."[103] Since laundry work was
a major employment of married women, areas in which the trade was concentrated attracted the attention of philanthropists concerned with the welfare of laundresses' children. In the Latymer Road area of Notting Hill,
this concern was translated into a model crèche. The following description
outlines how the nursery was operated and the philosophy that underlay its
establishment.

> Under the present conditions of life, and in the face of pressing necessity
> which requires many a working woman to leave her children in the care of
> others, the institution of the Crèche seems, indeed, to be one of the most
> urgent necessities of the time. As Lord Shaftesbury pointed out at the annual
> meeting . . . of this mission . . . it is very important that an institution of
> this kind should not be regarded in the light of a charity; the mother should
> be required to pay something, so that the movement will not have a pauperiz-
> ing influence.
>
> The Crèche in Blechynden Street is a model of its kind. The arrangements
> for the comfort and cleanliness of the children are in every way admirable.
> Each child, when admitted, shortly before 8 a.m., is undressed and washed.
> It is then dressed in clothes provided for the infants while in the nursery, a
> very necessary provision to secure that perfect cleanliness which is so abso-
> lutely essential to the health of the establishment. The Crèche itself consists of
> a large well-lighted and ventilated room upstairs, in which a number of cribs
> and cots are ranged along the walls, while swings of various sorts, toys, and
> other devices for the amusement of the children are to be seen on all sides.
> The usual daily attendance is about twenty-five babies of various ages, while
> as many as thirty-five have been received. The charge is sixpence a day for
> each child, and this includes food, while the child is well cared for, 8 a.m. to
> 10 p.m. if necessary.
>
> The mothers are fully conscious of, and thankful for, these advantages,
> and know that they would not get such treatment for their children elsewhere
> for twice the money charged at the Crèche. The foundations of good health
> and improved life for children are truly worthy objects for charitable help.[104]

Few other laundresses could have been as fortunate as those whose children attended this nursery; references to nurseries are sparse, and most of these do not occur until the end of the nineteenth century. It was only in 1906 that a campaign was launched in Acton—by this date the center of London's laundry industry—headed by Councillor E. F. Hunt, chairman of Acton's Public Health Committee, to lobby Parliament to pass enabling legislation to assist municipalities to establish and maintain crèches. In 1908, the campaign resulted in the establishment, under philanthropic auspices, of an Acton day nursery that was soon expanded and imitated in other London communities.[105]

Baby-sitting was probably the most common occupation of working-class children between the ages of seven and twelve, for employing outsiders could prove costly. Rates charged by landladies and neighbors to care for young children ranged from about four pence to eight pence per child per day, plus one pence extra for each hour of overtime work or one pence for every three pence overtime earned by the mother.[106] Child-care costs could take an enormous bite out of a small wage. "One woman earning 11 shillings for four days' work paid 1 shilling, two pence a day (4 shillings, 8 pence) to a neighbour for the minding of her two small children; another whose earnings ranged from 11 shillings to 14 shillings paid a day nursery . . . (3 shillings, 7 pence)."[107] High prices did not guarantee the laundress quality care for her children. One report concluded that the typical care given for four pence to eight pence per day to the children of West London laundry workers was far from adequate.

> The persons who have charge of the laundresses' children are generally aged people, living in squalor, and frequently it has been found that an elderly woman has had the charge of as many as seven or eight children in one dirty, little, unventilated room. The children, moreover, are very much left to chance; they have no proper or regular feeding; and the food given them is more often than not unwholesome. The result has been in Acton an exceedingly high mortality of infants under one year of age, directly attributable to the farming out of infants.[108]

With such costs, both fiscal and physical, for the care of preschool age children one is not surprised to discover that a laundress's older children, when not employed in laundry, household, and child-care tasks, were to be found playing in the soiled linen, perilously close to unguarded machinery, or unsupervised in the streets. "The children don't know what a mother is," lamented one laundress of her own children.[109] The laundress's children were pushed not only into the streets but also early to school. In

1912, it was alleged that in the poorer districts of London more children were in elementary schools at the noncompulsory ages of three to five than in the succeeding years of five to seven.[110] The inability to afford proper child care could have tragic or very nearly tragic results, as Eliza Warren discovered when she and a friend saved from drowning a child left alone with his small sister because his washerwoman mother could not afford the tuppence in advance demanded by a neighbor.[111] What it was like to be a laundress's child was described to Henry Mayhew by a young coster:

> Mother used to be out early washing in families—anything for a living. She was a good mother to us. We was left at home with the key of the room and some bread and butter for dinner. . . . She used to be at work from six in the morning till ten o'clock at night, which was a long time for a child's belly to hold out again, and when it was dark we would go and lie down on the bed and try to sleep until she came home with the food. I was eight year old then.[112]

Other mothers lost the struggle to care for their children and had to place them in the workhouse, or allow them to be placed as servants or sent as child immigrants to the colonies.

Poverty could place almost insuperable problems in the way of those who tried to be good parents. For poverty meant not only the mother's prolonged absence from home but driving the children from the home prematurely to support themselves or encouraging them to provide another contribution to the family income. Overwork often meant impatient, insensitive, and occasionally violent parents, with neither the time nor the energy to devote to their children. A. E. Coppard describes the change that poverty and destitution wrought in his laundress mother:

> In her widowhood my mother became something of a martinet; she had no time to be kind, my father's death having sunk us at once into destitution. At times she was subject to fits of wild maniacal laughter, at others to torrents of tears. In between she was always fighting against the persistent outwearing of every piece of clothing or boot we possessed, as well as the inevitable neglect we, her four youngsters, and the domesticity suffered from her twelve hour daily absence at a laundry where she had had to start out as a plain ironer . . . at twenty-seven pence a day.[113]

The pressure of poverty could also mean that infants were sometimes born to mothers who were unable to prepare for their arrival with adequate rest, nourishment, or medical care, and that babies were too soon separated from their mothers. Poor laundresses often worked right up until their confinements, as an Acton doctor recalled:

> 'One year I attended at least two hundred confinements, and, as these poor women were mostly employed at a laundry, they often remained at work too long.
>
> I always went immediately I was called and to my knowledge saved many a life by my prompt attention as, owing to their occupation and long hours of standing, these poor souls were very liable to dangerous sequelae.'[114]

While it seems that many laundresses made every effort to continue suckling their newborns, a great many returned to full-time waged labor before their babies were many weeks old. The Christian Social Union, as a result of an investigation of women engaged in home industries and in casual or irregular employment such as laundrywork and charring, learned that "a majority of women carry on their employment right up to the time of confinement," and resume working from ten to fourteen days after childbirth.[115] Factory inspectors were not able to intervene when women worked at home, but they did try to enforce the law prohibiting the employment of new mothers in workshops within four weeks of giving birth. However, prosecutions of laundries were rarely pursued because most of the violations that inspectors discovered were the result not of grasping employers but of the most biting poverty. A typical example was cited by an inspector in her annual report (1907):

> Presently I saw the baby arrive in the ironing room for the mother to nurse in the dinner-hour, being carried by Mrs. A's eldest girl, aged 12. I could not find that the woman had any food for herself, and all the circumstances of the case were infinitely sad. Mrs. A's husband was a labourer with no regular trade and had been out of work for the last two or three years. The only work he had recently done had been a 12 weeks' job under the Queen's Unemployed Fund at Chingford, and that had ceased about three weeks after the birth of the baby. Mrs. A. was aged 32 and had five children.[116]

When an infant's mother toiled at home, its hard-working mother lacked the time or energy to provide it with much stimulation or exercise and was "constantly tempted to give soothing syrups" to ensure periods of uninterrupted work.[117] Despite the many odds against laundresses, Clementina Black, in her study of married women's work, noted that "the immense majority were evidently . . . industrious decent women who were good mothers."[118]

Family and Social Life

Although laundry work was in some respects compatible with the domestic circumstances of married women, it could also have disruptive consequences for working-class family life. Intensive involvement in laundry work could alter the very structure of the working-class family. In particular, the importance of a wife's wage-labor in the family economy must have led inevitably to a blurring and sometimes a reversal of traditional marital roles. Working-class men normally dominated their households: they usually received a disproportionate share of food (often the only meat), clothing, and leisure—an allocation of resources that was justified by the family's dependence on the man's labor for their survival.[119] The authority of the working-class male was based primarily on his role as the principal breadwinner. However, seasonal or irregular work, inadequate earnings, or unemployment resulting from any number of causes could produce not only poverty but a loss of self-esteem and a despair, dulled now and then by bravado and the courage gained by drunkenness. Sometimes, as the husband's authority withered, so too did his initiative for finding work and his sense of an obligation to provide for his family.

Chronic underemployment and persistent seasonal unemployment explained the inactivity of many laundresses' spouses. Nonetheless, for a minority—a minority whose numbers were probably exaggerated by contemporaries—their wives' steady earnings undermined their determination to find other work. The literature about the laundry trade is full of allegations from middle-class as well as a few working-class observers that some husbands felt little obligation—at least after they discovered the abundance of the opportunities for laundry work—to "take money 'ome." Throughout all of North Kensington, for instance, it was said to be a local proverb that "the best ironer gets the worst husband." A local clergyman observed to Charles Booth that "to marry a laundress was as good as a fortune," while the Royal Commission on the Poor Laws was told in 1909 that "it is well known amongst the poor that men move to North Kensington for the purpose of being kept by their wives."[120] A union organizing meeting held in the same district recognized that "no class of women workers supported husbands more than the laundry-women did" and used this economic reality as an argument for unionization as a measure to improve wages.[121] Kensington was by no means the only area in which laundresses were found to be the family's main breadwinners; in Bath there were said to be "large numbers of idle men . . . who live upon the earnings of their wives. The wife takes in washing or mending, or goes out to wash—and by her exertions supports her husband and three or four children."[122] In Oxford, the washtub was the support of many a family and in one author's view produced "laziness and demoralization on the part of the man"; in nearby Headington Quarry laundry work, a major village industry, frequently took the place of male earnings as the family mainstay.[123] In some districts, the "laundresses' husband" was said to be almost a recognized profession, a view supported by the testimony of laundresses themselves. "My ole man ain't much good. I've got to keep him, it's true as he is too lazy to do any work hisself," reported one woman, while another testified to the Royal Commission on Labour that in Acton "nothing would induce the men to work in many cases, and their wives were obliged to go out."[124]

It is likely that in some families responsibility for paying the bills might have been allotted according to the ability to pay of family wage earners. In a suburban district where a huge amount of laundry work was done, a nurse familiar with the area observed that "it has become the established custom that the husbands pay only the rent and the baker's bill and buy the boots."[125] Similar economic bargains were probably struck in many laundry families. When the husband was unemployed, the bargain took on another aspect: if he could not find "man's work," there was still plenty of "women's work"—unwaged domestic work—to be done. Occasionally, husbands unemployed for months at a time might exchange places as housekeepers with their wives or, more commonly, mind the children while their wives worked.[126] Men infrequently cared for very tiny infants during the day but often attended to somewhat older children at mealtimes or baby-sat the sleeping children while their mothers washed clothes far into the night. One consumptive husband with five children, ranging in age from nine months to sixteen years, "was a devoted parent, who among other services, cooked midday meals for all his children."[127] Just as in many working-class households a wife assisted her husband in his work (for example, "shoemaker's wife" could be as much an occupational as a social designation), so too in many laundress's households a husband worked a half-day or two a week for his wife.

Many laundresses were tough and resourceful and, in the opinion of one witness before the Royal Commission on Labour, "the most independent people on the face of the earth."[128] One way in which laundresses expressed their independence was by sometimes demanding the right to begin work when it best suited their domestic circumstances, by slowing work to maxi-

mize overtime, and frequently by raw language and assertive demeanor.
Ted Willis, in his autobiography, describes the women who worked in the
laundry on the street where he grew up as a "tough and raucous lot."[129]
Toughness could often be an economic necessity for the laundress. If a
woman ran her own laundry business, a good business head was as important as good ironing technique if a profit was to be realized. A laundrywoman sometimes had to be an assertive debt collector: "When we got to
Mrs. Moody's in Thames Street," reported the daughter of a laundress,
"we wedged our feet in the front door lest it be shut in our faces without
the washing money; and our emotions were divided between the agonizing
uncertainty of Mrs. Moody's finances and the inexpressible relief of the day
behind us."[130]

Laundresses also had a reputation for hard drinking: they drank in the
pub, at home, at work, in the street; the "liquid lunch" was as much their
habit as that of the modern executive. "As a matter of fact," commented
one observer of women's work in 1894, "drunkenness appears to be more
common among London laundresses than among barmaids."[131] Their work
was at least as conducive to the comfort of drink as was that of the brickmaker, stoker, or coal heaver. The drinking habits of laundry workers were
encouraged by the hot and heavy nature of their work, by long hours, and
by the long-standing tradition of part payment in beer.

The following example illuminates the working environment in which
beer was perceived as being fully as necessary as soapsuds:

> On the mantlepiece stand half empty glasses, and the smell of stale beer is
> added to the other odours. The women, as they work, literally drip with heat.
> Amid such surroundings crowds of them pass their daily life. Here they
> stand, day after day, for hours ranging from ten to fifteen. They keep up their
> flagging strength with beer, which is sometimes supplied in addition to wages,
> but more often bought cheap and retailed dear by the proprietor. The habit of
> taking it is encouraged on account of the increased speed to which, for a
> time, it stimulates the women. It is not surprising that among laundresses
> intemperance is the rule, that the morality of the half brutalized toilers is
> below the average, that the women themselves speak of the life as "murder-
> ous," and often return home, "past eating, standing, or thinking," that rheu-
> matism is common, consumption a not uncommon complaint amongst
> them.[132]

The reasons laundresses drank extended beyond remuneration in beer,
and their drinking extended well beyond working hours. Saddled with the
primary responsibility of family support, these women demanded the tra-

ditional breadwinner's perquisite of the pleasures of the public house. Her home, her workplace, and her toil were as miserable as any in the working-class community; her economic power enabled the laundress to do her drinking openly rather than joining the "stair-head drinking clubs" of women excluded from the public house. The price of a pint bought tempo-rary psychological respite from harsh material reality: "Life took on a different look in the warm smell of fresh beer and sawdust; the gaslights turned full on, and everybody being friendly, at ease, and telling secrets to one another, and confidences . . . and she sighs with a sort of content-ment, and sips her beer, and there are six or seven hours between her and the scrubbing brush tomorrow."[133] It has become conventional historical wisdom, at least since the publication of Brian Harrison's *Drink and the Victorians,* to explain the working man's drinking habits in terms of an escape from domestic wretchedness: he fled from a cold hearth, a sparsely furnished and disagreeable home, squalling infants, and an argumentative spouse to the creature comforts of warmth, light, recreation, and sociabil-ity dispensed by the public house along with its inebriating product. The laundrywoman shared these needs. If throughout most of Victorian England the drinking place was indisputably a "masculine republic,"[134] in some laundry districts it became feminized: a Saturday night in Notting Dale found

> The beerhouse at the corner full; more women than men inside; much talk-ing but no drunkenness; hatless women with white aprons, rough hair and bare arms, with shawls round their shoulders. As they met the cold air com-ing out, two of them seemed first to realize that they had taken too much, and clutched at one another's shawls for support. . . . At St. Anne's Road and Latimer Road the first brawl, between a man and a woman—both drunk, being kept apart and sent home with great tact by a policeman. . . . In St. Anne's Road three young women of the laundry type, singing, arm-in-arm, reeling noisily drunk; one with a small baby in her arms . . . another woman drunk and noisy, and a few men equally drunk, but quiet, lurching home-wards.[135]

The liberal use of alcohol was further encouraged by consumer conserv-atism: householders demanded that laundry be picked up on Monday or early Tuesday and returned late Friday or Saturday, an expectation that produced enforced idlensss at the beginning of the week and overwork at the end. In keeping with this cycle, laundrywomen turned to drink on Mondays; in a sense, the laundering habits of the English bourgeoisie institutionalized "St. Monday" for thousands of washerwomen and ironers. If this was not enough, the predelictions of laundrywomen were rein-forced all too frequently by the routines of their spouses, whose work in brickyards and gasworks involved habits of drinking both at their strenu-ous work and in their seasonal idleness, which encouraged the drinking of the family laundry worker. One witness, a laundry proprietor, commented to the Royal Commission on Labour: "In Acton the women all drank but they worked; the men drank and did not work."[136]

In a small way, the laundress demonstrates the connection between social roles and economic power: where her work was peripheral, her social status in the family changed but little; where it was an important part of a dovetailed family economy, her social position moved closer to some sem-blance of equality with her husband; and where her labor was central and where her consciousness of her position was reinforced by the presence of many other women similarly placed, she could become socially dominant within her household. An entry recorded in the 1851 census is indicative of the domestic reality in many laundry workers' households. It reads:

> Jane—wife, head of the family, mangling woman, John—husband, turns my mangle.[137]

When a laundress kept her spouse, she had the power to terminate the bargain, and the threat to do so or mockery of the man's dependent status could lead to brawls—such as those that seemed to be so common in the laundry-dominated community of Notting Dale.[138] Most laundresses were driven to work by necessity; many deplored the necessity of going out to work; others, when asked (which was rarely), expressed pleasure in their occupation; some, valuing their independence, would probably have agreed with the woman who told one investigator: "A shilling you earn yourself is worth two given you by a man."[139] Because their work was onerous and often unpleasant, it should not be assumed that at least some of them did not take pride in the whiteness of their wash, in the sheen to which a shirtfront could be polished, in the beauty of a well-ironed and highly starched bit of finery, or in the ability to keep their families together and out of the workhouse by their own toil.

CHAPTER 2

————— ❧ —————

Regulating the Trade

The Political Climate

From 1895 to 1920 a series of legislative acts included the laundry trade within the compass of British public policy. These legislative initiatives, as much as the process of mechanization and the capitalization of the labor process, were to assist in the transformation of the laundry trade from a hand trade into a modern predominantly industrial enterprise. In the early 1930s, H. Llewellyn Smith wrote: "It may well be doubted whether in the same period any industry has undergone so great a transformation as has the laundry industry since the time of Charles Booth's original inquiry. The whole standard of the trade has been so raised, and the character of the workers and their working conditions have so improved that the laundry world of 1930 is as different from the laundry world of 1896 as could well be imagined."[1] By 1930, laundry workers could expect their labor to be accorded the status of any other industrial service sector employment. They could expect their working environment to be subject to regulations designed to help assure their health and safety, their hours of work to be subject to limitations similar to those of other occupations, and their wages to be maintained above legal minimum standards. For employers, legislative controls meant that the trade could no longer be branded a "sweated industry," stigmatized as a trade dominated by slatternly and often drunken workers and employers, or as a haphazard domestic by-employment; and, most important, uniform regulations helped to eliminate competition from unscrupulous entrepreneurs who had exploited their workers in order to undercut the prices of more ethical employers. Stimulation of investment by the industry in modernization was one conspicuous result of uniform regulation. Industrial change and legislative change were interwoven: here for the sake of analytical clarity they have been disentangled. (The process of mechanization and the changes it made in the laundress's work are discussed in chapter 5.) For the consumer, legislation provided an assurance that his or her laundry was washed and prepared in a sanitary and orderly environment. In the laundry trade, this dramatic transformation was not the consequence of systematic and straightforward progression; rather, it was brought about only after a long and tortuous struggle between the forces of reaction and reform in Victorian and Edwardian England. To unravel this tangled skein is the main objective of this, and the following, chapter.

It would be a mistake, however, to view the movement toward the regulation of the laundry trade in isolation, as a technical process of improvement, inspection, and public control, the significance of which was confined within a single industry. The changes that came about in laundries were part of a much broader spectrum of social reform which formed an impressive array of experimental social legislation. These measures were one outcome of changing ideas concerning the responsibility of the state for the welfare of its citizens. The period from the later nineteenth century until about 1920, and in particular the Liberal administration from 1906 to 1914, can be characterized as the critical foundation phase in the evolution of British social policy. These were years during which insurance against ill-health and unemployment, old age pensions, medical services, and school meals for children were introduced, years which saw a major campaign against "sweating" both in and out of Parliament, the fixing of minimum wages in some of these industries, and some attempt made to alter the distribution of income and wealth in society. It was also a time when part of the infrastructure of social administration was either put in place or expanded. The Department of Labour, for example, was formed in 1893 as "an Intelligence Department in all matters relating to labour" to provide the empirical data to guide the decisions of policymakers, while at the same time the increased Home Office Factory and Workshop inspectorate (including women for the first time from 1893) improved the effectiveness of measures enacted in the labor field. This wide range of social policy initiatives comprised what many historians have seen as the origins of the "welfare" or "social service" state.[2]

The factors behind this sudden flowering of social legislation are complex and interdependent: their relative importance remains a subject for debate among historians. One can examine the attitudes of members of Parliament and find, for example, influential Liberals such as Sir Charles Dilke, Lloyd George, and Winston Churchill whose advocacy of social reform was motivated in part by ideals of a future society in which the worst ravages of poverty would be eliminated. Looking closer one finds that similar ideals were shared by men on the other side of the House, particularly by supporters of the Labour Representation Committee (among whom J. Ramsay MacDonald was most prominent). Many other-wise bitter foes could be found joining forces—with each other, with trade unionists, or philanthropists, or feminists—in extraparliamentary lobbies such as the Anti-Sweating League or the Women's Industrial Council, which publicized abuses and lobbied for changes in social policy. Most historians would concede that to a significant degree social reform was a response to "pressure from below." Various measures were introduced and supported to curry electoral favor among now-enfranchised workingmen, to act as an antidote to socialism, to head off Labour-Liberal polarization or to prevent social unrest—as well as from motives of altruism.[3] The physical state of the working class provided another sort of impetus: pres-sure to improve the nation's health status in the interests of imperial pride—and better fed cannon fodder—produced policy initiatives (again often across party lines) geared to enhancing infant and maternal nutrition and child health, and assessing the impact of women's labor on domestic conditions and child care. As Richard Titmuss, one of the pioneering students of social policy and administration, wisely put it, "Welfare can serve different masters. . . . A multitude of sins can be committed in its appealing name. It can be used as a means of social control. It can be used as an instrument of economic growth which, by benefitting a minority, indirectly promotes greater inequality."[4] To puzzle our way through the knotted skein of early British social policy, it is useful to direct our atten-tion to a single strand. The laundry trade can provide an interesting case study to examine the interplay of individuals, social ideals, and pragmatic politics in the formulation of public policy.

Social reform would not have become a conspicuous feature of this per-iod in British history had increased information not stimulated concern about issues such as poverty, sweated labor, infant mortality, and women's work. During the last two decades of the nineteenth century, public atten-tion was directed increasingly toward the position of the poor and the conditions of work of the laboring people. The economic crisis of the mid-1880s created new concern about unemployment, and the pioneering social investigations of Charles Booth and B. Seebohm Rowntree that grew out of this anxiety exposed the cyclical, structural, and seasonal nature of much unemployment and demonstrated that putting aside funds for a 'rainy day' or a secure old age was an impossibility for most laboring people. These studies created for the first time (with the partial exception of Maynew's work in the 1850s) the data base necessary for meaningful discussion and policy formulation. In the view of Beatrice Webb, Charles Booth's investigation of London life and labor in which she participated stood out "as a landmark alike in social politics and in economic science. Prior to this inquiry, neither the individualist nor the Socialist could state with any approach to accuracy what exactly was the condition of the people of Great Britain."[5] She might have added that these studies served as a training ground for many of the civil servants and social activists who played an important role in the reforms of the period. Clara Collet's investigation of employment conditions in women's trades in East London, for example, stimulated interest in home work and women's trades, particularly those outside the range of factory and workshop legislation, and led to her appointment as one of four female commissioners to the Royal Commission on Labour and as Lady Correspondent to the newly formed Department of Labour in 1893.[6] From this approach also came the stimulus to the formation of the Women's Industrial Council, which set out in 1894 to document conditions in women's trades, to influence public opinion, to lobby for legislation to overcome masculine indifference to women's interests, and thereby to improve employment for females of the laboring classes. By 1913, the council had investigated 117 trades and provided expert testimony at numerous Royal Commissions and parliamentary committees.[7] The social initiatives of the period were pragmatic: they were based upon descriptive data that exposed problems in previously ill-documented occupations (particularly those in the rapidly growing service sector, such as retail shops, offices, and laundries) but also drew heavily on foreign examples of reform legislation. Germany, France, and New Zealand in particular provided legislative models for pension, unemployment, minimum wage, and factory legislation.

The prospect of an increased government regulatory role in the economy stimulated intellectual confrontation in a number of areas: between laissez-faire liberals and socialists, between feminists who sought economic and social equality and those "social feminists" who advocated protective legislation for women, between trade unionists who rejected increased government interference in the workplace and those who welcomed it, between those who thought that workshops in charitable institutions should be subject to inspection and those who thought they should be exempt, and between proponents of universal welfare measures and those who felt that government aid must be limited by means tests. Consumers, employees, and workers all debated the impact that individual measures of social reform were having, or were likely to have, on their own self-interest. The process of social reform was enormously complex. It must be examined in the context of late Victorian and Edwardian society, but the process should also be seen as part of the wider response of democratic governments to economic transformation. Most reformers wished to achieve social betterment within the framework of the existing capitalist system. Yet such reforms were brought about with the cooperation of those who advocated more fundamental economic and social change.

Through a study of the laundry trade, it is possible to isolate the pressures, personalities, and constraints involved in bringing about improvement and standardization of working conditions, safety, hours, and wages in one rapidly changing service sector occupation. By concentrating on a single industry, the attitudes of consumers, employers, and workers to successive legislative initiatives, an aspect of social reform that has received to date little scholarly consideration, can be examined. Finally, the implementation of changes in this predominantly female industry can reveal the interaction between middle-class and working-class women in the campaign for industrial improvement. With these questions in mind we can now turn our attention to the history of the regulation of the laundry trade.

The Struggle for Reform

Most of the laundry trade had been omitted—apparently unintentionally—from the terms of the 1867 Factory and Workshop Act. This act, by confining its attention to the preparation of articles "for sale," excluded from regulation all laundry work except that performed when new goods were prepared for the market. This inadvertent exclusion made the struggle to include the trade within the scope of factory and workshop legislation much more difficult in later years when new forces allied themselves with laissez-faire groups hostile to government intervention. In 1876, the Royal Commission on the Factory Acts, recognizing the anomaly in the law, recommended "that the definition of work to be regulated by the Act should include labour in or incidental to the washing, cleaning, or furbishing [of] any article."[8] At this time, however, opposition was so strenuous to any attempt to control the industry that no action was taken to implement the commission's suggestion. Owners of both steam laundries, which had begun to appear in small numbers in the 1850s and 1860s, and the much more numerous small, nonmechanized establishments joined together to oppose any enactment. Those with large laundries argued that the fluctuations endemic to the trade made it inappropriate to confine working hours to a uniform pattern, while those with small businesses, often situated in haphazardly adapted premises, feared the expense of meeting common standards.[9] On a general level, the commission heard evidence from individualists protesting "any interference with adult labour."[10] Factory legislation, by limiting the employee's freedom to sell her or his labor, they reasoned, actually harmed the worker's interests. It was alleged, both in Parliament and before the Royal Commission, that legal restriction of women's labor had particularly detrimental effects and a vigorous campaign was waged in committee by Henry Fawcett and other likeminded M.P.s "to omit the word woman" from the various clauses of the 1878 Factory and Workshop Act.[11] These women's rights advocates inferred that the impact of past government regulation had been to deny women workers their rightful opportunities: the law had discouraged their employment, had reduced the value of their labor, and had indirectly encouraged prostitution.[12] In 1877, a factory inspector flatly rejected the "monstrous assertion" that factory law "affords encouragement to vice and prostitution," citing evidence that in the industry where women's work was most stringently restricted—textile manufacturing—the proportion of women employed had steadily increased as had the level of their wages.[13]

The inspector's opinion, however, did not carry the weight and influence that adhered to the women's rights lobby, a pressure group that, especially from the 1870s, made its position widely known in the press, in Parliament, and, for a time, in organizations fostering women's unionization. The animosity of feminists, employers, and the broader laissez-faire lobby—abetted by the weakness and lack of organization of the forces favorable to legislation—ensured that the laundry trade continued as unfettered as before. After some years of an uneasy truce, the controversy raged again in 1891 over the desirability of enacting restrictions on women's hours and conditions of work. Factory laundries had become sufficiently numerous by the last decade of the century—in the metropolis at least—and sweated conditions so notorious in laundries large and small, mechanized and nonmechanized, that renewal of the debate over regulation was virtually inevitable.

The literature of the nineteenth-century women's movement richly documents the efforts of middle-class women to establish a place for themselves in the labor market.[14] In order to expand the range of creative and remunerative endeavor open to them, bourgeois women had to extricate themselves from middle-class assumptions: from the view that only two careers were appropriate for women—dutiful wife and nurturing mother; from the conviction that the home furnished the fullest scope for women's abilities; and from the notion that a "lady" should lead a sheltered life. Inspired by the nascent women's movement but frequently driven by material need, middle-class women sought to eliminate economic barriers, particularly those that made most professions a male monopoly. Their advocacy of women's legitimate claims developed as a corollary of contemporary liberal thought. In the social and political sphere, feminists combined the political liberalism of Mary Wollstonecraft, Harriet Taylor, and John Stuart Mill with the economic liberalism of Adam Smith to plead for their rights in the marketplace. The forces of the market, without paternalistic restrictions, should determine who gained work, under what conditions, and during what hours. The route to fiscal security, these women believed, was through equality not protection; for them laissez-faire meant freedom not exploitation.

The goal of equality between the sexes, while it could forge a strong bond among all women, created difficulties when that common goal was assumed to imply identical means of achieving it. "The mistake," reflected a contemporary, "that some [middle-class feminists] . . . have made is in transferring their own grievance to a class whose troubles are little known and less understood by them; in supposing that while they pine to spend themselves in some 'intolerable toil of thought,' Mary Brown or Jane Smith should also pine to spend herself in fourteen hours a day washing or tailoring."[15] Feminism and class interests produced tensions amenable to no easy synthesis. Further, the intensifying suffrage campaign created a dichotomy between feminists who put political equality first and the so-called social feminists who stressed the critical importance of labor reform. The laundry worker was very much at the center of this ineluctable, often bitter, even corrosive debate—debate that was at the core of feminist activism and is both a critical part of the social history of laundry work and at the same time an important case study in the history of feminism.

With the vigorous campaign in the 1890s to have the laundry trade included within the scope of factory legislation came a heightening of the differences between those feminists who thought that women's labor should be free of inegalitarian restrictions and those who believed that the most disadvantaged workers needed the assistance of law to assure them of a decent working environment. We can usefully begin by first considering some examples of feminist opposition to legal regulation of laundry work. E. J. Boucherett, for instance, who had been concerned for many years with the female industrial labor force, argued that restrictive legislation had driven women's wages down. Rather than inhibit all women for the benefit of a few it was better, she thought, "that a few delicate persons suffer in health than that hundreds should be exposed to the misery of being turned out of work."[16] In 1891, at the height of assertive lobbying for laundry regulation, Boucherett, along with Helen Blackburn, the co-editor of the *Englishwoman's Review,* founded the Women's Employment Defence League (which became in 1897 the Freedom of Labour Defence Association) to mobilize opinion against any extension of the Factory Acts. (Earlier bodies acting as pressure groups for women's work—such as the Society for Promoting the Employment of Women, which Boucherett had helped to found in 1859[17]—had focused principally on expanding opportunities for middle-class women.) Blackburn and Boucherett, as laissez-faire liberals, were suspicious of trade unionism in general and as feminists they were convinced that male unionists, who supported women's organizations that demanded legislative restrictions or equal pay, were acting from self-interested motives. Boucherett argued that extending the Factory Acts to laundries would mean the displacement of female labor by a combination of male labor and machines. Men were frequently employed in the washhouses of the steam laundries that by the 1890s represented an increasingly significant segment of the industry. She predicted that legislation would wipe out the small cottage laundry, leaving only "steam laundries, being worked by men, with only a small number of women ironers."[18] Employing logic that would be jarring to a Victorian textile worker as well as to a modern feminist, she accepted as self-evident that men were more suited to manage steam engines and thus would be preferred for work with power-driven laundry machinery. "It is said that in Glasgow alone," she added, "if Mr. Asquith's Bill became law, it would lead to the closing of such a number of small laundries that four or five thousand girls would be thrown out of employment. If only half of these were thrown out of work, it would still be a fearful thing."[19]

It was little wonder, then, that some men encouraged petitions, rallies, and resolutions in favor of laundry legislation. Their efforts, Boucherett alleged, misled the public and politicians about the true sentiments of laundry workers. As an example she drew attention to one meeting, cited in the press as having carried "by an immense majority" a resolution in favor of restricting the hours of laundresses, which was in reality a fraud; it had been dominated numerically by men and half of the small number of laundresses in attendance had voted against the resolution.[20] The provision of the 1891 Factory and Workshop Act, which proposed to make it illegal for an employer to "knowingly employ a woman within four weeks of her confinement," was perceived by laissez-faire feminists not as a measure that would guarantee a minimum level of welfare but as another attempt to put women at a disadvantage by labeling them as the weaker sex. This restriction would result, they believed, in the starvation of vast numbers of laundrywomen. "What is to become of these women," demanded Eunice Lipton, secretary of the Laundrywomen's Cooperative Association, "who are mostly breadwinners, if they are prevented from working for a month, God alone knows. I don't know." The unmarried mother would be driven to further degradation, Millicent Fawcett predicted, and widows and deserted wives would be forced to look to the Poor Law for assistance; while Dr. Garrett Anderson was of the opinion that "many women who work hard all their lives are quite able to work in less than a month after confinement, and whether they are or not, they ought to be left entirely to decide for themselves."[21] Feminist hostility to this provision did not stop its being passed but it did help to keep laundryworkers outside the terms of the 1891 Factory Act.

Suffragist arguments were also brought to bear against legislation for laundresses. It was inappropriate, declared Mr. C. B. Stuart Wortley, M. P. for Sheffield and strong supporter of women's rights causes, for Parliament to enact measures for an unenfranchised class. (His argument conveniently ignored the implications for all the prior measures which had done just that.) "The time to say whether this legislation [to control the laundry trade] was justified or was founded upon the great bulk of public opinion of those whom it principally affected would arrive," he announced in the House of Commons, "when, and not until, the House extended the Parliamentary franchise to women."[22] Feminists' appeal to the fundamental liberal principle of no legislation without representation was paralleled by their invocation of the stolidly individualistic axiom of a person's right to control her or his own destiny. Legislation limiting the laundry employee's right to work was seen as a clear violation of this axiom. Helen Blackburn pointed to the necessity of making distinctions among the various elements of factory legislation. It was, she thought, laudable to support initiatives that required employers to safeguard the health and safety of workers through such measures as fencing of machinery or improving ventilation since these were matters beyond the direct control of the worker; it was also acceptable to impose some limitation on the employment of minors as they were not as yet "legally free agents," but it was essential to resist "arbitrary restrictions placed by law on the self-regarding actions of persons of mature years and sound mind."[23] The law could turn virtue into vice. Under Factory Act regulation, the diligent efforts of the poor laundress to support herself and her family by working as long and as hard as her strength allowed, "hitherto regarded as a virtue," would now be "turned into an offence."[24]

In 1893, the Women's Industrial Defence Committee, another women's rights pressure group, issued a widely quoted report that illuminates quite effectively the range of arguments brought to bear against laundry regulation. Laundresses, the report stressed, were "an independent set of women . . . quite able to take care of themselves;" the skilled and intelligent (ironers and packers principally) were opposed to any extension of the Factory Acts that might affect their labors; and furthermore, the report went on, the woman without a character, the woman given to drink, as well as the married woman with a sick or unemployed husband, "all find their chief chance of honest earning at the washtub" and no legislative obstacles should be put in their way. Laundresses, the committee emphasized, liked irregular hours and needed to work as many hours as possible. Furthermore, in their view, long hours and poor conditions were less taxing in the "easy and pleasant" social atmosphere of the small laundry than in a factory. Finally, the expense of complying with regulations requiring the fencing of machinery, improved ventilation, and other arrangements would sound the death-knell of small laundries and thus further restrict employment.[25] Misguided welfare legislation, these feminists argued, could have tragic consequences for many laundresses. Seen from this viewpoint, survival-of-the-fittest capitalism meant opportunity not oppression.

The committee's approach, in common with many others, implied that an absence of legislation would reverse or slow the trend toward mechanization in the industry. Despite their advocacy of laissez-faire, many of these protesters betrayed a profound uneasiness about industrial change— and an element of traditionalism in their assessment of the labor of working-class women. In their defense of individualism, initiative, and self-help, many feminists tended, perhaps unconsciously, to downplay or reject structural changes in the economy that might undermine the power of these values. Productive work unhampered by legal restriction was the goal of middle-class women in professional employment; to transfer these values to their support of working-class women was natural, if somewhat misguided. Organizations such as the Women's Industrial Defence Committee, along with the Laundresses Cooperative Union, and prominent suffragists like Millicent Fawcett and Ada Heather-Bigg, supported by a few men including the member for Hammersmith (a constituency with a great many laundries), and a private citizen who owned slum properties in an area where many small laundries were located mobilized petitions against laundry legislation. The most significant of the petitions presented to the House was signed by 2,115 persons (of whom it was claimed that 1,878 were workers), protesting against the inclusion of a laundry clause in the 1895 Factory and Workshop Act.[26] Meetings in defense of leaving laundries unrestricted were held at several locations in London, where it was argued that any limitation on hours would impose great hardships on "the poor widow and lone woman who manage to earn a scanty living that enabled her to keep out of the workhouse."[27] Everywhere the petitioners and speakers argued that it was their aim "to protect industrial workers, especially women workers, from the imposition of legal restrictions which would diminish their earning capacity, limit their personal freedom, and inconvenience them in their work."[28] The depth of the feminist feeling of many launderers and property owners may be somewhat suspect—even the independent laundrywoman's primary parliamentary defender prefaced his remarks about the plight of the poor widowed laundress by ingenuously announcing that "he had been requested by several laundries in his constituency to do what he could to prevent their inclusion in this Bill."[29]

Opposition to legal limits also came from women who devoted their careers to the welfare of working women. One such woman was Emma Paterson, ardent suffragist and founder of the Women's Protective and Provident League (later the Women's Trade Union League), which worked for unionization and self-help among women, particularly those in sweated trades. In the view of one male unionist she was "the only great woman the English Labour Movement . . . produced."[30] Paterson, while favoring the Factory Acts as far as they dealt with the restriction of child labor and the enforcement of good sanitary conditions, was convinced that the limitation of women's hours of work was prejudicial to their opportunities for employment. So strong were her convictions that she appeared before the Royal Commission on the Factory Acts in 1876 to advance her views and gave publicity to similar stances in the *Women's Union Journal,* of which she was editor.[31] Paterson's enthusiasm helped in the creation of a laundress's union in Notting Hill,[32] but her individualism and domination of the female trade union movement was important in keeping this and other trades outside the compass of legislation until after her death in 1886. Edith Simcox, Paterson's chief lieutenant, in a paper on the "Organization of Women's Labour," read at the Trades Union Congress conference in 1875, condemned legislation that reduced wages by a reduction of hours.[33] Both women sought the improvement of working conditions through trade union action and feared that regulation limiting hours could induce a complacency damaging to unionization. Emma Paterson's dynamic leadership of the women's trade union movement helped to bring about the strange spectacle of socialists and individualists, workers and employers, feminists and traditionalists metaphorically linking arms in opposition to government regulation of the laundry trade.

On the other side of the debate, the campaign to aid laundresses in the 1890s marked an important shift in policy on the part of many reformers who had been working to organize women workers and alleviate sweated conditions. Unionization of unskilled women had proved a difficult and discouraging enterprise: unions shakily formed in times of industrial crisis melted away in periods of calm. (The problems involved in organizing laundry workers will be examined in chapter 4.) With its efforts to have laundry work placed under legislative protection, the organization at the center of this work, the Women's Trade Union League, now under the leadership of Emilia Dilke, acknowledged that it was only through the law that the first steps toward assisting the most exploited women in the workplace could be taken.[34] This shift away from the league's earlier laissez-faire policy (espoused during Emma Paterson's tenure of office) was a tacit recognition of these difficulties. Decent conditions, and in particular sensible hours of work, now seemed to many activists to be essential preconditions for reform—preconditions that had to be realized before any stable labor organization could be hoped for in the sweated industries. Most of the league's membership had concluded by the 1890s that "it is cruel mockery to preach Trade Unionism and Trade Unionism alone . . . to the laundrywoman standing at the tub eighteen hours at a stretch."[35] The league, buttressed by its parliamentary allies, notably Sir Charles Dilke, John Tennant, and John Burns, who labored for years on behalf of laundrywomen, was instrumental in gaining the appointment of female factory inspectors (the first was the league's treasurer, May Abraham [later Tennant]). The inspectors' findings, along with the results of an investigation of the trade undertaken by the league, the Fabians, and the Women's Industrial Council, provided the hard evidence regarding the state of employment in laundries throughout the country, and this evidence eventually convinced a majority of Parliament of the necessity of legislating for the trade. But it took more than the words of an inspector's report to push the weight of inertia.

The battle to regulate laundry work was long and tough. It was waged by means of deputations, surveys, and rallies to influence members of Parliament. Both sides argued that they had the best interests of laundrywomen at heart and sought out powerful adherents who could make their views seem most authoritative. Both the Laundresses' Cooperative Union, which resented any curtailment of their right to work, and the Amalgamated Society of Laundresses, which stressed the desire of their members to come under the Factory Acts, claimed the broad support of their fellow laundresses. The Amalgamated Society's ambitious and systematic survey of their peers produced results that lent weight to their efforts to convince uncommitted M.P.s. In 1891, the society canvassed 67,506 London laundresses, 65,939 of whom, it was alleged, were found to be in favor of the Factory Acts being applied to their occupation. The society published its results, itemized by district, listing the names of head canvassers in each area, and specifying the six aspects of the operation of the acts that were explained to laundresses before their views were solicited.[36] The value of the survey was enhanced, noted Gertrude Tuckwell, Secretary of the Women's Trade Union League, by the fact that it was taken "not by ladies, but by the laundresses themselves." Two years later a canvass of the laundries in Hammersmith, revealed "that the overwhelming opinion of the Laundresses in this thickly-populated district are in favour of inclusion."[37]

Effective surveys could yield valuable evidence, but they could not by themselves attract much public or press attention or create significant political pressure. What statistics could not do, lobbying and publicity might. In June 1891, an all-out campaign was initiated to try to force an inclusion of the trade within the Factory Act of that year. Laundry owners and managers were lobbied on the merits of legislation for themselves as well as their workers; small bands of laundresses met with employer after employer, assisted by the ladies (the term applied to middle-class female supporters) of the Women's Trade Union League, very often in company with its Secretary, May Abraham, a spirited organizer and agitator who made the plight of the laundresses her special cause.[38] Others marched to Parliament to lobby M.P.s and the Home Secretary, Henry Matthews.

Their activities attracted the notice of *The Times*: "During the past week a deputation has waited on 85 members of Parliament, with the view of gaining their adhesion to a movement which has been set on foot, for securing the extension of the Factory and Workshops Act to laundries and laundresses. Seventy-three of the 85 have promised their sympathy. . . ."[39]

On 14 June, the laundresses, in company with railway workers and with the support of the London Trades Council, mounted a joint "monster rally," which, having assembled on the Thames Embankment, marched 20,000 to 30,000 strong (according to press estimates) to Hyde Park. The laundresses, revealing a flair for publicity, colorfully advertised their views. Some laundrywomen harangued the crowd, others advertised their craft with displays of exquisitely "got up" finery, while still others provided practical demonstrations of their virtuousity with a variety of irons.[40] Three platforms were set up in the park by the laundresses from which speakers addressed those in attendance; and at each gathering the following resolution was carried simultaneously "amidst loud cheering:" "This mass meeting of laundresses and organized workpeople, having regard to the terribly bad sanitary conditions of a large number of laundries, the excessive hours of overtime worked by laundresses, and the exposure of women and girls to unfenced and dangerous machinery, calls upon the House of Commons to include laundries under the Factories and Workshops Act, and thereby extend to laundresses the same protection given to other female operatives."[41] The Women's Trade Union League was represented by May Abraham who chaired one of the platforms, but reformist support was much broader than this. Tom Mann urged the approval of male unionists for the laundresses' campaign, saying that there were a vast number of women "in this great city engaged in laundry work and compelled to labour under the most unhealthy conditions, some 14 hours a day, 15 hours a day, and even 18 hours a day," who deserved the support of men who had, perhaps, in the past "paid too little attention to the women." To clinch his case Mann added that the majority of these women were "widows of respectable mechanics" with families to support. Women union activists, such as the secretary of the Women Ropemakers' Association, who moved one of the laundry resolutions, came to stand beside their sisters. One of the most prominent adherents of the cause was the laundress's son, John Burns, who, to loud cheers, avowed that "he would rather be the possessor of that lineage than be the descendant of any baccarat-playing scoundrel."[42] Unfortunately, even the colorful John Burns was not enough to convince the home secretary to lend his government's weight to the laundresses' petition, and his cold response was roundly mocked by *Punch* both in caricature and verse.[43] The 1891 Factory Act passed without any mention of laundry work. But if the reformers had failed in their immediate objective, they had succeeded in attracting considerable interest to the plight of laundresses.

Information and Investigation

After 1891 the forces of social feminism turned to the investigative. In abandoning laissez-faire, the women's trade union movement came to recognize that the key to social reform lay in solid information. A government could only be expected to act when it had evidence to support its actions. An obvious opportunity presented itself with the appointment in 1891 of a Royal Commission to investigate the conditions of labor and to make proposals for necessary legislation. The fact that the commission failed to consider women's work seriously and apparently did not initially contemplate hearing women witnesses provoked a strong and immediate response. Emilia Dilke, in an article entitled "Women and the Royal Commission," contended that there was a special need for an inquiry into women's labor issues, including the proportion of married to unmarried women in such industries as laundry work. "All these points want special attention with a view to bringing out the physical consequences to the women themselves and the children born of them as well as the effect of their labour on current rates of wage in the industrial market," she argued.[44] In response to the agitation in March 1892, the commission appointed four female assistant commissioners: Eliza Orme, Clara Collet, May Abraham, and Margaret H. Irwin. Their work, *The Employment of Women,* which was published as part of the commission's findings, was praised as "the first attempt on the part of the Government, or any other agency to make a systematic inquiry in the conditions of women's industrial work in this country."[45] Theirs was not, however, an unqualified triumph. Beatrice Webb castigated the Royal Commission on Labour as a "lamentable fiasco" and, while noting that the women's report, along with that on agricultural labor, formed the most valuable portion of the findings, considered that the lady commissioners had been destined to failure by the enormous extent of their task. The four of them had been "directed to investigate the whole range of women's employment from one end of the kingdom to the other."[46] The appointment of female commissioners may have been tokenism, but it marked an important beginning for women workers, particularly those in unregulated industries.

Whatever the general limitations of *The Employment of Women,* laundry workers could be heartened by the pages Clara Collet devoted to their work. Her investigations focused on hand and steam laundries in London and provided the first thorough comparative documentation of conditions of work, wages, and the attitudes of both employers and workers to regulation. The great bulk of her evidence clearly pointed to the need for legislation. Her survey of steam laundries, for example, showed that daily hours of work in all of them were beyond the limits pertaining under existing factory enactment.[47] Her work stimulated an interest in ascertaining whether these London findings were replicated elsewhere. Another of the assistant commissioners, Margaret H. Irwin, acting for the Women's Protective and Provident League of Glasgow, conducted an investigation in 1893 of the conditions of work in Scottish laundries which substantially confirmed Collet's London data. On receiving Irwin's report the league's council concluded that "therefore, in the opinion of the Women's Protective and Provident League, there is an urgent necessity that laundries should, without delay, be brought under the Factory and Workshop Acts with a view to the limitation of the hours of labour, and the securing of healthy conditions in the buildings in which the work is carried on."[48]

They further resolved to request all trade societies and those concerned with the welfare of women and children to cooperate with them in urging the government to act. Through the pages of a government blue book and a trade union sponsored investigation, some of the horrendous conditions in laundries became more widely known. But the reports of royal commissions are all too often shelved and the reports of "interested" groups ignored. This information, therefore, might not have resulted in legislation had not a concern about laundry employment extended into the administrative arm of government, that is, into the civil service.

It is never easy—indeed, it is probably impossible—to make definitive judgments concerning the pressures that move legislators. However, any student of modern democratic governments will have observed the influence civil servants often exercise with their ministers. When the civil servant is charged with the duty of administering the political decisions of the legislature, he or she may frequently play a crucial role in helping to determine the detailed shape political initiatives may take. At times, as in the period considered here, when legislators are motivated by a unfocused desire to improve the living and working conditions of their fellow citizens, civil servants can help to transform a rather vague sentiment into a coherent operational form. In my view there is an evidential causal link between the personnel of the Home Office, in particular the factory inspectorate, and the evolution of laundry legislation. The year 1893 proved to be a meaningful one for laundrywomen—and all women workers. In this year, the Department of Labour was formed with a mandate to investigate working conditions. In June, the Home Office appointed the first two female factory inspectors and in November a local authority appointed its—and the country's—first two women sanitary inspectors. These women brought to their duties a general commitment to reform and a particular commitment to objective research and social investigation as the pathway to that reform. They were investigators, empiricists, and pragmatists. There is little evidence that they brought much in the way of theory to their jobs, but in their devotion to their laboring sisters they were by definition social rather than laissez-faire feminists.

The first women sanitary inspectors were appointed in Kensington, a part of London noted for its workshop laundries: thus the inspection of these premises formed a major part of the inspectors' duties.[49] The Kensington Vestry's Medical Officer, Dr. T. Orme Dudfield, showed himself, over a long career, to be one of the most progressive of London's Medical Officers of Health; he frequently advocated to his local authority ways to maximize use of existing health and sanitary legislation, and through his annual reports, he provided "exceptionally useful and instructive comment on the progress of sanitary work, not merely in Kensington but in the metropolis generally."[50] (The ratepayer-dominated vestry did not always welcome his suggestions warmly.) Dudfield also took it upon himself to stress the important role that women inspectors could play in sanitary administration. He urged that since laundries and other workshops where women were employed suffered from great overcrowding and often appalling conditions, these establishments should be subject to systematic inspection. Women were best suited to this work since the duties involved were, he indicated, often of "too special and delicate a nature to be discharged by male inspectors." The solid training received under Dudfield's supervision along with the detailed knowledge they gained of women's trades— particularly dressmaking, tailoring, and laundry work—were to serve well the first two women inspectors, Lucy E. A. Deane and Rose E. Squire, and helped to form the ideas they took with them into their subsequent work as inspectors of factories and workshops in the Home Office.[52] Squire's career provides a good example of the impact factory inspectors could have on the formation of public policy.

Squire's initial assignment as inspector for North Kensington gave her intensive knowledge of that area's very numerous laundries and the women who worked there. The laundresses she came to know in the course of her inspections were, she found, "mostly middle-aged and draggled, down-trodden creatures, ill-paid, and constant sufferers from rheumatism and from ulcerated legs due to long standing."[53] She was quick to recognize the dual implications of the work: its conditions made the women wretched and its casual sweated nature attracted primarily those who had the least chance of finding alternative employment.

Through her work she was able to achieve some hygienic improvement in its most elementary form—cleansing, drainage, and ventilation—but even these simple and relatively inexpensive measures were only brought about over the opposition of owners of slum properties who were also members of the local council. Once some of the most flagrant sanitary evils had been partly remedied, she found that other matters not then covered by legal remedy pressed themselves upon her attention. Employees, seeing a woman inspector for the first time, told her their grievances concerning mealtimes, hours of work or dangerous equipment and were disappointed to learn that she could do nothing for them.

Recognition of the limitations of her work led Squire to resolve, first, to become a factory inspector herself, and second, to advance the cause of laundresses by lending the authority of her detailed local knowledge to the campaign to bring their work under government regulation. Through these efforts she became acquainted with Sir Charles Dilke, M.P., and his niece, Gertrude Tuckwell, best known for her work in the Women's Trade Union League, a relationship that, Squire later reflected, "was followed by years of close association in the combat with industrial evils." In common with other female reformers, Squire was irritated by the necessity of having to call upon men to voice women's grievances in Parliament: men who, in her view, were "ignorant for the most part of the meaning of the words they uttered," and who, before speaking in Parliament, had been briefed with only "a few hasty sentences [of] first-hand information" by herself and other inspectors and trade union leaders.[54] Despite these difficulties, the empirical data supplied by Squire and her colleagues, along with their clear-headed analysis of the worst abuses and their potential remedies carried great weight in finally bringing the laundry trade within the Factory Acts. That they conceived of their role broadly made the work of these investigators especially influential. They not only supplied the "horror stories" of industrial abuses that fueled the rhetoric of sympathetic members of Parliament, they also documented with care the nature and extent of support for proposed legislation among employers and workers. Their reports on the views of laundry employers, for instance, signalled to M.P.s a shift of opinion among a broad spectrum of employers toward an acceptance of regulation, and a consequent lessening of the political costs of regulatory legislation.

Perhaps what finally broke the back of parliamentary opposition was the recommendation in October 1893 by R. E. Sprague Oram, Her Majesty's Chief Inspector of Factories, that laundries be placed under the Factory Acts in order to secure "ameliorations in the conditions of those employed therein."[55] There was, Oram pointed out, a great need in laundries throughout Great Britain to take measures to fence engines and dangerous machinery, to improve ventilation as a means of regulating temperature in ironing rooms and of removing steam from washhouses, to limit the hours of work in the trade, and to place some controls (under special provisions) on laundry work carried out in convents and other charitable institutions. The chief inspector's conclusions and recommendations were drawn from a series of special reports undertaken by his inspectors. The most detailed and important of these investigations were those carried out by the two new female inspectors, May Abraham, who visited hand and steam laundries in London, Liverpool, and Dublin, along with convent laundries in Dublin and hotel laundries in London, and Mary Paterson, who inspected Scottish laundries and those in the north of England. Their reports stressed the long and irregular hours worked in laundries, linking these hours with both poor health and exhaustion-related drinking on the part of employees. They also drew attention to the broad array of poor conditions that were shown to have further deleterious effects on the health and safety of workers.[56]

These women did not simply record conditions impassively, they openly advocated reform in laundry work through governmental means: they were, then, active agents of public policy. The inspectors' links with extra-parliamentary advocates of reform predisposed them to advance regulatory rather than free-market approaches to the problems they encountered. The strength of these associations drew criticism from those opposed to government intervention. "Is it right," asked E. J. Boucherett,

> that men or women who have been secretaries or presidents or avowed supporters of trades-unions should be appointed to be Labour Commissioners or sub-Commissioners, factory inspectors or sub-inspectors, all of which appointments are of a judicial character? Ought not the fact that a man or woman has been the distinguished and energetic secretary of a trades-union, or the brilliant advocate of trades-unionism, to be regarded, not as a recommendation, but as a disqualification for these offices?[57]

No matter how well intentioned, such appointees could not be impartial, she argued. Beyond this, she perceived that the role of such inspectors extended beyond the enumeration of legal transgressions and the listing of unhealthy practices to the framing of the recommendations upon which home secretaries acted. Boucherett was right: the female inspectors' assumptions and perspectives were indeed influential, and in the case of the laundry trade, their particular knowledge of and concern for the welfare of women who supported themselves by labor at the washtub or ironing table helps to explain the inclusion of this industry within factory legislation in 1895, two years after their appointment.

If the home secretary trusted the advice of his civil servants, he still might not have acted (or gained the support of his cabinet colleagues) had he not decided that the political climate was now ripe for regulation of this industry. When inspectors Abraham and Paterson recorded the growing support of employers, particularly those with large mechanized establishments, for more regular hours of work and supervision of health and sanitary conditions,[58] they were sending their minister a clear political signal—one which was readily verified by other means. For example, a National Laundry Association meeting in London in September 1893 passed the following resolution: "that this public representative meeting of the trade is of the opinion that all Laundries—or places where Laundry-work is carried on for gain—should be included under the Factory Act, due provision being made to suit the special requirements of the trade."[59] This motion was passed by more than a two-to-one majority. Other sympathizers wrote their endorsement to trade journals. This stance represented a considerable shift of opinion since 1891 when industry support for Factory Act regulation came primarily from a handful of the owners of the largest and most modern laundries, such as Spiers and Ponds in Battersea, who wished both to run their own businesses with more regularity and efficiency and to do away with competition from those (usually small) establishments that worked the longest, most irregular hours and often gave their workers additional work to take home. These firms had learned that good conditions could literally yield dividends through increased productivity and orderly management, and now they sought to influence the undecided opinion among their peers. They argued that fair-minded traders needed the Factory Acts to raise the reputation of their industry and to free the ethical businesses from the competition of notorious "sweaters." The *Laundry Record,* a trade journal that represented the most technologically sophisticated portion of the industry, gave extensive publicity to the debate over the Factory Acts and threw its weight behind those favoring regulation.[60] By 1895, these efforts had apparently produced many converts. A letter in *The Times* in June 1895, signed by representatives of five laundry trade associations, stated that "hundreds of trade meetings have been held," all without opposition to the Factory Acts being expressed.[61] Although it is impossible to gauge numbers with any degree of accuracy, probably by 1895 there was a substantial body of industry support for regulation—although certainly some owners must have felt that they were simply yielding to the inevitable.

In framing final legislation, the Home Secretary, H. H. Asquith (East Fife), took due note of the "special requirements" of the trade that industry owners and petitioners had emphasized needed to be respected in any regulations: that is, the need for flexibility in working hours to accommodate both fluctuations in work from hotels, ships, and similar establishments and the rigid weekly rhythm of household laundry requirements that created a pressure of work at the end of the week and seasonal patterns of intensive working. The government's Factory Act in 1895 made provision for flexible working, long days on a regular basis, and thirty days overtime yearly. At first the government had hoped that an experiment could have been made to bring laundry work within the ordinary statutory limits and thus reduce the excessive (up to eighty-five hours) weekly hours worked in the trade.[62] In conceding to industry pressures on hours, the government decided that it could ignore the other principal way in which influential industry support for legislation was conditional: that is, it chose to ignore the warning expressed by industry deputations, reported in the press and recorded by factory inspectors, that industry endorsement was contingent on universality of regulation.[63] Instead, the government yielded to pressure from laissez-faire feminists and others who argued that the independent laundrywoman would suffer if she were forced to conform to uniform standards of safety, sanitation, and hours of work: it exempted from regulation all laundries employing less than three persons who were not family members.

As soon as it became clear that the government meant to exclude small laundries from its bill, larger employers sent deputations to Parliament and letters to the press protesting against this discriminatory provision. This was one issue around which employers could make common cause with trade unionists, as the *Laundry Record* was quick to point out. Resolutions urging uniform regulation of the industry were passed by such diverse bodies as the Barry Dock Liberal Workmen's Club and Institute, the Mildmay Radical Club, the Women's Trade Union League, the Dundee Trades

Council, the Marylebone Women's Liberal Association, and the London County Council.[64] The periodical, the *Queen*, pointed out that the implications of the government's action would be "that precisely those women for whom some protection is most necessary—that is to say, married women, the mothers of young children—will be left in their present plight; left to burn the candle of their physical strength at both ends, and to work all day, and sometimes all night, during one half of the week at the washtub or ironing-board in order to be able to work without ceasing during the other half for the benefit of husband and family."[65] Even the journal's further argument—that this unlimited toil tended to increase the propensity to "loafing" among laundresses' spouses—fell on deaf ears in the corridors of power.

A Flawed Compromise

Finally, after years of campaigning on the part of those who were concerned with sweated labor and women's work, the laundry industry was included under the provisions of the 1895 Factory Act. The legislation, a classic political compromise in the face of opposing pressures, was, however, distressingly incomplete and ineffectual. Although regulated laundries were to conform to standards concerning health, safety, and sanitary conditions, those establishments most in need of such regulation were exempt. Moreover, by failing to bring laundry hours in line with other industrial employment, the law ignored what many inspectors found to be the most serious source of abuse in the industry. The laundry clauses of the act were described in 1897 as "one of the great disappointments of experimental legislation."[66] This was none too harsh an assessment of legislation that not only exempted large segments of the trade from any control whatever but which also allowed, as perfectly legal, sixty-hour work weeks, days of toil stretching from early morning to midnight, and Sunday working in the "regulated" portion of the industry. Flexibility became licence when: "A woman, for instance, who has two hours off a day for meals, may work from eight in the morning till midnight on Wednesday, Thursday, Friday and Saturday, without having worked the number of hours permitted by law, and this without overtime."[67]

The defects in the initial legislation stemmed as well from two other issues, one of which was consumer self-interest and conservatism. Consumer self-interest had first initiated broad public interest in the laundry trade and support for controls over sanitary conditions in laundries when, in 1877, there was widespread discussion of the extent to which disease, especially smallpox, could be spread in establishments where washing was done by poor women themselves infected, or where there was disease in the household. In a special report that year, the *Lancet* highlighted the problem and pointed to the distances disease could travel when transmitted via the wash.[68] Heeding the warning that infection could spread easily from mean streets to modish ones, public support for a cleanup grew, and the sanitary provisions of the regulations applying to laundries were among the most successful. This same self-interest, however, worked against the laundress when it came to the limitation of her hours of work. Throughout the nineteenth century, it had become the accepted pattern for work to be sent to a laundry on Monday or Tuesday and returned on Friday or Saturday, a system that created enormous pressure at the end of the week and idleness, especially for ironers, early in the week. Moreover, ships, hotels, and restaurants required that laundry be done with great dispatch and at odd hours, which resulted in much night work. Citizens, even those who were ready enough to support controlled hours of work in textile factories or mines, proved hostile to similar limitations when they involved a change in their own habits or in personal inconvenience. It was argued, for instance, that a prohibition of Sunday working could seriously inconvenience a lady who might suddenly have to go abroad.[69] The weekly washing cycle proved to be most intractable. Employers reported that "even an offer of cheaper rates have not induced the public to depart from ancient custom."[70] Employers, with the support of factory inspectors, concluded that only a legislative limitation of hours could induce consumers to alter their habits.[71]

There were others, however, who believed that the evils of working conditions were insufficient to justify "Draconian legislation to change their [the consumer's] habits and practice." Henry Matthews, M.P., in opposing any legislation for laundries, thought that "there was almost a divine law which compelled Englishmen to wear a clean shirt on Sundays, and to obtain it he must send the shirt to the wash before Thursday."[72] There was much support for Matthews' point of view, although the Fabian Society noted that "this argument exalts a domestic custom to the dignity of a law of nature. . . . There is no reason in the nature of things why families with a normal supply of linen should not have their 'washing' called for on a certain day of the week, and returned on the same day in the following week."[73] Sensing an ally in the middle-class consumer, the Women's Industrial Defence Committee found it useful to support consumer conservatism, arguing that no Factory Act would succeed in changing the customs of the British public, and thus, of course, that it was useless to pass legislation.[74] The government got the message. For too many voters the Englishman's laundry schedule was as sacrosanct as his tea-time; the benefits of legislative intrusion were felt to be far outweighed by the political costs.

A further narrowing of the scope of the legislation was the result of opposition from religious bodies and charitable institutions hostile to governmental interference in their affairs. The large number of such institutions (many of them homes for "fallen women") which carried on laundries to defray expenses, and to teach inmates both a trade and self-discipline, objected to state interference on the grounds that it was prejudicial to discipline, that inmates would be needlessly upset, that any posting of workers' rights might cause insubordination, and that their institutions regulated themselves. For some the mere suggestion that there was a useful role here for government was taken as a slight on the good intentions of those who ran them. As one M.P. put it, "[these institutions] were kept going by ladies whose lives were devoted to works of the noblest charity, and who eked out their want of fortune by the small assistance which they could derive from these laundries . . . [They] viewed the intrusion by the Government Inspector with feelings of pain and almost horror. . . ."[75]

The home secretary and the chief inspector of factories were both well aware of the delicacy of this issue, and H. H. Asquith, when introducing the Factory Bill to the House in April 1895, noted that the provisions for convent and institutional laundries would be "somewhat more elastic" than those for other laundries because of the religious and disciplinary nature of their management, and he explicitly indicated a willingness on the part of the government to amend the bill further to overcome such objections as might be raised. He thought, however, that the principal difficulty surrounding the issue had been largely removed by the appointment of female inspectors.[76] The government was probably unprepared for the storm of protest that broke when the bill received detailed clause-by-clause consideration in the Grand Committee on Trade, and it was besieged with letters and petitions from convents and homes, clergymen and philanthropists, Anglicans and Roman Catholics. The keenest parliamentary opposition came from Irish M.P.s who feared, in the words of one M.P., that the "convent spirit" would be damaged by the "factory spirit." The virulence of their protest probably owed as much to the general antipathy of the Irish Catholic establishment to the intrusion of an English, predominantly Protestant government in Irish affairs as to the sensibilities of the mothers superior with regard to the management of their inmates. The government bowed to these various pressures and modified its bill. Institutional laundries remained outside the framework of mandatory legislation until 1907.

Some argued that institutional laundry work was only a minor portion of the industry and offered no real competition to those involved in commercial laundry work. But this was not entirely the case. Laundry work dominated the cash-producing activities of charitable institutions and often yielded substantial returns. In 1902, the Home Office published a listing of some 204 religious and charitable institutions in which laundries were carried on, with the caveat that its compilation made no pretense at completeness.[77] The enumerated institutions included only those "which take in laundry from outside by way of trade or for purposes of gain" and not places where a training laundry only met the institution's own needs. In addition to the large number of homes for "fallen women," institutions for poor, orphaned, or disabled children also ran laundries. For example, the Wandsworth Common Deaf and Dumb Residential School ran a hand laundry to train girls from thirteen to sixteen years of age to earn a livelihood by laundry work.[78] These latter laundries escaped compulsory industrial and reformatory school inspection because their inmates were in no way offenders.[79] Most of the institutions with laundries seem to have been chronically underfunded, and, as a result, income from the laundry was of central importance to the enterprise's economic viability. In 1901, the Magdalen Asylum in Edinburgh earned £5,847 from laundry work as compared with £493 from other sources. Other laundries with smaller gross receipts from laundry work earned a similar proportion of their total incomes from this source.[80] Although these laundries may not have represented a significant percentage of all laundry work, nonetheless their ability to undercut the prices of commercial laundries—because they paid their workers no wages—must have had serious implications for laundry workers competing for the same market. Certainly commercial launderers were loud in their denunciations of this unfair competition.

On 1 January 1896 the Factory and Workshop Act of 1895 took effect, bringing the laundry industry for the first time within the scope of factory legislation. That such an important service sector industry—one of considerable size and rapidly increasing industrialization—should have remained for so long beyond the reach of the sort of measures which had applied to textile factories for many decades, and that the battle for its inclusion under regulation should have been so long and tortuous, provides an important case study of the interplay of the forces of reaction and reform in Victorian England. The tensions between these forces did not end with the passing of this incomplete and inadequate piece of legislation. The victory was too slight to give solace to the advocates of reform and the exemptions too slender to deter opponents from redoubling their efforts. The laundry trade was to remain as solidly a part of the debates over the development of social policy in the early decades of the twentieth century as it had been in the later years of the nineteenth. The enactment of ground-breaking legislation may be viewed as much a beginning as a culmination. How the industry changed under the impact of legislation, how the legislation itself was administered, amended, and expanded, and how the issues of concern in the industry altered over time—with shifts in the thrust of broader social policy, with the impact of war, with changes in the central concerns of reformers, feminists, and women workers—will form the focus of the following chapter.

CHAPTER 3

———— •◦• ————

Amelioration, Administration, and Public Policy

The law, when applied to the conditions of employment of people who were among the most downtrodden of a nation's labor force, could be a means of emancipation: a vehicle through which a body of workers might secure better health, a pleasanter and less hazardous workplace, and more hours of leisure. Legal mechanisms could be creative as well as protective; they could establish the conditions, both psychic and physical, which enable the worker to develop her fullest potential as an individual and as a citizen. Beatrice Webb seems to have had such objectives in mind when she wrote of the benefits of legislative intrusions into the workplace:

> Everyone knows that the Lancashire woman weaver, whose hours and condi-
> tions of work are rigidly fixed by law, enjoys, for this very reason, more
> personal liberty than the unregulated laundrywoman in Notting Hill. She is
> not only a more efficient producer, and more capable of associating with her
> fellows in Trade Unions, Friendly Societies and Cooperative Stores, but an
> enormously more independent and self-reliant citizen. It is the law, in fact,
> which is the mother of freedom.[1]

While one can probe the extent to which Beatrice Webb's appraisal was colored by a tincture of paternalism or tinted by a roseate faith in the power of legislative innovation, hers was a perspective shared by a great many others. It was shared by those who had tried and abandoned the advocacy of self-help alone; it was espoused by reformers who hoped the working woman would devote her newly won time and energy to her family responsibilities; it was supported by those who saw in such provisions the chance for a more permanent and vital unionism, and also by those who chiefly saw the amelioration of the industrial conditions of women and girls as an end in itself. The concern here is to show how the efforts of a wide variety of civil servants and reformers cultivated the legal soil in which a better life for laboring women might take root. In the laundry trade, it is possible to observe closely the tending of a single legal allotment: making factory and workshop legislation applicable to a service industry was seen as an experiment, if a long needed one, and as such the growth of this legal area was attended with more than usual interest.

The Impact of Legislation

Under section 22, the Factory and Workshop Act of 1895 made all commercial laundries employing more than two nonfamily members subject to provisions of the general Factory Act governing safety, sanitation, accidents, and the powers of inspectors, as well as to those prohibiting the employment of children under the age of eleven and of women within four weeks of childbirth. In addition, steam or power laundries were required to install fans or other devices for controlling temperature in ironing rooms and removing steam from washhouses, and to separate stoves used for heating irons from rooms in which ironing was performed. The laundering of clothes in buildings where it was known there was infectious disease was made subject to a fine of up to ten pounds. Other special provisions allowed launderers considerable elasticity in determining hours of work: adult women could work fourteen hours a day, sixty hours a week, and two hours of overtime on thirty days a year.[2]

In announcing the new provisions in his annual report, the Chief Inspector of Factories, Mr. Sprague Oram, welcomed the inclusion of laundries under government regulation, something he had advocated in his 1893 report, and advanced the opinion that the flexible scheduling of working hours would "enable the laundry sections to be enforced without inconvenience to those concerned."[3] Alongside his optimism, the chief inspector had to record the skepticism of some of his inspectors. While applauding the safety and environmental clauses of the laundry section, a number of inspectors characterized the hours clause as "weak," "senseless," and "to be regretted." Captain R. M. Smith, factory inspector for Sheffield, forecast "great difficulties in giving effect to the beneficent intentions of the Legislature" because of the absence of a set daily period

of work, an omission that negated what he saw as one of the best safeguards of the Factory Acts; this omission would, he predicted, make the
task of proving the actual number of hours worked nearly insurmountable
and conviction impossible. A Birmingham inspector pointed out that "the
hands might be told to come in at 6 a.m., and kept waiting for hours
before being employed, and then worked the limited number of hours,
possibly into the early hours of the next morning and yet it would not be
illegal."[4] The findings of these and other inspectors, along with official and
unofficial reports and testimony before government commissions, had
identified excessive and irregular hours as the main blight on the laundry
industry; their concern was the logical product of that knowledge.

Despite these reservations, there were many who had high hopes for the
new legislation; indeed, one inspector noted that the laundry clause was
the measure most popular with the public. Greeting the new legislation
with enthusiasm, Evelyn March-Phillipps observed: "The laundry-worker
may take heart. Broken-down women, like the one who exclaimed, 'I'm
going to make shift to hold out a bit now, for the Factory Act is coming,'
will have a chance to recover the health and strength strained beyond
endurance by days and nights of exhausting pressure, amid conditions
calculated to sap the strength of the strongest."[5] Rose Squire recorded in
her autobiography the excitement she felt when the clauses of the act were
being examined in a parliamentary committee: "These were not in my
case academic questions, but were seen as strands woven into the fabric of
life of countless women and girls."[6] Squire, through her work as a Kensington sanitary inspector, had developed a close acquaintance with laundry
workers and their problems. As a result she was one of the strongest supporters of legislation to bring the industry under factory inspection;
indeed, she became a factory inspector herself in an effort to be of greater
service to working women.

In January 1896, laundries first came under government regulation,
and in the same month, Squire began her work as H. M. Inspector of
Factories and Workshops. Her first charge was to assess the success of the
initial year of regulation and inspection of that industry. "The result," she
recorded, "cannot be said to be satisfactory." With this terse statement,
Squire began a report that was permeated with disappointment: the disappointment of workers, of inspectors, of concerned citizens, and of progressive employers. As some inspectors had predicted, the latitude and
obscurity of the measures relating to the period of employment proved
unworkable. Legislation designed to raise the standards of an industry

seemed, paradoxically, to do quite the opposite; instead of using the best employers (who voluntarily worked hours similar to those in textile factories) as the benchmark for the whole industry, the new act gave the sanction of law to the late hours and long days previously regarded as the unnecessary evils inherent in an unregulated industry. Laundresses, Squire recounted with sympathy, responded to the legal fourteen-hour day with an "outburst of indignation;" they said that they would "like to see how men would stand fourteen hours of this work in heat and steam."[7] Owners of progressive modern factory laundries complained that the law allowed work to be carried on until far into Saturday, something that they wished to avoid but often had to accept in the face of consumer demands and competition from other launderers.[8] Many laundry workers were incredulous that a half-holiday was not compulsory under the new legislation. "Women anxious to do their Saturday cleaning at home, and girls who had a vision of 'an afternoon out like the dyers and cleaners' are alike dissatisfied," noted Inspector Squire.[9] Other inspectors agreed that the legislation concerning hours had brought workers little advantage. Where the act was enforced and its spirit observed, "packers and sorters alone benefitted by a net reduction in weekly total of hours that for them [had] often exceeded seventy hours."[10]

Initial evaluation of the other provisions of section 22 were considerably more optimistic. The new Chief Inspector of Factories, Arthur Whitelegge, found that "a great deal has been done to improve structural conditions (e.g., fencing, ventilation, flooring, proper placing of stoves)"; and other members of his staff, while reiterating the negative comments on hours, provided evidence that sanitary provisions had been of value, that ventilation in particular had been much improved, and that many owners of factory laundries had accepted the act "with good grace, and have carried out instructions with commendable alacrity, and often at considerable expense and inconvenience." The most optimistic inspector noted that "the lot of the laundry operative had been much improved and it would be difficult to point to any industry (save that of brickmaking), the conditions of which have been more affected for the better than that of laundry work."[11] Progressive employers were anxious to conform with the law; many were installing new machinery or opening new factory organized premises and welcomed information that enabled them to operate their businesses in the cleanest, most orderly, and professional manner.

Sensitive to the public's fears of laundry-borne disease, many new or renovated laundries not only adhered strictly to the sanitary requirements of national and local regulation but christened themselves "model" or "sanitary" laundries. Cleanliness was the main stock in trade of launderers, and their advertising stressed the high sanitary standard and modernity of their premises, the healthy appearance of their workers, and often encouraged prospective customers to inspect their premises.[12] It was in their commercial interest to overcome what some felt to be "the unjust prejudice against laundries" and to stress the differences between themselves and smaller, often unregulated, establishments. The differences were very real; inspectors observed that the best conditions were to be found in purpose-built or renovated laundries of which there were relatively few before 1900 in the center of the trade—West London and the south of England. In northern cities long used to the regulation of textile factories, many laundries had voluntarily established conditions and methods of working superior to legal minimum standards. In hand laundries, the situation was less reassuring. Hand laundries, even those large enough to come under regulation, were not subject to the clauses concerning ventilation, drainage, and separation of stoves for heating irons. Indeed, one official pointed out that hand laundries would benefit most by keeping stoves apart from workrooms. "In these workshop laundries the ironing rooms are small, hence, on the one hand, the women are exposed to a scorching stove, and on the other to the cold draughts of open windows. This happens, of course during the winter as well as the summer, and the hands work under these conditions till 12 at midnight, and often till 2 or 3 in the morning."[13]

A year's experience yielded, from those charged with its administration, some plaudits for the laundry section's health and safety measures—where they could be fully implemented—but many more reservations about the limited applicability of the act, and much consternation about the uselessness of the law to effect much improvement in hours of labor. Observers outside government came to similar conclusions: investigators for the Industrial Subcommittee of the National Union of Women Workers, seeing the new law as amateurish, were of the opinion that "the application, by the measure of 1895, of the Factory and Workshop Acts to the laundry appears to rank as one of the great disappointments of experimental legislation;" in the view of the Webbs "the genuine public sympathy . . . with the laundress . . . has resulted in nothing but sham legislation of an entirely illusory character."[14] The Christian Social Union appointed a committee to observe the working of the laundry provisions. Thoroughness marked the committee's deliberations; laundries were visited, in both busy and slack periods, employers were interviewed, and workers were seen both at their work and in their homes. Considerable improvement was disclosed "in the matters of Ventilation, Sanitation, and Machinery" but the researchers learned that "the condition of the workers with regard to hours does not appear to be at all improved" and that exemptions seriously curtailed the law's benefits.[15] Whether the tone was one of disappointment, outrage, or measured criticism, all observers of the act's operation were in agreement that the law was least successful in controlling hours of labor.

Greater knowledge of the law and its provisions, along with repeated inspections over a period of years, made many laundries safer places to work in, but inspectors found their efforts to encourage the working of regular and moderate hours to be "extremely disheartening." In 1901, the inspector with responsibility for a district with the nation's largest concentration of laundries wrote in her annual report: "After six years experience of the effect of the present regulations, it is impossible not to feel greatly depressed by the result; the elasticity of the law has tended to encourage rather than check these unsettled hours and, graver still, makes it almost impossible to administer with equal fairness to all."[16]

The product of compromise and vacillation, the legislation was in many ways counterproductive. The problems created by the special flexibility given to laundries in setting hours went far beyond the sixty-six hour workweek (with overtime) it made possible. The rules were difficult to administer, seemed to abet various undesirable tendencies in the trade, and certainly placed laundry workers at a comparative disadvantage relative to other industrial employees. Among the laundress's disadvantages were that she might be asked to work on Sundays, that she was not guaranteed a Saturday half-holiday, that her hours of work might be altered daily, and that she could be required to work at night—all without her employer in any way infringing the law. When Edward Cadbury and George Shann investigated sweating in 1906, they uncovered some of this legal discrimination against the laundry worker: "Night work for women and children is abolished except in laundries, where, provided they do not work above a certain number of hours at one time, women may work at any time day or night. . . . As each industry came under the [Factory and Workshop] Act night work by women in it was prohibited, except in the case of laundries."[17] Other observers concluded that the employer's freedom to spread permissible working hours over any portion of a day was an innovation without parallel in the country's industrial legislation.[18] Inspector Mary Paterson, reporting on the north of England and Scotland, provided evidence of women regularly working from 7:00 a.m. to 11:30 p.m., their meal hours arranged so that the act was complied with. In one case, the employer argued that the protracted daily period of work was necessary because so much of the work arrived and left by an evening train.[19] One laundress expressed annoyance at the inconvenience as well as the fatigue of such hours; when she finished work she found all the good shops closed, and had to buy inferior merchandise at the small shops that remained open late; despite being a widow, she said she would prefer to accept less money in order to get shorter hours of work.[20]

Shortcomings entailed by the failure to establish the parameters within which work might be performed had been long known as one inspector pointed out:

> As the Commission of 1876 remarked, experience has proved that the only way to enforce a law against overwork is to provide not merely a maximum period of labour in the day, but maximum limits within which such a period may be taken; and as Dr. Kay observed in 1832, "Whilst the engine runs the people must work. . . . The animal machine, breakable in the best case, subject to a thousand sources of suffering—is chained fast to the iron machine, which knows no suffering and no weariness."

The principal lady inspector endorsed the need for tighter control but suggested that "the force to which the human machine in this industry is chained for action is not so much the iron machine as the blind, unlimited force of the consuming public's desires—so good a force when regulated, so disastrous a force when mastering the productive capacity and life and health of bodies of individual workers."[21] Workers' lives could be further disrupted by the practice in some laundries, especially seaside and resort laundries and those specializing in ships' laundry, of having workers sleep on the premises. "Such a place," noted Margaret Ethel MacDonald, "is the firm whose forewoman told us they never worked later than 9 p.m., but who afterwards said that three hands slept in as they might be wanted at any time to carry out telegraphic orders arriving in the middle of the night from hotels, & c."[22]

Unscrupulous employers used the law to make a mockery of the holidays to which workers were entitled. The half-holiday was frequently given on Monday rather than Saturday (because the work had not arrived or only the sorters were needed), thus depriving the laundry workers of the same free time as her fellows in other employment. Such was the legal flexibility that for any of the four Monday bank holidays, or for Good Friday, two half-holidays might be substituted: Monday mornings thus could be legally entered by employers in the "notice" as statutory holidays. As Inspector Lucy Deane drily remarked, "to the women however the permission to regard as a statutory half-holiday a morning which in any case is not, as a rule, a working period is but a scant boon." The weekly period of work also made holidays illusory since it was common for employers to require the full sixty hours work by lengthening the remaining days to make up for time lost by a holiday. In other laundries, Sunday work was simply substituted for the bank holiday.[23] Of course, not all employers sought to take advantage of all the loopholes. Although the special concessions of the hours clause had come about as a result of employer pressure, by 1903, the chief female inspector, Adelaide Anderson, was able to record as a source of hope the "steady growth of a strong section of employers who have set their minds on inaugurating a more rational system of employment in conformity with ordinary factory hours."[24] This reformation began in the north of England and in Scotland, where abuses of labor time had been much less common than elsewhere and where long-standing textile factory regulation set the general standard and undoubtedly armed the work force with expectations for regular and reasonable hours. Some enlightened employers supported the work of inspectors, devoted considerable time to discussing reform with them, and publicized the merits of shorter, more consistent hours in their trade journal.

Where employers were less enlightened the law's laxness, according to the National Union of Women Workers, reduced "to a nullity the Inspector's power of enforcing any limit of hours at all."[25] Inspectors were not quite as ineffectual as that—twenty-four cases prosecuted against laundries in West London in 1899 all resulted in convictions—but this occurred in an area where one inspector gave "the greater part of her time to West London laundries," although as one official reported, "to take proceedings against an occupier of a laundry is truly a venturesome task."[26] A prosecution was taxing for both the inspector and the worker-witness. To be successful, a worker had to remember accurately every hour of the day's work, including every quarter of an hour taken for meals—a daunting task when the work had been carried out weeks earlier and when every day of the week's work may have begun and ended at different times. Workers in separate parts of a laundry could all have different work schedules on the same day so that detection of illegal overtime involved "more careful sifting and more prolonged enquiry than in any other workplace;" two inspectors recounted that it took them four hours to inquire into the hours of working at a single large laundry, which had five divisions or departments. Each section of a department might have its individual schedule of working. In one laundry employing 300, for example, there were twenty-six different schedules in force on the day the inspectors visited. As a consequence, and despite considerable overwork on the part of inspectors, prosecutions "which could easily and advantageously be undertaken in any other trade have to be abandoned."[27] Sometimes employers or forewomen resorted to locking the gate to detain workers after legal hours, until work was completed, and to avoid detection.[28]

Regulations concerning overtime were not only difficult to administer, they were also hard to explain to employers and workers alike. In many of the better-run laundries, it had been assumed that overtime was being worked when labor continued after 8:00 p.m. or occasionally 9:00 p.m., but under laundry legislation, work might go on until midnight one day without involving overtime, while a shorter subsequent workday might include two hours of overtime. Employers were frustrated by the need to declare overtime at the beginning of the day because, if they reached the end of the week without requiring more than sixty hours of their workers, they had handicapped themselves by unnecessarily using part of the limited annual number of allowable days of overtime.[29] Other frequent and often hard to detect infractions included the lack of adequate time given for meals and the exceeding of the "five hours spell," which prohibited working more than five hours without a break. The latter was especially intractable as a result of worker collusion; on Saturdays, in particular, employees anxious to finish work would exceed the limit and conceal the infraction. In smaller laundries, a combination of passive endurance and loyalty too often resulted in connivance in order to hoodwink the inspector—a psychological reluctance to oppose the employer that is still encountered by inspectors and union organizers in women's trades.[30]

By 1906, whatever the weight of specific factors, any improvement in hours was marginal. The Board of Trade Earnings and Hours Inquiry of that year disclosed that in London the average number of hours for female laundry workers in a full week was 53.7 hours in power laundries and 51.9 hours in hand laundries, but more than a quarter of the women and girls worked 60 hours.[31] These figures did not take into account flagrant violations of the law, or the fact that individual days might be unconscionably long without the weekly limit being excessive, nor, most important, did they encompass the greater part of the industry that was still outside the law.

Finally, the law concerning laundry hours had ancillary deleterious effects on the workers and the industry. Some large laundries where legal limitation of hours was readily accepted contracted out part of their work to small, unregulated laundries, either on a regular basis or when there was a sudden press of work. The Christian Social Union's investigating committee discovered that: "A large quantity of work is given out from the larger Laundries to those exempted. Mangling, Servants' washing, Glazing of Collars & c. are done in these exempted Laundries, so that not only is there serious overwork, but the members of the public whose work is thus given out have not the protection they hoped to ensure against infection & c. when they send their linen to inspected Laundries."[32] Excessive hours not only produced fatigue and increased the possibility of injuries, they also exposed unescorted young women to the trials of walking home very late at night. Late working for the urban laundress might mean missing the last available mode of public transport and thus having a very long tramp indeed. A girl of fourteen might work at any hour in a laundry, although she could not have done so had she been a cotton weaver or a bookbinder. Since this provision was the consequence of conscious policy aimed at customer convenience, one report alleged that the "House of Commons deliberately permits the rough and untrained laundry girl, after standing long hours in the heat, to be turned into London streets or suburban lanes at any hour of the night, in such a way that not even the most careful mother could possibly keep an eye on her coming and going."[33] If reformers stressed the moral danger, the laundry women probably emphasized the cost: fares were more after the departure of the last workmen's train.

Moreover, some felt that the laxity of the law encouraged casualization of the industry. Employers often complained about their workers' irregular habits and lack of punctuality; yet long and exceedingly irregular hours attracted those who could not negotiate employment on more favorable terms. These were the workers without bargaining power—frequently drunkards—whose work influenced that of their fellow workers. These were the workers engaged daily at the factory gate, the workers prepared to work all day on Sunday, the workers who would work almost any hours if "fortified by the . . . visits to the laundry of the pot-man from a neighbouring public-house with the beer cans slung from a pole carried in each hand" and the workers whom the managers will allow "to sleep on the tables they have been ironing on all day." The problem was not theirs alone, for, as one complainant stated, "When respectable peoples comes

[sic] [to] work a proper day and wants [sic] to leave at a proper time they are told they are not wanted—other people can fill their places." No one pretended that such laundries were in the majority, but they were sufficiently numerous to exacerbate the casual nature of the industry and, by lengthy working, to reinforce consumer expectations that could not be met by laundries run in a more humane and orderly fashion. In fact, progressive employers urged the appointment of more inspectors and the extension of the law to all laundries because they believed that only uniformity of regulation and certainty of sanctions could accelerate the modernization of this service laundry.[35] Those charged with administering the law, however, while supporting augmentation of their numbers, concluded at an early date that the law needed to be changed and that "no vigorousness in administration can secure perceptible results in diminution of laundry hours, nor make Inspectors hopeful of eventually dealing with the workers' incessant complaints of prolonged days and late hours."[36] When the act had been in force for six years, Inspector Deane reiterated the tendency of the law to inhibit rather than to foster industrial improvement: "The result is disastrous even from the point of view of the industry itself, which if properly organized would be capable of offering really desirable employment to skilled workers, instead of being as it too often is, the last resort of the idle and the intemperate."[37]

The Campaign for Comprehensive Regulation

Conditions in the laundry trade were the focus of continuing public debate. The industry was kept in the public eye by inspectors, reformers, and leading employers, all of whom drew attention to the strengths and failings of the factory legislation and eventually lobbied for reform. Organizers supported state action when unions were floundering and workers hard to enlist; progressive employers preferred government paternalism to cutthroat competition; reformers of various ideological hues endorsed effective legislation as an aid to equity, social betterment, or the protection of maternal and infant health. Together these groups ensured that the shortcomings of laundry legislation would not go unnoticed. Concerned private groups publicized legislative problems through their own studies, by highlighting the findings of inspectors, by comparing the experience of other industries and other countries, and by working together to encourage amendment and extension of laundry regulations. The Scottish Council for Women's Trades, for example, requested the assistance of the Legal

Committee of the Women's Industrial Council to promote a bill to amend the 1901 Factory and Workshop Act to make laundries subject to the same rules and hours as other controlled workplaces and to extend the law to cover charitable and institutional laundries. Together they were able to secure the support of Cameron Corbett, M.P., who introduced the measure as a private member's bill, which, while it did not reach discussion in the House, elicited a government promise of future legislation. When government action was not forthcoming they followed up with deputations and written proposals for reform.[38]

At the same time, vigorous measures were taken to increase the effectiveness of existing laundry regulation. The Industrial Law Committee and other reform groups familiarized workers with the law and provided free legal advice and an indemnity fund to compensate any workers victimized for giving testimony to an inspector. At the center of this work was the Women's Trade Union League, which, according to a historian of the league, writing in 1909, two years after the law had been amended, "instituted a supervision of the hours of work, the proper guarding of machinery, ventilation, air space, and general sanitation which has so supplemented the factory inspectors' work that conditions of work in this occupation have improved greatly in the last fifteen years."[39] This special monitoring was perceived by the league as a means of gaining for poorly organized workers some of the benefits accruing to women workers in highly unionized industries.

In a period of gradually increasing public sympathy for government assistance to society's most disadvantaged citizens, reformers and inspectors worked to expose and document the circumstances of those workers least able to help themselves. Even lukewarm supporters of the welfare state could support government protection when laissez-faire was inoperative. Laundry labor in closed institutions was one such situation. The laundress who was also the inmate of a charitable institution was seen to be a worker particularly in need of her government's care. This worker did not choose her occupation and received only room and board for her labors; she was usually young, underprivileged, ill-educated, and often physically weak or mentally handicapped. Since those who employed her did not welcome prying eyes, especially official ones, and since they were devoted to her best interests, her workplace had been exempted from all regulation. Unfortunately, convent walls do not make a machine safe nor good intentions clear the air of steam or shorten hours. Having identified what seemed to be a conspicuous and untenable omission, inspectors and lobbyists worked to break down hostility toward the inclusion of charitable and church institution laundries in factory act regulation. The biographer of the first female principal inspector noted that May Abraham was especially distressed "that any cloak of religion should be thrown over the sweated conditions of some of these places." Her successor, echoing Abraham, remarked that regulation was particularly imperative to monitor the labor conditions of institutional inmates who "lack the self-protecting habits of normal industrial workers."[40] While publicists drew attention to the evidence, the inspectors went beyond administering the law to acting forcefully to change it.

Charitable and institutional laundries aroused strong feelings whenever the prospect of their being brought into line with factory act legislation was discussed. In 1894 an inspector found that, although she was received with courtesy, most matrons of institutions that she visited were hostile to the idea of mandatory inspection, even though the laundries they managed were usually clean, and none worked more than factory hours each week, and frequent breaks (normally compulsory church services) were the rule.[41] Members of Parliament were reluctant to risk giving the impression that they were impuning the good intentions of those running such institutions by suggesting through legislation that there were abuses that needed correcting. However, their failure to regulate the entire industry seriously undermined the support of commercial launderers for a law which they believed forced them into a disadvantageous competitive position.[42] Commercial opposition seems to have been strongest in Liverpool, where launderers felt that institutional competition was cheating them of lucrative shipping contracts, which could involve 10,000 to 20,000 items per voyage. While these launderers' fears may have been exaggerated, there were at least ten institutional laundries there in 1902, and the Liverpool Magdalen Institution announced in its *51st Annual Report* that it had updated its laundry with modern machinery "to undertake the washing from ships, steamers, factories, hotels, cafes and hospitals, both promptly and efficiently."[43] The flatwork that predominated in such contracts was regarded as especially suitable institutional work since its simplicity was appropriate for inmates who tended to be very young and often feeble-minded as well.

For a second time, in 1901, the government tried to include institutional inspection among the amendments to the Factory and Workshop Act. Home Secretary Ritchie, like his predecessor in 1895, expressed his government's readiness to legislate provisions to inspect these laundries and its willingness to modify the regulations to meet any objections: "These provisions are intended to protect workers in laundries from being overworked, and to see that they work under sanitary conditions, and I cannot for the life of me see why these provisions should not apply to laundries in religious institutions of any ordinary character."[44] The debate that followed was a duplicate of that of 1895, with reformers like Sir Charles Dilke and H. J. Tennant arguing for regulation as they had six years before, while many Irish M.P.s, such as John Redmond of Waterford, emphasized the need to exempt institutional laundries (Redmond even quoted at length part of the earlier debate in support of his views).[45] "Frequently," John Burns reminded his colleagues, "charity covers a multitude of industrial sins;" he urged his "Irish friends" to accept a form of regulation that, he was certain, could be supervised by a female inspector of the Catholic faith. Where others favorable to regulation had stressed the unfairness to commercial launderers of continued exemption of charitable and small domestic laundries, Burns pointed out that any such handicapping of private enterprise would mean laundry girls would be kept for longer hours at low wages in order to compete with the exempted categories.[46] Although most of the antiregulatory speeches in the House came from Irish M.P.s, the home secretary informed the House two months after his initial introduction of the bill that he had received many representations against institutional inspection from England as well, so many in fact that despite his own views in the matter he found it necessary to drop the laundry clause.[47] He held firm through the spirited attacks that followed—there were vituperative exchanges between advocates of both sides, which came at times dangerously close to racial and religious slurs—and remained unimpressed by assurances from other members that they had letters of support from managers of charities and from commercial launderers to more than match the hostile petitions. As A. J. Balfour explained it, the government found itself with a factory act consolidation bill on 99 percent of which there was general agreement, but "on the 1-100th of which there is profound, bitter, implacable dissent." Where there was so much consensus, he stressed, any government would be most imprudent to risk that consensus by supporting the anomalous divisive measure.[48]

Aggressive lobbying won out in the end. The Factory and Workshop Act of 1901 did not include laundries in religious and charitable institutions. Indeed, it did nothing to change the enactments relating to laundries, beyond slightly strengthening the powers of local authorities to enforce sanitary conditions in domestic laundries not under the Factory Acts. In the course of the debate in Parliament, inspectors' findings and reformers' arguments had been frequently cited in favor of improving the legislation, but to no avail. Laundries that were carried on in the name of religion and moral reform, as the advocates of regulation quickly realized, were not simply workplaces in which safe, sane, and sanitary modes of working should be assured, they were also institutions that occasioned ideological, religious, and moral warfare. When a government with a safe majority and substantial internal commitment to welfare legislation would not pass a regulatory measure amid such controversy, reformers could not but recognize that theirs was an uphill battle.

More members of Parliament clearly needed to be won over to the necessity of institutional regulation. To achieve this the managers and supporters of institutions needed to be convinced that they had nothing to fear from inspectoral visits and, quite possibly, much to gain. The female inspectorate, with the support of the Home Office, followed two distinct routes to this end. First of all, the Principal Lady Inspector, Adelaide Anderson, made a special inquiry into the methods of regulating similar institutions in other countries, and subsequently in 1902, she conducted comparative visits to the majority of British institutions prepared to receive her. Following her visits to laundries in France, Belgium, and Germany, Inspector Anderson was able to report not only that regulation appeared to work well in those countries but that the British exemption from control of religious and charitable workplaces was anomalous: "England stands hitherto alone in reserving for convent laundries or other charitable institution laundries an exceptional exclusion from regulation. I would draw attention specially to my classification of the various kinds of laundries I personally inspected in France and to the fact that I saw the law applied equally in all."[49] In France, no distinction was made between laundries carried on for gain and those used for technical training; it sufficed that manual labor took place for the law to apply. The law was more far-reaching than that in effect for any British laundries: night work for women and young workers was prohibited; work was not allowed more than six days a week; daily hours were regular and included a minimum one hour break during which all work must cease; and the employment of women, children, or young persons at unguarded machinery was illegal. Here the large number employed in institutions (48,432 in 1900) convinced the authorities that such workplaces, if unregulated, would be a source of unfair competition (*concurrence deloyale*). At the same time, the fact that the majority of institutional workers were under eighteen years of age drew attention to both the need to protect them against accidents and dangerous machinery and the necessity of limiting working hours to leave time available for their education. Investigation had disclosed not only long hours and poor conditions but also that women frequently left the convents at the ages of twenty to thirty without being able to read or write and were incapable of earning their livelihood (often because their work had been restricted to a tiny portion of a task).

This experience, in a predominantly Roman Catholic setting, provided Adelaide Anderson with what she called "a helpful object lesson." Very real problems had been much relieved in France by the universal application of ordinary industrial legislation, and these benefits had been achieved without incurring the hostility of religious orders or upsetting reformatory or religious discipline. (Belgian and German experience had proved less relevant since in the former the industry was small and domestically based, while in Germany there were no institutional laundries of any size or importance and the whole industry was very small since "home washing is still the rule, household linen not being readily trusted to outsiders.") Genuine social benefit had been achieved without political cost and without disruption of institutional routine. Inspector Anderson made sure that British politicians and the matrons of institutions got the message. To both she emphasized the opportunity to increase the welfare of workers particularly in need of protection. Inspector Anderson's visits to institutions were often able to allay fears, for her explanations frequently smoothed away difficulties, and in many well-run places, she could show that the law would only require changes such as the fencing of stoves or the guarding of machinery, which were entirely oriented toward the health and safety of the inmates. To achieve these objectives, she stressed, it would not be necessary to interview inmates, a step matrons felt would interfere with the reformatory process.[50]

The second measure undertaken was designed both to demonstrate to institutions the advantages of inspection and to circumvent the absence of legislation. In January 1902, the Home Office sent a circular to religious and charitable institutions that were known to run laundries, inviting them to accept voluntary inspection, an action that, the circular intimated, would be taken by all those who valued the welfare of institutional inmates. To soften further the perceived threat posed by inspection, the circular pointed out that a female inspector could be sent and that the existing laundry enactment was flexible enough to permit great variations in working arrangements. Finally, it was emphasized that the assistance and advice of inspectors could serve the interests of those establishments farsighted enough to avail themselves of it: "The Inspectors' duties were not merely confined to seeing whether regulations . . . are actually carried out. Their visits are often of considerable value to those in charge of laundries, by giving them opportunities of consultation with the Inspectors and of gathering from them suggestions of better arrangements and appliances based on the wide experience of the Inspectors as to what has found to be practicable and useful in similar circumstances elsewhere."[51]

In all, 117 institutions (roughly a quarter of the number registered under subsequent legislation) acceded to the Home Office's request and received inspectors into their laundries. This action, which often proved to be the beginning of a human relationship between people whose mutual concern was the interest and well-being of the women sheltered in these establishments, did much to obliterate resentment to "Government interference." Gaining voluntary support was critical; even under mandatory regulation evasion would be easy in closed institutions. Gradually, more managers and mothers superior came to recognize the benefits of shorter hours, of work breaks, and of more safely arranged workplaces. Over and over again inspectors discovered that sincere and caring matrons had virtually no idea of the dangers to which they were exposing their charges. Feeble-minded or very young, untrained girls were asked to feed an unguarded wringer or calender; hydroextractors were operated uncovered; driving belts were left unfenced; workers were permitted to leave their hair loose near indrawing machines, and work was carried on in a damp, unventilated, steamy, and hot environment. Matrons came to express "a livelier and more practical interest" in the visits of inspectors once they discovered that they brought with them much pertinent knowledge— knowledge which, often by means of such simple measures as rearranging equipment, could yield greater productivity and profit as well as reduce the strain of labor.[52]

Yet, despite hopeful signs, voluntary inspections were limited because they were not only incomplete, but also often in conflict with the aims and constraints of the institutions. Repeatedly inspectors were told that improvements essential for the health of the workers had not been carried out because of the expense. A great many institutions were underfunded; figures from the Annual Charities Register for 1901 showed that in many institutions income received from laundry work many times exceeded revenue from all other sources.[53] In fact, underfunding frequently governed the choice of laundry work as a reformatory employment since it was relatively inexpensive to set up, immediately remunerative, and required little training. Fiscal need often made institutional laundry work worse than it need otherwise have been. Inmates might work long hours, particularly when completing remunerative shipping contracts, in poor or unsuitable conditions; some were assigned to laundry work even though they were too frail or undernourished for such heavy labor, or despite a drinking problem (institutions were scarcely helping an alcoholic by training her in a hot, thirsty, and heavy trade in which part payment in beer was a common practice). Sometimes inmates were chosen more for their suitability for laundry work than for their need, and officers were hired for their laundry skills and devoted more time to laundry than reform programs. In the York Penitentiary Refuge, a home for "fallen" women, where the assistant matron was a laundress whose main task was to operate the laundry and instruct the girls in the art of washing, starching, and ironing, it was found that "the work is far too heavy for the girls and occupies their time too exclusively." Despite a desire to vary and enrich the routine, the institution's records make it evident that the work continued to dominate both the time of the inmates and the receipts of the institution.[54] Too strong a need to place profit before the proper training of young workers, either in the laundry or in basic literacy, and too little incentive to attempt other occupations, were among the problems most frequently encountered by inspectors.[55] Another problem, by no means found everywhere, was that of prevailing attitudes toward reform and discipline. Some institutions maintained rules of silence, provided little exercise, few if any holidays, and deliberately prolonged work to keep inmates from mischief and ensured a monotonous routine and drab clothing in the cause of subduing evil and reforming character.[56] The managers of these laundries believed that factory hours would undermine their efforts at reclamation.

Fortunately, the advent of voluntary inspection coincided with some rethinking about the whole issue on the part of church leaders and the managers of institutions. Bishop Creighton, the Bishop of London, argued "against utilizing the services of proteges in Penitentiary Institutions for the making of profit in any sense. . . . Such [long] hours in a laundry are, of course, not 'educative' for feeble-minded girls; . . . the need presumably is as great for the application of the minimum standards [of] . . . health and safety as in many private laundries."[57] The bishop's view was endorsed by Rev. Arthur Brinckman, Chairman of the Church Mission to the Fallen, whose thirty years experience with such institutions had alerted him to long hours and "the temptation to overwork the girls," and had made him a strong supporter of inspection.[58] So much had attitudes changed by 1907, aided by the publicity given to the issue by the Industrial Law Committee and others, that an interdenominational deputation from charitable institutions in which laundry work was undertaken, headed by the Bishop of Stepney, presented the Home Secretary, Mr. Herbert Gladstone, with a number of proposals for bringing institutional laundries under inspection corresponding to that to which commercial enterprises were subject.[59] The back of the opposition had been broken. Later that year Parliament passed a new Factory and Workshop Act that included provisions for the mandatory inspection of charitable institutions. The legislation allowed institutions to vary their pattern of working as long as it was in general conformity with commercial hours, and, as the Archbishop of Canterbury said during the debate in the Lords, no "institutions properly conducted need fear anything from inspection."[60] Despite some residual opposition from Irish M.P.s, the inspectors' work had broken down most apprehension about the machinations of a distant and monolithic government while their services as "management consultants" came to be viewed as a positive bonus.

In the years immediately following the implementation of the 1907 Factory and Workshop Act, inspectors professed themselves well pleased with the results: "I am deeply impressed," wrote inspector Tracey in her report for 1909, "with the beneficent effect of the Acts on the industries carried on in these homes. In fact, I might go further and say that inspection under the Act has been a blessing to the whole work of the homes, and those in charge are amongst the readiest to acknowledge this rather unexpected result."[61] Once the door had been opened to new ideas, some managers and matrons began to reevaluate their programs. When inspectors mentioned the inadequate diet in some institutions, the lack of outdoor exercise, or unearthed other problems not covered by their legal mandate, institutions were increasingly likely to respond positively. Others unilaterally experimented with other forms of work, sometimes at the instigation of the matron or medical officer, and many abandoned some of their punitive practices, allowing girls greater freedom, more attractive clothing, and increased holidays and outings; some also changed their names from the degrading "Homes for Penitent Females," "Fallen Women," or "Waifs and Strays" to "Homes of Hope" or other simple names that would not label the girls when they left.[62] Factory inspectors were fortunate that their initiatives to bring charitable laundries under regulation occurred at a time when a broader reassessment of the nature and organization of residential institutions was beginning to take place; from the 1890s changes took place in the British workhouse system that were to lead to the specialized, more humane institutions which replaced it.[63] At the same time, their advice and attention undoubtedly accelerated the process of change. Their primary campaign had worked; it had achieved its aims of bringing institutional laundries under public scrutiny, and it had done so not by strong-armed machinations but by a process of gradually gaining people's confidence and by bringing very real benefits to these workplaces and their workers. Meanwhile these efforts helped to open many well-meaning but conservative philanthropic bodies to new methods and attitudes toward reformation and the care of the physically and mentally handicapped.

Health and Safety in the Workplace

With the beginning of laundry inspection, in January 1896, came disturbing confirmation that a laundry could be a dangerous and unhealthy place to work. Workers' health could be compromised by the damp, steamy environment, long hours, and much standing, but, more dramatically and tragically, accidents could end a woman's ability to support herself and leave her permanently disfigured. Danger was increased by rapid and too often ill-considered technological change. The comparatively recent development or use (some of the technology was employed earlier in a few specialized laundries and in the United States) of a large variety of powered equipment meant that effective guards had often not been developed, particularly for the most up-to-date machinery, while its installation and use by those with only rudimentary knowledge of maintenance and operation further exacerbated their dangers. In addition, "do-it-yourself" adaptation of familiar equipment often had startling results. A laundress recounting the circumstances of her injury observed: "Since the guv'nor tied the old box-mangle up to the new engine, she has taken to leapin' back and forrards [sic] that alarmin' and that suddenlike, that it's a wonder I've not been caught out sooner nor I was."[64] The ever-increasing quantity and variety of laundry machinery ensured that occupational health and safety in the laundry trade became an immediate and continuing priority of the inspectorate. But before much could be achieved, inspectors had to learn more about the nature and causation of laundry accidents and to test the capacity of the factory act to reduce the incidence and severity of injuries.

In 1899, partly to achieve these ends, the Factory [Inspectors] Staff Committee recommended that a special district be set up in the West

London boroughs under the superintendence of one inspector, who would take entire charge of steam and hand laundries in order to provide a showcase of what could be achieved by the most intensive use of existing regulations and to focus attention on both those measures that needed changing and on the value of extending regulation to exempted workshop laundries.[65] (Laundries within the purview of the district were those in Acton, Chelsea, Chiswick, Fulham, Hammersmith, Kensington, Marylebone, Paddington, and Westminster.) The district was a good area for study since it contained 10.5 percent of the total number of workers employed in regulated mechanized laundries in the United Kingdom (from the 1901 census); the average number of employees per laundry was only slightly less (29 compared with 30.2) than that for the country as a whole; and, more important, the area exhibited both an accelerated growth in the introduction of mechanized processes and the greatest possible variety in industrialized laundries.[66] The number of power laundries grew by more than 42 percent in the West London District between 1900 and 1910. The experimental district made practicable the close and thorough examination of the circumstances of accidents in order to isolate the most dangerous machinery, to pinpoint the workers most at risk, and to establish those laundries with the highest incidence of accidents. The lessons learned here were to be of benefit to the entire industry.

Out of the plethora of evidence presented by the inspectors over a number of years, one can extract several major findings concerning laundry accidents. First, the great majority of accidents occurred in the operation of power-driven ironing machines of all types and in the use of wringers. The indrawing rollers of wringers and ironing machines were the most dangerous (other ironing machines such as shirt and blouse ironers did not generally involve the same mechanism). Of a twelve-year total of reported accidents, 62.5 percent were attributable to these machines.[67] Many accidents permanently maimed the victim by crushing and burning (in the case of ironing machines) fingers, hands, and arms. "The loss of the tip of a finger does not make an imposing show on the accident record," wrote an inspector of the supposedly "minor" variant of such injuries, "but it may prove a handicap to the worker throughout life, for the most sensitive part of the hand may have been thus lost."[68] Laundry accidents, in the assessment of the principal inspector, stood out among all the injuries sustained by women workers: "There are no machines which come into the ordinary experience of the Factory Inspector more dangerous than those of the type so common in laundries, in which the process of wringing, drying, ironing, or mangling is carried on by means of rollers."[69]

Acting rapidly on these findings, every occupier in the district was instructed concerning the proper guarding of these machines, negligent employers were vigorously prosecuted, and experiments were begun to devise more effective and less readily tampered with devices. The latter endeavor involved active collaboration with laundry engineers and some of the largest employers; this localized work gained in significance and, in 1910, a conference on laundry safety was held as part of the Laundry Exhibition held at the Royal Agricultural Hall, Islington, which was attended by engineers, representatives of the factory inspectorate, and representatives of trade associations. The discussions resulted in substantial agreement on methods of safeguarding the major types of ironing machines, especially the ubiquitous flatwork calender, and the framing of what subsequently became a Home Office *Memorandum on Fencing of Machinery and Prevention of Accidents in Laundries.*[70] The statistical analysis made by the inspectorate is difficult to use since fluctuations in numbers cannot be attributed clearly to growth in the number of laundries under regulation, or intensity of inspection, or variations the reporting of injuries. Nonetheless, it does seem that special efforts to have guards installed and maintained did reduce the incidence of these accidents, especially given the enthusiastic cooperation of some of the largest laundry concerns.[71]

Second, the division of labor in factory laundries meant that the youngest workers were most at risk; girls and young women were most commonly employed on flatwork ironers while older women predominated in the hand processes—washing of delicate items and hand ironing of fancy work; men were employed most often in the washhouse or in delivery and collection. The principal lady inspector recorded that the detailed accident reports crossing her desk revealed that most accidents were sustained by those under twenty-one years of age.[72] The danger to these young workers was exacerbated by their inexperience, by the design of guards that often allowed their smaller fingers to slip beneath them, and by their own insouciance. In fact, attitude—that of employers and workers alike—was another significant factor in accidents. There was minimal perception by either group, prior to intensive publicity in the West London District, that "doing the wash" involved risk. Workers suffered for their assiduousness when they reached under a guard to smooth the work; the relatively slow motion of the machines conspired to give an impression of innocuousness.[73] When accidents did occur, employers were inclined to blame the carelessness of the worker even when the machine was unprotected. In France, Inspector Anderson pointed out, young workers were not employed on dangerous or unguarded machinery, and in Germany, employers were liable to special penalties "if accident arises, particularly to a young worker, through causes which he might reasonably have prevented by proper organization of work or other safeguards."[74]

Findings based on the special district highlighted two further sources of accidents: the physical arrangements of laundries and the hours worked. For these comparisons it was not necessary to go abroad. Inspectors who had worked in the district found that accidents were more frequent than elsewhere, even when in other places less attention had been devoted to preventive measures. In both Glasgow and Paisley, Inspector Deane found, not only were there fewer accidents, there were none of the little crowded factory laundries so

> common in the [West London] district. In none of those [laundries] I visited did I find the little rooms crowded with machinery—bought, not second, but third or fourth hand—so placed that threading one's way through it is difficult. The hours were shorter and more regular, I think. I heard of no cases of employment on Wednesday, Thursday, and Fridays from 8 a.m. to 9:30, 10 and 11 p.m. respectively with no work at all on Mondays and Saturdays . . . a state of things not uncommon in this district.[75]

Similarly, in Norwich, laundries were safer though less often guarded, apparently because of more regular hours, more appropriate buildings, and both fewer young girls employed and less time-related pressure. The West Riding of Yorkshire owed its "comparative immunity from accidents" to comparable conditions, noted Inspector Squire, while in Kent the absence of piecework relieved workplace pressure and consequently mishaps were fewer. Institutions, where hours were either shorter or more relieved by breaks and where supervision was close, also had better safety records. Another inspector noted the great contrast between Irish shirt and collar finishing laundries, where injuries were few, and West London laundries where the same machines were used and more often were guarded. Since these Irish laundries dealt in new goods, it was essential that young workers be properly trained and the work carried on at a more leisurely pace to prevent the spoiling of work.[76] Thus, accidents were partly attributable "to the reprehensible though not illegal custom of employing young girls monstrously long hours at the dangerous work of feeding [often] unguarded calenders," an opinion amply verified by studies showing the intimate relationship between fatigue—commonly toward the end of the five-hour spell—and industrial laundry mishaps.[77] In addition, these conditions were aggravated by unthinking, inefficient transformations of small row houses into mechanized laundries by people who neither fully under-stood the nature of their equipment nor were able or willing to maintain it properly.

If such conditions were to be found in supposedly regulated laundries in the nation's most painstakingly supervised area, what horrors might be found in unregulated laundries? Obviously, inspectors could give no defin-itive answer. However, they could demonstrate that their investigation of complaints revealed considerable numbers of hazardous workplaces that turned out to be exempt "domestic" laundries. These laundries were often full of unfenced ironing machines in dark corners, and unprotected motor belts for washing and wringing machines—all in unsuitable quarters and all safe from official scrutiny. They could not be regulated because no more than two employees not family members were regularly engaged. The scope of the law needed to be expanded, the inspectors argued forcefully; most laundries were small concerns, and of all the workers employed in those laundries only 36.5 percent (according to the 1901 census) worked in inspected workplaces.[78] Further, even in those domestic laundries where no machinery was used, workers were just as vulnerable as those in regulated laundries to the health hazards of standing for long hours in heat, damp, and steam, and there seemed to be no reason to exclude these laundries from the aid that legislation could offer.

Laundresses were more susceptible to consumption, ulcerated legs, and bronchial problems than their fellow workers in other industries. To add weight to her own findings, the inspector for the special district cited a paper read to the British Medical Association on the "Incidence of Phthisis among Laundry Workers" in which the author, Medical Officer for Batter-sea, Dr. McCleary, found that in 1899 and 1900 admissions to the Isle-worth and the Wandsworth and Clapham Infirmaries showed a higher incidence of the disease among laundry workers than among other women workers (10.9 percent vs. 4.3 percent and 8.7 percent vs. 5.3 percent of all admissions respectively). Young workers were most liable to the disease: in the Wandsworth and Clapham Infirmary 11.9 percent of those admitted were afflicted compared with 2.6 percent for other employed women and 4.2 percent for those without paid employment.[79] Rheumatic joints were made worse by the work. One elderly laundry worker observed that "though we had boards to stand on, we could not keep our legs dry; sometimes we were wet up to the shoulders with steam."[80] Leg ulcers and varicose veins afflicted laundresses more than other workers, even though most forms of factory employment were done standing. Others complained of headaches and sore eyes from poorly maintained gas-operated machines or gas-heated hand irons (some cases of carbonic oxide poisoning were recorded), while the sorting of soiled and perhaps infected linen incurred definite, though not readily measurable, health hazards.[81] The reports from the special district assailed readers with examples of health problems in an inadequately regulated trade, but it was sometimes as compelling to let workers speak for themselves: " 'I don't know that it's anything partic- ular as carries us off, but we are just wore out in no time.' 'There's nothing like this life for wearing you out.' 'We're old women at forty.' 'It's a harder life than any, is a laundry.' . . . 'For one strong one that'll stand it, there's a many and many fair wore out by it before they lived half a life.' "[82]

From a Fair Day's Work to a Fair Day's Wage

Assessing the work of the West London District, Lucy Deane concluded: "The history of this subject is another refutation of the theory that indus- trial conditions would automatically improve on the sole initiative of public opinion without any troublesome legislative interference."[83] In 1907, West- minster finally concurred and passed a new Factory Act, which was almost entirely a laundry regulation measure. It extended the law to workshop laundries and institutions, made hours of work somewhat easier to police, and prohibited workdays longer than thirteen hours and labor past nine at night. The debate in Parliament on this measure was vigorous, but it was in general free of the acrimony that had characterized discussion of earlier legislation. Members of Parliament had accepted the need for greater pro- tection for laundry workers, often citing the findings of inspectors in sup- port of their conclusions; perhaps they were also influenced by the assessment of a British Association report, which found no adverse effect on wages in regulated laundries. M.P.s continued, however, to be very solicitous of the conservative requirements of the laundry customers.[84] For example, the act permitted a laundry manager to designate three days a week (other than Saturday) as extended workdays so that most customers' work could be done at the same time of the week. The only improvement was that the days and hours to be worked had to be registered in advance and could only be changed once yearly, which made detection of illegal working easier. To assist the large employer, a special order allowed the designation of different hours for separate departments, thus permitting packers and sorters, for example, to work long hours on different days from ironers. Flexibility was granted to institutions via a provision that permitted alternate schemes of working if these were approved by the secretary of state as equivalent to the normal hours as specified by the act.[85]

In the wake of better regulation, the industry was changing. An inspector of laundries in West London observed the trade's evolution: "From being purely domestic it is becoming highly organized and scientific, and may rank in the future as one of the best and most skilled of women's industries. The Act of 1907 has helped to this end, for it has improved the conditions as regards hours of work, and it has helped to attract a better and more intelligent class of worker."[86] The 1907 act was not, however, greeted with universal applause. Margaret MacDonald complained that the workers' welfare had not been given the priority it deserved by the framers of the legislation; the amendments, she felt, were "still dominated by the old idea that laundry proprietors and customers must have special arrangements to suit their convenience." Clementina Black concurred, seeing no reason for customers' desires "to be regarded as an immutable law of the trade." Flexible arrangement of working hours initially made the law more difficult to explain to workers and employers, and these same provisions meant that inspection continued to require more time than other trades, and workers, so inspectors reported, were unhappy that the new law had done nothing to guarantee them a Saturday half-holiday.[87] The Women's Trade Union League, fearing that the many permitted patterns of work would put insurmountable obstacles in the way of detecting illegal overtime, petitioned the Home Secretary Herbert Gladstone to abolish differing hours in separate departments of a laundry. J. Ramsay MacDonald, M.P. for Leicester, urged the House to annul the order that made this possible. The motion was defeated by 175 votes to 26.[88]

After two years in force, however, the new legislation had produced far fewer problems than either anticipated or first encountered. By the end of 1909, the fencing of laundry machinery was more rigorously enforced in West London while a special systematic inspection in the rest of the country showed a clear decrease in laundry accidents—from 437 in 1908 to 409 in 1909. The decline in accidents was of greater significance than the figures first suggested, the principal inspector pointed out, because the amount of machinery in use had increased substantially over these years.[89] (Mechanization of the industry and its timing are explored in chapter 5.) The next year (1910) witnessed a further reduction in accidents, and properly guarded machines had become "invariably the rule," though sometimes the machines were not carefully enough installed for maximum effectiveness.[90] Hours, although they continued to be longer than in other regulated trades, showed considerable improvement. Many large laundries worked from 8:00 a.m. to 8:00 p.m. and rarely made use of either overtime or extended working. In West London, most of the laundries took advantage of the extended working scheme—85 percent of the factory laundries and 61 percent of the workshop laundries—but inspection was made easier by the fact that most chose the same pattern. There the order allowing different hours of work in each department was much used, but intense competition meant that employers were quick to report other launderers abusing the system.

Cases of serious contravention of the law nearly all occurred "either in country districts where workers find it extremely difficult to give evidence against their employers, or in seaside and hotel laundries where the work tends to be especially seasonal, and where living-in frequently increases the temptation to overwork the employees."[91] A stronger act had benefited a majority of workers, but overwork continued in small laundries where the hired hands would be dismissed at the approved hour but family members often worked on behind locked doors.[92] The poorest laundress, her health or her family keeping her from outside work, labored on, her numbers and circumstances quite often unknown to the inspector. Her choices were stark. Most often she chose overwork over starvation or the breakup of her family. With the passing of the act, "upon which they had pined so much faith," workers inundated inspectors with complaints by every post, many of which they could not handle. By far the largest group of such complaints related to low rates of wages and nonpayment for overtime—economic matters beyond the scope of factory legislation.[93]

Factory legislation, whatever its value, did nothing to eliminate the low wages prevalent in much of the trade and only a little to curb its long hours. The factory acts improved working conditions, but they were not a panacea for economic ills. Labor organization overcame sweating in some portions of the trade, as we shall see in the next chapter, but the setting of minimum standards of payment across the whole industry was only achieved in 1919 when the industry became subject to the provisions of the Trade Boards Act.

The enforcement of minimum wages by governments was a highly controversial tool of public policy. Such overt state intervention in the marketplace was bound to be contentious in a capitalist democracy. Discussion of the issue did not even divide cleanly along laissez-faire versus collectivist lines. Sir Charles Dilke and Lady Emilia Dilke, in their respective roles as member of Parliament and chairman of the Women's Trade Union League, argued that minimum wage regulation should be a logical corollary to factory act legislation, while J. Ramsay MacDonald and Clara Collet, their allies in so many other labor causes, vehemently opposed government intervention to establish minimum wage rates.[94] MacDonald argued that "the humanitarian heroics of Wages Boards as a remedy for sweating break down, as all other heroics do, when faced with the facts of life." In his opinion, such approaches did nothing to attack the root causes of the problem and, in any case, the Australian experiment with wages boards upon which proposed British legislation was based had achieved little.[95]

The most vigorous lobbying for minimum wage legislation came from a pressure group called the Anti-Sweating League. The league had been formed in reaction to the Board of Trade's 1906 wages inquiry and the Select Committee on Home Work, both of which had revealed appallingly low wages in a number of industries. Laundry work was numbered among these industries, although the initial attention of the league (whose membership included such prominent citizens as Gertrude Tuckwell, George Bernard Shaw, H. G. Wells, and G. K. Chesterton) was directed toward the plight of the home worker. In 1906, at the instigation of the *Daily News*, a Sweated Industries Exhibit was held at the Queen's Hall, London. This exhibition dramatically demonstrated the hardships and distressing conditions of the men and women at the bottom of the industrial totem pole. The spate of investigative reports, mainly on home work, which were disseminated in the wake of this highly successful publicity campaign accentuated the pressure for government action.[96] The first Trade Boards legislation, introduced in 1909, was substantially a response to the impressive efforts of the Anti-Sweating League. The setting up of Trade Boards, which required representation from employers, workers, and government, introduced a social policy that assumed new responsibility for the economic welfare of the people without entirely displacing private enterprise. When the act first took effect on January 1910, it covered four trades: tailoring, paper boxmaking, chainmaking, and machine-made lace finishing, and contained a mechanism for future expansion to other trades.

Many laundry workers' employment was "sweated;" that is, it was paid at a rate that yielded them "insufficient to enable an adult person to obtain anything like proper food, clothing and house accommodation."[97] However, there was little immediate pressure to include the industry under the Trade Boards Act because the work was neither predominantly done at home, nor, by this date, largely nonmechanized, and because, for some workers, wages might be relatively good, especially in unionized workplaces. In 1911, the *Daily News,* which had organized the 1906 exhibition, highlighted low wages in the trade, but employers were quick to protest that the trade paid good wages and that occasional low income was solely the result of lack of ambition or lack of skill on the part of individual workers or the unfair competition of a handful of price-cutting employers.[98]

The first concerted attempt to have the trade included under the legislation did not take place until 1913 with pressure coming from two main sources: the London County Council, and the important London laundry district of Acton. Both had the support of the Anti-Sweating League and the National Union of Women Workers. The London County Council, largely at the insistence of John Burns, the Councillor from Battersea, had established the practice of including in its contracts a "fair wages" clause by which it paid either trade union rates or rates "generally accepted as fair in the districts where the work is carried on." In 1913 when the council tendered for contracts to do the washing needed for its schools, no such rate existed in the laundry trade. The council, upon discovering this, appealed to the National Federation of Women Workers (NFWW) and to the Launderers' Association for their support in requesting the establishment of a Laundry Trade Board. The former body, along with the Women's Labour League, the Fabian Society, the Women's Trade Union League, and the Anti-Sweating League, proffered its enthusiastic endorsement, but the employers denied the council their approval. The London County Council and the NFWW petitioned the Board of Trade to move to control laundry wages, while in a letter to the press Gertrude Tuckwell and others stressed:

> Nothing can exaggerate the fact that the London County Council find it practically impossible to undertake this laundry work by any other means than the machinery of a Trade Board. It is the first time that a public body has taken such a step [urging the establishment of the Trade Board], and such an application must necessarily carry a great weight both with the Government and the public.[99]

The interest the letter writers predicted materialized; representatives of an estimated three to four thousand Acton laundry workers wrote to J. J. Mallon, secretary of the Anti-Sweating League, voicing their support on the grounds of their dreadfully long hours which, they said, damaged not only their health but also the care of their homes and families. George

Vine, of Shepherd's Bush and Acton, president of the Launderer's Association, countered that long hours were not the fault of the employer but of the customs of the public, and added that the threat of a Trade Board would only encourage the ingenuity of engineers in developing new machinery to displace workers.[100] The Acton Urban District Council, now the most important laundry area in the metropolis, held a public inquiry to ascertain whether the locality should urge the government to extend the Trade Boards Act to the whole of the laundry industry. The council decided in the end "that no good would be served" by calling a town meeting to urge such a course of action, but in the process of reaching this decision, considerable press attention was directed to the industry. Local workers and employers appeared before the special committee along with representatives from the Launderers' Association, the Anti-Sweating League, the National Federation of Women Workers, the National Union of Gas Workers and General Labourers, and both the senior lady inspector (now Rose E. Squire) and the inspector in charge of the West London District. Prominently reported was the evidence that 18 percent of the members of the National Union of Women Workers in the area earned less than twelve shillings a week. The workers, feeling betrayed by the council, threatened a strike as soon as the busy season began. Employers, for their part, denied allegations of sweating, and also argued that the trade was unsuitable for Trade Board regulation. Some employers felt that a stigma attached to Trade Board regulation, while others pointed out that there was no precedent for such regulation of a service industry—one in which wages represented 50 percent of gross receipts. Because the laundry employer was selling a service that customers could perform for themselves, it was argued that it was more important than in nonservice industries that an employer be able to tailor his rates (and hence wages) to the purses of the people in the community he served. A single scale of payment would thus wreak havoc. Many proprietors feared a repetition of the situation that had existed earlier under the Factory Acts, when (to their minds) unfair competition resulted from incomplete regulation.[101]

The latter fear appeared to be justified when, in 1913 and 1914, a select committee of the House was urged to establish a Trade Board to regulate wages of only those workers employed at calendering and other steam ironing machines. The employers, who reputedly subscribed five thousand pounds to a fund to fight inclusion, defeated the first attempt by pointing out that the use of the term "steam" laundry equipment discriminated unfairly among employers using different sources of power. The following year, the word steam was omitted but attention remained focused on machine ironing, perhaps the worst paid of all laundry work (32 percent of adult workers earned less than ten shillings while only 15 percent earned more than fifteen shillings).[102] But the proposal failed again. The *New Statesman* blamed the ineptness of the Board of Trade, which, it alleged, made little effort to add new strength to their case when facing an especially well-organized employers' lobby. Whatever the reasons, the select committee once again pronounced the evidence insufficient to warrant the issuing of a provisional order; wages in the industry were thus left untouched until after the war.[103]

In 1919, the laundry industry became subject to Trade Board regulation under circumstances which disarmed some of the earlier employer opposition. The Laundry Trade Board applied to the entire industry; lower minimum rates were established for two particularly low wage areas (the north of Scotland and Cornwall); a combination of union activity and large laundry catchment areas, made possible by increased use of motorized vans, had almost equalized prices; and, finally, an amended Trade Boards Act in 1918 had removed the phrase that was thought to attach a stigma to industries under minimum-wage regulation.[104] The war had had its effect too: laundresses who had experienced the superior wages and conditions in munitions works were not anxious to return to sweated conditions and were supported by the War Cabinet Committee on Women in Industry, which recommended the immediate establishment of a "reasonable subsistence wage" for all adult women.[105] It was not until July 1920 that rates were fixed for males (excluding outside workers such as vanmen)—rates that were roughly double those for women.[106] Despite the clear sex discrimination in wage scales, apparently Trade Board rates generally benefited laundrywomen. According to the major contemporary historian of the British Trade Boards system, the most striking evidence that legislation helped to increase wages in the laundry trade was that the real wages of adult women increased 75 percent between 1914 and 1922.[107] A further improvement was that overtime was payable after forty-eight hours of work or after five hours on a Saturday.[108] The implied "normal" forty-eight hour week, though not a legal restriction, eventually brought about a reduction in the hours worked by most laundresses.

The Trade Boards were welcomed for the benefits they brought to many workers, but they did not mean improvement for all. In the short run, some workers suffered because of a reduction of the numbers employed, a result of both Trade Board intervention and a sales drive by American

Table 1. Female Laundry Workers' Wage Rates, 1919

Age	Trade Board rates per 48-hour week s. d.	Court of Arbitration awards per 48-hour week s. d.
Under 15	12.0	11.0
15 and under 16	15.0	16.0
16 and under 17	19.0	19.0
17 and under 18	23.0	24.0
18 and over	28.0	28.0

Source: Dorthy Sells, *British Trade Boards System: A Study in Industrial Democracy* (Washington, D.C.: Brookings, 1939), 90.

Table 2. Variations in Minimum Time Rates of Female Laundry Workers, Nov. 1919–July 1922

Date	Normal hours per week	Wage per week at 15 years or under s. d.	Wage per week at 18 years or over s. d.	Cost of living index number*
Nov. 1919	48	12.0	28.0	225
Nov. 1920	48	12.0	30.0	276
May 1921	48	13.0	32.0	228
Dec. 1921	48	12.0	30.0	199
July 1922	48	10.0	28.0	184

Source: Dorothy Sells, *British Trade Boards System: A Study in Industrial Democracy* (Washington, D.C.: Brookings, 1939), 91.
*From *Labour Gazette,* where July 1914 equals 100.

manufacturers of laundry equipment, although it was thought that numbers had started to expand again by the later 1920s.[109] Evasion of the law was comparatively easy in the smallest laundries—establishments that suffered most from competition with highly industrialized concerns. In 1920, the Ministry of Labour ruled that the board could only fix rates for hours worked, thereby allowing employers to reduce wages legally in the slack season. In addition, the combined votes of employers' representatives and appointed members of the Laundry Trade Board were able to establish moderate time and piece work scales over the opposition of employee representatives.[110] Finally, the minimum rates established were so modest that they fell below the wages of many workers in large mechanized laundries. For this reason, the best organized employers, who were usually the most industrialized, accepted the act with few complaints. In 1922, National Federation of Launderers survey found that 49 percent of the employees in a sample of 157 member laundries were being paid above the rate required by the board; Trade Board regulation aided most those whose wages were particularly low and whose workplaces were readily monitored.

The lot of the laundry worker in 1924 was still less than ideal. The labor was among the most arduous: it required long hours of standing and an endurance of steam, heat, damp, and the smell of other people's dirty linen. Nonetheless, the work was much pleasanter than that endured by her counterpart in 1894. Even the poorest solitary worker doing a bit of her neighbor's wash could now quite often do her work in a tolerably well-equipped public washhouse. It was shorter, safer, healthier work, work with the dignity and safeguards of other industrial work. In some ways, even the perception of the work had altered; from the last resort of the unskilled elderly widow or married woman saddled with a spouse who would not or could not support her, it had become simply part of the increasingly important service sector of the economy, work that any woman, or man, might consider. The history of regulation of the laundry industry shows clearly the debt owed to policies that from the 1880s had begun to devote increasing attention to social welfare—to the role of public policy in "leveling up" the economic and social opportunities of citizens. Laundry work became part of a broader process of social amelioration and experimentation.

A washing dolly, also known as a peggy, possing stick, or laundry punch, was used to loosen soil from garments in a manner that combined the agitation actions of a modern washing machine with those of a butter churn. The dollies illustrated above are only three of several designs, the most common of which was a wooden dolly that resembled a four- or five-legged stool topped with a handle. Dollying was arduous work, reserved for heavy articles such as sheets or blankets, and was sometimes performed by men.

Irons heated internally, either by charcoal placed on a grill inside the iron or by a piece of heated metal, were an alternative to the more common flat iron. Some laundresses preferred them, but considerable judgment and dexterity was needed to handle slugs of hot metal or prevent charcoal from soiling freshly laundered goods. Illustrated above are two charcoal-heated box irons as well as a small tally iron, which, when heated by the poker shown, was used to give a finishing touch to ruffles and frills.

The collection of flat irons illustrated above shows the range of sizes and shapes of irons that might have been used in hand laundry work, from the heavy goose iron (pictured beside the clothes sprayer) to the tiny finishing irons. Simple flat irons or sad irons, however, were used most often. Sad irons had handles or covers that could be removed from an iron that had cooled and reattached to another left heating on the stove.

An 1888 advertisement for the London Co-operative Laundry and Cleaning Company.

This view of the Faversham Sanitary Steam Laundry Co. Ltd., and the two following, are taken from one of the firm's advertising brochures, and are reproduced courtesy of the Kent Archives Office.

CALENDER, &c., ROOM.

PART OF IRONING ROOM.

CHAPTER 4

———◆•◆———

Self-Help, Sisterly Help, and Industrial Action

Laundry work was first and foremost heavy manual labour, and it was the means, whether primary or secondary, of earning a living. It was also the primary mechanism that defined the lives and social circumstances of those who earned their livelihood by its performance. Laundry workers, in common with other laboring people, tried in various ways to influence the conditions under which they worked. They did so as individuals, as members of unions, as supporters of efforts to control wages and working conditions through public policy. They did so on their own and with the support of middle-class organizing bodies. In what ways—and how successfully— were laundresses able informally to alter their working circumstances?[1] Did their organized efforts result in any significant victories? The efforts of middle-class women had done much to make the laundry a better place in which to earn a living, but were there any ambiguities to these sisterly relations across class lines?[2] This chapter attempts to answer these questions and to describe more fully the workplace circumstances of a major service sector industry.

The Fight for Industrial Rights

Laundresses enjoyed, particularly among their employers, a reputation for sturdy independence. One laundry proprietor spoke for many of his colleagues when he testified before the Royal Commission on Labour that "laundresses were the most independent people on the face of the earth."[3]

This attribution of "independence" was a slur rather than a compliment. The laundress, by definition a service worker, displayed little of the deference that was expected of the servant, of the laundry maid in the great house, or of any indoor domestic servant for that matter. Many were so resistant to any sort of industrial discipline that one proprietor, a man with colonial experience who had invested in a laundry after his return to England, was led to remark to a factory inspector "that he would rather continue to manage a hundred coolies on a West Indian estate than ten girls in a laundry."[4]

Laundry workers influenced the nature of their workplace situation both through action that altered the structure of employment and through demeanor that changed the tone of workplace relationships. The grueling and too often sweated, casual nature of laundry work often attracted rough-mannered and tough women, although, as Margaret MacDonald noted, some laundry workers were among "the most refined and intelligent girls whom one could find anywhere in London."[5] The former workers sustained themselves through long hours of heavy, unpleasant toil with coarse jokes and banter, quantities of beer and sometimes a pinch of snuff.[6] One author who had worked as a young man in the laundry-dominated area of North Kensington noted that even in a Notting Hill billiard room he encountered "nothing in the way of language nearly as bad as the women in the laundry used habitually."[7] In some small laundries, the proprietor who worked alongside the employees was as acid-tongued and rough-mannered as the rest, but elsewhere assertive behavior and a general abrasiveness can be interpreted in part as a symbolic affirmation that a laundress's endurance had earned her the right to ignore the proprieties observed by those of higher economic and social status. Of course, the extent to which any such behavior involved a clear-cut situational disrespect (to use Erving Goffman's term) is impossible to gauge. Sometimes laundresses' aggressive behavior was a defensive reaction to exploitation. The inspector who listened to the complaints of the proprietor quoted above observed that he was one of a growing number of absentee laundry owners who bought laundries in the hope of gaining "a small fortune" and installed a manager who shared in the profits to insure this. Such owners, this inspector reported, complain of workers' unmanageability, but they "are most surprised when accidents occur owing to the absolute ignorance on their part of the danger of machinery. They are equally surprised when cautioned that their manager has been employing the workers beyond their legal limit."[8] Disrespectful behavior was certainly a protest in such situations and must have helped to forge a bond among workwomen and to enhance the distance between themselves and their employers. Employers were not hurt financially by raw language, though the reputation gained for the trade by the most vocal and disrespectful workers might explain why some "parents and school mistresses concerned for the welfare of young girls are adverse to the laundry."[9] How important this was is not readily assessed, but the character of much of the labor force inclined some to the view that laundry management was not a job for the faint-hearted. One inspector with extensive knowledge of and sympathy for the laundry worker put it this way: "They may at present be characterized as a hard-working, impulsive, short-tempered body of women, the control of whom, under the existing irregular conditions which have been thoughtlessly and unnecessarily encouraged, is not to be lightly undertaken by a man without a fair amount of physical and moral courage."[10]

Easily the most commonly voiced complaint against laundry workers by management concerned the workers' frequently successful efforts to determine their own hours of work. Official and unofficial reports are full of evidence that laundresses did not readily conform to the pattern of working desired by employers. "That they are peculiarly irregular in their habits it is impossible to deny," admitted a factory inspector, while Clara Collet, summarizing the results of her investigation of the laundry trade for the Royal Commission on Labour, noted that "all the employers unite in saying that it is impossible to induce their laundresses to come punctually, a large number persistently coming late."[11] The laundress's unwillingness to work in an orderly fashion was used by some employers to justify their opposition to factory legislation. Not only did employers not want the restriction of hours that would come with legislation, according to a deputation in 1895 from the National Laundry Association to George Russell, M.P.; "Laundry workers, too, preferred to work irregularly, and it was impossible to get them to work for a week after Good Friday."[12] When workers testified to working punishingly long hours, sometimes without meal breaks or even all night long, some employers responded by blaming the workers, citing their unpunctuality and their lack of willingness to work early in the week.[13] (Employers were equally ready to use the defense of customer tyranny and conservatism to justify long hours.) On the other hand, those employers who welcomed the regulation of laundry hours also sometimes reported the lack of punctuality and irregular working habits among their workwomen.[14]

These irregularities cannot be attributed entirely to a deliberate attempt by laundresses to modify their permanent working environment. Those laundry workers who objected to any limitation of working hours were most often casual employees, driven to work by temporary financial desperation, who needed to earn as much as possible. One proprietor explained the circumstances of such employees: "Some women, good hands, who were formerly constant workers, only work when their husbands are out of employ; these hands are anxious to make as much time, piece-work, as they can; it is the only way of feeding the little ones when the husband is unemployed."[15] For long-term laundry workers the motives were different. While they too worked long hours and were often their families' main or sole support, their celebrated unpunctuality was largely a consequence of their attempt to combine domestic life and family responsibilities with paid employment. It is significant that many reports specify that the tardy employees were married women. Three-quarters of one launderer's hands were married women; "They were supposed to come at 8 a.m. but rarely did so," he grumbled, while a more understanding laundry manager explained that "there are many domestic reasons that prevent women beginning work at a punctual and stated hour, and in consequence they are glad to work on later to make up for lost time in the morning and again at the dinner hour."[16] Married women had all the familiar domestic tasks to perform in the morning: older children to get off to school, smaller tots to deliver to creche or caretaker, and the family's dinner to prepare. Some "often prepared the dinner for the children in the morning before they went to work, and the children ate it in the streets," while others lost time in the middle of the day suckling infants brought to the laundry.[17] Creches often did not open until 8:00 a.m. or were far from the woman's workplace, making a late start at work inevitable for many laundresses.[18] In the smallest and poorest laundries in which married women predominated and where the owners' personal circumstances were very like those of her employees, flexible working seems to have been most readily accepted and accommodations were commonly made for the nursing of infants in the laundry. In this segment of the trade, confrontation between capitalist and worker was not much in evidence, and since status differentiations were ambiguous, industrial relations were rarely seriously confrontational.

In larger establishments, most employers were less ready to make concessions. Indeed, they frequently fined workers for being as little as five minutes late. In one Lancashire laundry, where work started at 6:00 a.m., fines were imposed at three minutes after 6:00 and sometimes amounted to "as much as 1s. 6d. out of a wage of 4s. 6d."; in London fines of one pence for the first five minutes and two pence for each five minutes thereafter were reported to be common.[19] A few launderers permitted their married workers to begin work half an hour later than other employees,[20] and, after the passage of the 1907 Factory Act, it is likely that some of the laundries which adopted a 9:00 a.m. to 9:00 p.m. pattern for working (instead of the more usual 8:00 a.m. to 8:00 p.m.) did so to accommodate married women. In rare cases, very large laundries engaged a male relief staff to perform machine ironing at night when there was a particularly heavy press of work, such as a large ship's order.[21]

Large hand laundries catering to an elite clientele had the greatest incentive to make concessions since they were highly dependent on the talents of the experienced finery ironer, who was most often a married woman. (In contrast, employees in highly mechanized laundries, whose circumstances will be discussed in the next chapter, were predominantly young, single, and easily trained or replaced.) Their skill gave the best ironers some real bargaining power; it allowed them to enforce for themselves some real measure of control over their industrial role. Unlike the washerwoman, or the famous handloom weaver, they were not displaced (at any rate in this period) by the machine. These experts had always been employed on the most delicate and complicated work, and their services were still indispensable in most general or household laundries. These workers, though they may have gained by joining a union, were far from powerless in their unorganized dealings with laundry owners and managers. With such pivotal workers, employers could find that fines were a tactic of industrial discipline that might well backfire. Faced with the great "difficulty of inducing ironers to come punctually," one employer found it more effective to offer a gratuity (payable at the end of a nine-month period so as to exclude casual workers) of one shilling a week "to those ironers who are both regular and punctual in their attendance," and another went so far as to offer a prize of three pounds to the employee who had been in the laundry for three years without losing time and a 10 percent bonus for all employees who were punctual during the busy months from April to July inclusive.[22] The importance that was attached by management to the attendance of these workers may be gauged by reflecting that the three pounds prize would have represented perhaps 5 percent to 6 percent of the annual income of a quite proficient ironer in regular employment throughout the year (assuming no drastic reductions in pay in the slack periods). Highly valued workers, then, were able to induce employers to use incentives rather than repression in their efforts to implement industrial discipline.

Sometimes workers further tried to limit the length of their working days. While it was alleged that some workers deliberately slowed their work in order "to have to work overtime," married women more often preferred a limitation of hours in order to spend more time with their families, adding that "they could save more money at home than they made by overtime working."[23] Additional child care costs, which could equal the overtime pay, combined with the necessity of shopping at the few stores that stayed open late and charged more, made overtime a losing proposition for many. The most astute workers recognized that their industrial power was greatest when employers were under greatest consumer pressure. It is not surprising, then, to find workers resisting pressures to intensify their labor. According to one observer, "They will not work during the London season longer than 11 o'clock for anybody I believe. As they describe it they are worked out, and no doubt they are."[24] This was the most profitable part of the employer's year and workers were unwilling to put themselves out unless they were given some special consideration. "It is the greatest difficulty in the world," noted the proprietor of a cooperative laundry,

> to get them to have less than an hour (mealbreak) in the middle of the day. It is quite a favour on their part to have only half an hour in the London season. If I were to go into the laundry and ask them as a favour I believe they would work for me. I am a little popular with them, as sometimes when I have been there I leave 2s. or 3s. for some beer for them privately, they hear it is from me, and if I were to go up and ask them they would do it, but they would not do it for our manager. They are very exacting in that respect. I do not know that I ought to call it something for I think it is quite right myself.[25]

Laundresses were a hard-working lot on the whole and responded positively to employers who displayed some concern for people as well as profits. The employer cited above professed a deep interest in women's work and testified that when he opened the laundry he "took it up as much as a philanthropic matter as anything else with some enthusiastic ideas with regard to some reformations that ought to be made";[26] if true, he was not representative of the majority of employers.

Laundresses may well have had a further indirect industrial power. Some of them had the implicit power that derived from the two-wage household. As we have seen, the domestic economy of the working class family frequently depended on a complex dovetailing of employments, but, on the other hand, there would have been times when several members of a household were simultaneously employed. This could help to give one worker the economic support that was a prerequisite for vigorous and protracted industrial action. For example, the ability of building workers to exert control over the labor process through the informal mechanism of the workgroup, which has been ably documented by Richard Price, may well have been aided by the support of their laundress wives. One contemporary observer detected what, in his view, was a very real connection between the militancy of building workers and the employment of their female relatives as laundresses: "A very large proportion of this labour (laundry work), perhaps nearly one-half, is done by the wives and sisters and daughters of London bricklayers, and London bricklayers' labourers, hence that strike lasted so long some years ago, because hundreds of their wives kept the men through it."[27]

In a similar fashion, laundresses whose spouses were for the moment in full employment could enjoy enhanced bargaining power. Of course, some working-class men objected to their wives working except in periods of economic emergency, but laundresses, whose labor offered no threat to male employment prospects and was "domestic" in character and frequently more regular than that of their men, may well have received more masculine support than many other working women.

Laundresses' efforts to impose controls over their hours and conditions of work received the support of many male-dominated labor organizations. As long as laundresses were working as many as sixteen hours a day, male workers certainly would have found it more difficult to press their case for a workday limited to eight hours. Giving aid to laundry workers in their campaign for decent working conditions could also be viewed as a means of assisting the widows of working men in their formidable struggle to support themselves and their families, a point made by Tom Mann in 1891. In that year, the London Trades Council gave its active support to the demonstration in Hyde Park in favor of including laundry work under the Factory Acts, while a year earlier the Trades Union Congress, meeting in Liverpool, had devoted special attention to organizing women in trade unions, one result of which was the formation of a laundresses' union in Liverpool with the backing of the Liverpool Trades Council and the Liverpool Society for the Formation of Women's Trade Unions. The banner of the Laundresses' Union formed part of the procession on the final day of the TUC conference, although technically the union was not formed until sometime later.[28] Evidence of labor movement endorsement of laundry workers' efforts at organization can be traced as far back as the 1830s when the Owenite press recorded organizational efforts in many women's trades, including laundry work; the Owenite center in London also provided meeting space for women's union meetings (an appropriate place to meet was often a problem for women workers), and, in 1834, the *Pioneer* reported the success of two strikes by laundresses in London.[29] The London Trades Council "gave strong support to the new movement for the organization of women workers" when the Women's Protective and Provident League was formed in 1874, and two years later a member of the council reported unanimous support for the new movement at the Glasgow Trades Union Congress conference (although it should be added that the council's enthusiasm for the women's cause was not always unqualified).[30]

Laundry workers probably also received encouragement and advice from organized labor on a casual, informal, day-to-day basis. Unfortunately, however, the bias of the historical record toward both crisis and dramatic change means that evidence of active collaboration is primarily found at moments of union formation or industrial conflict. When laundry workers in Acton organized unions, they were supported by the local branch of the Gasworkers' Union, which sent representatives to organizing meetings; the Liverpool Laundry Workers were backed in contract negotiations by the Warehouse Workers' Union; in Fulham gasworkers encouraged laundrywomen to form a branch of the National Union of Women Workers and at the same time invited male laundry employees to join the Gasworkers' and General Labours' Union; in Longton the Pottery Workers union offered similar encouragement to organizing laundry workers, while in Tilbury dockers came out to urge laundrywomen to form a union and affiliate themselves with the Dockers' Union.[31] For the most part, laundresses had little experience with organization, negotiation, or industrial action and scant knowledge of the law: this made the assistance of other labor leaders especially valuable. The laundry workers of York in 1913 were fortunate in the staunch backing they received from local labor organizations and sympathizers both when they formed a union and, a few months later, when they decided to test their new found solidarity in a strike. Their initial unionization had had the encouragement of the local trades and labor council but, more significantly, when the laundresses struck, they did so with the backing of the Gasworkers' Union, the National Union of Railwaymen, and a sympathetic local councillor, Will Dobbie, also the prospective Labour candidate for York. These groups gave vital assistance to a fledgling union which had neither bargaining skills nor strike funds and, along with a representative from the National

Union of Women Workers, represented the workers in negotiations with their employers. This help created more of a balance of strength at the bargaining table to which the employers brought not only their power as owners of capital but also the assistance of lawyers and representatives from the Northern Counties Laundries Association and the Federation of Laundries Association.

That this union, which had scarcely had the time to inscribe the names of its members, was successful in gaining an improvement in hours and an increase in wages undoubtedly owed something to the quality and enthusiasm of its outside support. The laundresses' case was drawn to the attention of the citizens of York through a large demonstration in the marketplace, enlivened by the music of the York City Band and addressed by labor leaders. One York councillor emphasized the "miserable, sweated conditions" under which the laundry workers toiled and urged the public to support these workers despite the measure of personal inconvenience that might ensue.[32] In York there was considerable public sympathy for the laundresses, who earned between ten and fifteen shillings a week in summer and as little as eight shillings in winter. An amicable agreement was reached with the employers, in part because some employers recognized that a citywide union could benefit them. The industry was highly competitive and labor-intensive, and an across-the-board union standard of hours and rates of wages could provide a laundry proprietor with some security against price-cutting by competitors. Support of the laundresses by their male fellow unionists was apparently straightforward, and perhaps was best expressed by a representative of the Fulham Gasworkers' and General Labourers' Union who stated: "They did not want men and women to be crucified on the altar of capitalism."[33] That the laundresses' cause was readily endorsed because it posed no threat to men's jobs was left unspoken.

Perhaps the hardest fought industrial struggle waged by laundresses took place in Hull in 1920 when a determined band of laundresses, an estimated 300 to 400 strong, held out for six weeks in a strike for a minimum wage of two pounds per week and recognition of their union. The strike was precipitated not only by the employers' refusal to pay more than twenty-eight shillings a week (the Trade Board minimum established the previous year), but also by the dismissal of sixty-two laundresses who refused to work overtime. The support of organized labor in Hull for the strikers went well beyond mere lip service: all the unions affiliated with the Hull Trades Council raised levies to provide strike pay for the laundresses

and a number took up additional collections. Work in the laundries continued during the strike in a desultory way with the aid of blackleg labor,
some of whom were smuggled past the pickets in clothes baskets.[34] Blacklegs were initially easy to employ since at the time the strike was called
there was considerable unemployment in Hull among women, especially in
shoemaking, dressmaking, millinery, and jam making, but the strikers
soon claimed to have "converted" many of the blacklegs to their cause.[35]
The employers took an intransigent approach, demanding that the women
return to work and apologize before any of their demands would even be
considered, and, heartened by press reports of consumer annoyance at the
inconvenience, they resisted attempts by the Lord Mayor and a representative from the Ministry of Labour to mediate the dispute.[36]

Despite the prospect of a long strike the laundrywomen were buoyed in
their militancy by a strong and unified labour front, and encouraged by a
successful public meeting addressed by Joe Cavanaugh, Chairman of the
Hull Trades and Labour Council, and the support of union leaders from
London, including Margaret Bondfield. They were also sustained by their
indignation at what they saw as the transparent hypocrisy of one of the
leading laundry managers, who was both an alderman and one of the more
respected members of the Methodist Church. Picketers taunted this adver-
sary with endless renderings of his favorite hymn, which included the
refrain "Dare to do right, dare to be true. . . . Stand by your conscience
and battle till death," and found in the coincidence of a major Methodist
conference in Hull a marvelous propaganda opportunity.[37] A labor periodical described the laundresses' strategy:

> There was a procession of the brethren to the Wesleyan Church. Now the
> strikers have nothing against religion but they have much against humbug.
> So they formed up and joined the end of the procession. By taking a short-
> cut, they got to the Church first, so that the embarrassed worshippers, with
> the blushing Alderman in their midst, entered the church between two lines
> of strikers, who in the most orderly manner followed them in, and took pos-
> session of the front seats. Rather an ordeal for the Alderman—but not so
> difficult as for a rich man to enter into the Kingdom of Heaven.[38]

Whether pinched in pocketbook or conscience, the employers finally came
to terms with their workers. With the aid of the Transport Workers' Federation, the laundresses were able to negotiate higher wages, shorter hours,
recognition of their union, and the dismissal of all blacklegs, along with an
undertaking on the part of the employers that no new employees would be
taken on until all the strikers had resumed work.[39]

Despite the success of industrial action by organized laundry workers in Hull and York, it should not be assumed that strike action by laundresses was always so enthusiastically conducted, that such action was consistently undertaken by organized workers, or that unionization was easily achieved or readily sustained. On a number of occasions, women working in laundries showed themselves to be capable of launching direct collective action in response to poor wages or working conditions without the support of a union or the active assistance of others in the labor movement. Successful strikes were undertaken in Notting Hill and Westminister in 1834 by non-unionized laundresses; in 1893, workers at the Leamington Steam Laundry stopped work to protest against low wages—as little as three farthings an hour for apprentices—while similar actions were taken by laundry workers in the village of Wootten in 1913 and in Dublin in 1916.[40] The action of the Leamington Spa laundresses failed, at least in part because, at the instigation of the employer, police constables were called in to assist nonstriking workers past the pickets, but their protest at least revealed the other side of the firm's hyperbolic advertising claim that "our employees work shorter hours than at any other place in the district, and in well-ventilated and healthy premises."[41] The laundry's proprietor, Sidney Tebbutt, a knowledgeable innovator in the area of steam laundry equipment who had created on his premises a new "Model Sanitary Laundry" in which working conditions were probably superior to those in many other laundries, attributed the strike to the rowdyism of an undesirable element among his workers. He asserted confidently that "there is no place in the town where there is such a respectable, contented, and happy lot of girls as in our laundry."[42] Needless to say, the "undesirable ones" were not re-employed. That such collective action was often readily broken by employers should cause no surprise. What is remarkable is that spontaneous direct action by workers with limited skills sometimes resulted in concessions by their employers.

Victories achieved by spontaneous action, however, were often precarious, for they were rarely followed by permanent organization. Unpremeditated work stoppages were often defensive reactions to altered working conditions—to attempts to cut wages, to the introduction of new machinery, to unfair or excessively authoritarian behavior on the part of managers and forewomen—rather than assertive efforts to improve pay and working conditions. In such circumstances, workers often had little knowledge of or sympathy toward the union movement in general. Such instances of industrial action are best seen as outbursts of indignation directed toward the alteration of circumstances of the moment rather than as evidence of a

broader conception of workers' rights and goals in the workplace. Leslie
Woodcock Tentler, writing about wage-earning women in early twentieth-
century America, concluded that much of women's collective protest in
that country was similarly ephemeral in nature. A young laundry worker
who was also an ardent trade unionist recorded her frustration with the
impermanence of spontaneous action at her place of work:

> One day, however, we had a little recreation. A new manager had taken
> charge of the floor, who had very little experience in the laundry business.
> But soon enough he began to suggest and enforce new rules. We did not
> object as long as our pay did not diminish; however, as soon as there was an
> indication of diminishing our pay we were all provoked and immediately
> decided to quit, and to go the boss at once. How romantic that spontaneous
> outburst was! What fiery interest it aroused in all of us! Everyone was ready
> to sacrifice her job—of course her job, since there was nothing more precious
> to any of us who were ready to sacrifice for the principles of humanity, of
> human rights . . . in a solid group, to the amazement of the rest of the
> workers, we marched down to the office at the end of the floor. As we reached
> the office, the boss came out pale and trembling. . . . I being one of the girls
> in the front row, spontaneously began to tell him our demands, surprising as
> it may be, without losing my self-control. He listened, asked a few questions,
> which were promptly answered, and in about fifteen minutes, we, victorious,
> walked back across the floor. The girls were satisfied, but not I.[43]

Essentially defensive action of this sort, while it may have reinforced laundry workers' reputation for assertive behavior, did not necessarily increase
the likelihood of permanent unionization.

The difficulties inherent in the unionization of women workers have
often been noted. The episodic, secondary nature of much female labor, it
has been argued, militated against effective organization, and many wom-
en's orientation toward home and family resulted in both an expectation of
short-lived work force participation and a lack of career commitment.
Laundry employment did not necessarily fit this pattern. Many laundresses worked in the industry for many years, both before and after marriage, and were the primary support of their families. Therefore, it is
crucial to look beyond these facile hypotheses to explain the pattern of
unionization in the laundry trade. The first significant feature that
emerges from the literature is the timing of organization in the laundry
industry: unionization took place almost exclusively in the last years of the
nineteenth century and the first quarter of the twentieth. There are several
different reasons for this particular chronology. Union organization was

simply not relevant as long as most laundry workers were either employed independently or in very small community laundries; as a consequence, there was little unionization until the industry included a substantial number of sizeable units. Among the earliest unions were those in laundry-dominated areas; in 1877, for example, laundresses formed a union in Notting Hill, one in Hampstead in London, and another in Brighton.[44]

In common with most organizations of laundry workers, these unions were formed with the assistance and encouragement of one of the umbrella bodies concerned with women workers, in this case the Women's Protective and Provident League. In fact, most unionization of laundry workers took place during the lifetime of several organizations whose raison d'etre was the betterment of female workers. The Women's Trade Union League, originally founded as the Women's Protective and Provident League, existed between 1874 and 1921 (in the latter year it was absorbed into the Trades Union Congress as the Women's section), while its offshoot body, the National Federation of Women Workers (NFWW), founded in 1906, survived until 1920, when it amalgamated with the National Union of General and Municipal Workers. The Women's Industrial Council was active between 1894 and 1919, almost the same period of time during which there was a separately organized female factory inspectorate (1893-1920). The very existence of these bodies was symptomatic of a growth in the general concern for the working conditions of sweated workers and for the special circumstances of women workers. At the same time, this new concern revealed a growing appreciation both of the economic significance of the expanding service sector and of the need to provide some industrial protection, whether through legislation, inspection, or trade unionism, for the citizens, often women, who were employed in this sector. The years when there was the greatest growth in unionization among laundry workers were also the years when there was considerable union activity among other women employed in service occupations, such as shop assistants, waitresses, some kinds of domestics, and bedmakers at the Cambridge colleges.[45] In common with many laundry workers, these women often formed unions under the auspices of the National Union of Women Workers, although women shop assistants might also be part of shop assistants' unions with both male and female membership.

Unionization closely followed auxiliary efforts to improve the working conditions of laundry workers through legislative means. When the first concerted efforts were made to convince legislators to include laundries under the Factory Acts in 1890 and 1891, numerous unions of laundry workers were established; in 1891 the Amalgamated Society of Laundresses was formed with branches in Kensal Green, Hackney, Wandsworth, Battersea, and North and South Fulham.[46] The unions, while they served to make a political point, were shortlived. Clara Collet, testifying about London laundresses' unions before the Royal Commission on Labour in 1893, stated: "I doubt whether there are now even 60 paying members in the whole union. Passive submission is not, however, a characteristic of the laundresses as a class, and the cause of the apparent failure of the Trade Union is probably due to impatience and lack of education."[47] By the next year, Charles Booth reported that the union had become extinct.[48] The difficulties encountered in forming and sustaining unions among laundresses provided, as pointed out above, the primary impetus to a shift in policy on the part of the WTUL—a shift from an exclusive concern for unionization and self-help to an emphasis on the campaign for legislative regulation and protection. This change of strategy perhaps accounts for the paucity of evidence of unionization during the first decade of the twentieth century, the period when major reforms were enacted to regulate the laundry industry. Laundresses had pinned their hopes on the new legislation and on the spirited efforts of the female factory inspectors. As a result, they may have felt less pressing need to organize. This does not, however, mean that laundry workers were unaware of the potential advantages of unionization when their interests were being directly threatened. In 1902, a laundry worker in Blackburn wrote to Lady Emilia Dilke at the Women's Trade Union League asking for assistance in forming a union branch. "The reason," she explained, "that has made me broach this subject now, is (that) I was speaking with the proprietor of the laundry in which I am presently employed and he was talking of lowering the prices of the articles which are sent to the laundry, which means that the proprietors will be obliged to compete and in the end would mean the lowering of the workpeoples' wages."[49]

Significant encouragement to laundry unionization came in 1913 and 1914 in the wake of a series of articles in the *Daily Herald* about sweated conditions in laundries, the Acton inquiry into laundry conditions and wages, and the vigorous support for organizing laundry workers by the WTUL, the NFWW, and the Anti-Sweating League.[50] In addition, an amendment to the Health Insurance Act required all workers earning less than £160 a year to join an approved society for the payment of benefits (including maternity benefits). These provisions gave the National Federation of Women Workers an opportunity to recruit new members, among them laundresses. Indeed, the federation found it necessary to both expand its staff to thirty and move to more spacious quarters in Mecklenburgh Square. (The financial pressure of paying both the insurance contribution and union dues, however, did drive some workers to approved societies not affiliated with a trade union.)[51] Bolstered by public and union support and encouraged by the success of some of their sister laundry workers, laundresses in Willingborough, Wootten, and York struck for higher wages, while many more in Sheffield, Stourbridge, Barrow-in-Furness, and London were able to improve their wages and working conditions at the bargaining table.[52]

Laundresses were also receiving sympathetic attention from journalists. Under such charged headlines such as "Laundry Serfs" and "Slaves in the Launderies," the *Daily Herald* (whose editor, George Lansbury, proved to be a keen advocate of the laundresses' cause) ran a series of articles in 1913—followed by a spirited correspondence—that drew attention to the long hours and poor wages in many parts of the industry, and emphasized to middle-class customers the social costs of the bouts of price-cutting which occurred periodically in this highly competitive and labor-intensive industry. Experts from both management and labor cited wage rates from different laundries throughout the country; it was easy enough for each side to find figures to suit its purposes in an industry characterized by a bewildering complexity of time-rates, piece-rates, and pay scales, as well as by much part-time and take-home work. The war of figures was put into perspective when seen in the context of a worker's needs, experiences, and opinions. "I work from 8:30 in the morning till 8:30 at night," wrote "Laundry Serf" to the *Daily Herald*:

> I am a general ironer, and on one day for ironing 72 pieces, one coat and a dress, I earned 2s. 3d.
> Will anyone suggest how we can organize into a trade union? We shall not get better wages until we organize for a strike. I will start at once if anyone will help me.
> The Laundry Association, she says, ought to be burned.
> I have for the last three weeks been working in a laundry here in the north of London. You can earn about 2d. an hour, and not that on some of the work when it comes out of wet starch.
> You have got to be very smart. What can a woman earn to keep herself and a girl of ten years who is delicate? We are slaving to keep the Fat Man in cigars and wines. Hoping someone will organize.[53]

Such publicity, especially when it was backed by the activities of professional union organizers, did produce results, but these tender shoots of labor growth required careful nurturing and frequent replanting. In Acton, there had been a spate of union formation in 1911, but by 1913, a number of the branches were much in need of resuscitation. There was also a recognition that existing unions could not achieve much more until the small laundries, where the most sweated conditions were found and which offered the most severe competition to fair-minded employers, came to embrace trade unionism.[54] Despite difficulties, progress was made. Laundry workers in Stourbridge, Wolverhampton, Bristol, Sheffield, Stratford, Westmoreland, Barrow, and Willenhall were able to negotiate favorable settlements, while in London and nearby centers, such as Brighton, the National Federation of Women Workers negotiated a scale of minimum wages with the Launderers' Association that was binding on their members throughout the London District.[55] In addition, the last months of the war saw a flurry of union organizing in such cities as Gloucester, Aberdeen, Hull, Cheltenham, and Manchester.[56] In 1917, the prospects for laundry workers seemed rosy enough to one member of the National Federation of Women Workers to lead her to comment, both optimistically and prophetically:

> Really the laundry trade should be a most satisfactory and beautiful trade for women, given the right conditions. Older women can continue at it long after they would not be considered suitable for other work.
>
> It is the trade that more women go back to than any other. After girls marry, if they have been skilled laundresses, they very often take it up again as piece-workers or daily workers. It is work many women will wish to take up after the war.[57]

Women did return to laundry work after the war, their attitudes often profoundly altered by wartime experiences. However, many of the old problems remained. The very advantages of the work were obstacles to unionization: workers who returned to the trade only in time of family need were hard to organize and were often driven by necessity to accept wages well below union rates. A union organizer in Brighton reported that the greatest difficulty in organizing workers could be attributed to

> married women doing casual part-time work at laundries. As their personal interest in the laundries is much smaller than that of the single full-time worker, they are very apt to think that the Union does not matter to them. This is a great mistake, for however short the time they work may be they need a strong union to keep up the rates, and moreover the very casual nature of their work encourages employers only to pay time rates, instead of a guaranteed weekly wage, and this is much to the detriment of the full-time workers.[58]

One response to punishing hours and low pay by a few laundresses was to set up on their own in cottage laundries, and this individualistic solution often served to place downward pressure on the wages of their fellow laundresses. Independence rarely yielded the hoped-for benefits. The lot of the small laundress in the nineteenth century had been miserable enough, but in the twentieth century, it could be disastrous; many a laundress unwittingly put herself on the same footing as the sweated seamstress trying to compete with factory output. "While it is natural that the workers should want to be their own masters," reported the *Woman Worker*, "there are a great many objections to home laundries. 'The houses,' says Mrs. Busby (a union organizer), 'were built for homes, not workshops, and without the proper appliances and in competition with large laundries the women have had very hard times. It is monstrous that because they are working at home their customers should expect them to wash garments for half-price, but so they do.' "[59]

Despite these difficulties, many a postwar laundry worker, her consciousness often raised by her experience of better working conditions and of unionization in munition works, returned to her trade demanding a better deal and prepared to join a union to support her demands. One thirty-nine-year-old laundry worker, who had been employed in laundries since the age of eleven, recounted her wartime experiences and the new determination that grew out of them. Her pay in a laundry in the northeast of London had been so low that, as she told a meeting of laundresses,

> When I had my baby I found I could not pay 8s. a week to have baby minded and go out to work on that, so I went into munitions. I was on aeroplane work on the carburettors til last February. I came out of that. Of course, through that I joined the Women's Federation (NFWW).
>
> We had never heard of laundry work being organized in North-East London, because it had never been organized there; so I have put in these few weeks to organize my mates. Everyone came in, practically. . . . Listen to me fellow-workers. Every fellow-worker should be your friend, and you should do what you can for your friend.[60]

Laundry workers were among the large numbers of demobilized women who, despite high rates of unemployment (by March 1919 just over half a million women were officially recorded as unemployed), took their wartime experience in trade unionism with them into their postwar jobs and effected a considerable expansion of union organization.[61] A major meeting, run by a committee of laundry shop stewards, was held with great success at Central Hall, Westminster in May 1919 to encourage solidarity and unionization; laundresses packed the hall and vigorously applauded the speakers, most of whom were laundry workers, although Margaret Bondfield and George Lansbury of the *Daily Herald* also addressed the meeting. The women's speeches were case histories of long hours, of poor wages, and of women supporting husbands and children on small and uncertain incomes. The war had meant for these women not only experience with unions but also the responsibility of caring for fatherless children and maimed husbands and sons. The wife of a disabled soldier expressed the indignation of many of her fellows:

> Has anybody suffered more in this accursed war than the laundry workers? You all know what I've got lying in a Belgian grave, and you all know what I've got come home to me.—(cries of "A blind husband!") . . . I'm proud of him, he has done his bit. . . . We girls, we women we've worked. There was money enough to slaughter our boys—There's money enough to keep them! If England can keep all those millions of men to be slaughtered fighting— then England can keep the working man and the working women; and it is a crying disgrace to women that so many married women have got to work, or see their little children go down in hunger.[62]

This new militancy, born partly of the knowledge that so many women would now be permanently the sole support of their families, helped to make laundry organization flourish and was aided by the inclusion of the industry under Trade Board regulation. Trade Boards had been advocated to provide some basic protection for workers whose lack of skill made it difficult to sustain trade unions. As Clementina Black put it in 1907, "Labour organization is only of value when you can control the supply of labour and when you can make up a sufficient fund to support the workers when they refuse to work for low pay."[63] Both of the points she cited were clearly problems for laundry workers. Trade Board regulation established the minimum laundry wages which had been campaigned for over many years, and, at the same time, the necessity of having workers' representatives on the boards themselves provided a strong incentive to union formation. The pages of the principal women's union periodical are full of announcements of the formation of new laundry unions from Gateshead to Bristol and of collective agreements that included such benefits as tea urns, mess rooms, washing facilities, and full payment for bank holidays— benefits that were only made possible by the new security of the basic wage rate.[64] In Manchester, the Amalgamated Union of Co-operative Employees reported in 1919 that "practically all the eligible laundry workers" in that city had been persuaded to join the union.[65] "When approached with the arguments that membership in a union would ensure direct representation upon a Trade Board, that strong organization increases the probability of obtaining fair rates from a Trade Board," reported the author of a book on British Wages Boards, Dorothy Sells, "the average worker responded favourably" and "quite a substantial trade union membership of laundry workers was . . . acquired."[66] So active was unionization that the WTUL appointed an organizer whose sole duty over a three-month period was to establish unions in the laundry industry.[67]

In the final analysis, however, the failures and inadequacies of the Laundry Trade Board may have been as much of a stimulus to united action as its successes. The twenty-eight shillings wage rate initially set by the Laundry Trade Board was carried by the vote of appointed members and employers over the objections of workers' representatives. Anything less than thirty-five shillings a week for adult laundresses in urban areas, workers' representatives asserted, would only perpetuate sweating—this time with legal sanction. "Thirty shillings now," argued the *Woman Worker*, "is equal to 12s. 6d. in pre-war value—just about the old sweated rates in laundries which made a Trade Board necessary; and this sweated rate is to be the new national rate!"[68] Enraged by their victimization, organized laundresses across the country reacted vigorously. In London, laundresses held another "sensational" meeting at Central Hall, Westminster to call "upon the Laundry Trades Board to revise the present inadequate rates immediately." They demanded a two pound minimum weekly rate for timeworkers and pieceworkers, and a week's holiday annually with pay in addition to statutory holidays.[69] Within a month, similar protest meetings had been held "in all districts including Newcastle, Sheffield, Manchester, Aberdeen, Hull, Bristol," while the *Liverpool Post* reported that "the trade generally through-out the country is said to be in a state of ferment" and that "the livelihood of 130,000 operatives" was, in the view of the secretary of the Anti-Sweating League, "imperilled" by the failure of employers to agree to a Trade Board minimum rate of thirty-four shillings.[70]

In the absence of worthwhile Trade Board standards organized laundry workers set out to achieve a guaranteed weekly thirty-five shilling base income by means of industrial action. Action by Willesden laundry workers was to prove the model for much of the country. In Willesden, a part of London with considerable laundry concentration, a number of demonstrations and mass meetings were held demanding a two pound minimum wage for a forty-four hour week and protesting against the ineffectual performance of the Trade Board. When no response to their demands was forthcoming from employers, over 1,000 Willesden laundry workers went on strike. Their objectives were threefold: higher wages, recognition of their union, and reinstatement of shop stewards victimized during an organizational drive the previous year. After five days of hard bargaining, a committee of employers assented to recognition of the union, reinstatement of the leaders, and a thirty-five shilling weekly wage. Most important, the employers' association, representing many of the largest metropolitan laundries, agreed that the settlement would form the basis for settlements for the whole of London.[71] The terms of laundry collective agreements negotiated over the following months suggest that the Willesden precedent was largely adhered to. In an open letter to the laundry workers of Willesden, the members of the Southend Branch of the NFWW sent "thanks . . . for your brave stand during the late strike, and their heartiest congratulations for the great benefits you have gained for the whole of the laundry workers all over England by your splendid victory."[72]

Any remaining confidence in the worth of Trade Board regulation was dealt a severe blow by a surprise ruling by the Ministry of Labour that Trade Board power was limited to setting rates of wages for hours worked, thereby making a guaranteed weekly wage unenforceable.[73] The wage floor concept remained, but it could no longer ensure the laundry worker of an irreducible minimum income in slack periods. Collective industrial action had greater potential to achieve positive results through negotiated wage rates. In addition, the growth of umbrella organizations among both workers and employers meant that collective agreements in one locality could frequently become the accepted standard for negotiations elsewhere in the industry, considerably smoothing the course of industrial relations. While of course some employers continued through intimidation, dismissal, or blacklisting to discourage unionization, the more perceptive recognized the benefits to them of standardized union wage rates in a highly competitive industry.[74] By the 1920s the self-help of laundry workers and the sisterly help of union organizers, other unionized women, and middle class supporters had combined—aided by wartime experience, the impetus of the Trade Board, and the stimulus of press attention—to increase worker solidarity and confidence and to produce measurable benefits in many a workplace.

Uneasy Partnership: Laundresses and Middle-Class Supporters

The relationship between working-class laundry workers and the middle-class women who espoused their welfare was not, however, without ambiguity and tension. Informed by a feminist consciousness, groups such as the National Federation of Women Workers and the Women's Industrial Council brought together women of diverse backgrounds to advance the economic and industrial rights of women. This forging of a common cause achieved, as we have seen, considerable success in enacting better legislation, advancing unionization, and educating laboring women as to their rights in the workplace. At the same time, the bourgeois women who were the leading members of these organizations, though radical in their feminism, accepted other aspects of the dominant culture at face value. These values could sometimes be at odds with the goal of bringing about economic independence for working women. Predictably, many such women were advocates of ventures such as penny banks, Working Girls' Clubs, Temperance Unions, and other uplifting endeavors consistent with social and economic self-help.[75] In fact, moral influence was deemed to be of such importance that the job of laundry superintendent was recommended to educated women by one author as social work—the opportunity to extend "a guiding kindly hand"—as much as a means of earning a living.[76] Though perhaps alien to some working-class cultural norms, these ventures did not undermine broader social and economic objectives and benefited some working women.

On the other hand, the traditional view of the role of women in the workforce and the family that permeated much of the activity of the Women's Trade Union League and the Women's Industrial Council was potentially detrimental to the economic position and rights of working-class women. Shackled by such values, these organizations were unable to effect any significant reorientation of women's place in the industrial system.

Middle-class reformers failed to use their very real influence to press for inclusion of women in nontraditional occupations. Even within the archetypically "woman's" occupation of laundry work, they made no effort to ensure equality of either access to or pay in those positions that in factory laundries came to be dominated by men.[77] Still more destructive of the interests of laundry workers was the widespread acceptance that women's most important role was that of wife and mother not wage-earner. (Laundry work was one of the two occupations—the other was charring—in which single employees were outnumbered by their married and widowed co-workers.) Women who were very prominent in the campaign to bring laundry work under factory legislation, Margaret MacDonald and May Abraham Tennant among them, were often equally active in the drive to keep mothers out of the labor force.[78] While many recognized that much paid female labor was an economic necessity and a few accepted that a woman might be "extremely proud of the fact that she need not ask her husband whenever she wanted a copper," most agreed that "the paid labour of married women . . . leads inevitably to great loss of infant life, and lasting injury to the originally vigorous survivors."[79] Social disapproval, mothers' and widows' allowances, minimum wages for men, legislative prohibition: all these measures were proposed at various times to curtail the paid employment of married women. A novel approach was taken by one philanthropic group in Dundee, called the Social Union, which ran Nursing Mothers' Restaurants to provide free meals to mothers of infants under three months of age. "One object of the restaurant," recorded a factory inspector, "[is] to discourage married women's work. At three of the restaurants it is the rule that no free dinners should be granted to mothers who have returned to their work."[80] Few would deny that hours and conditions of work experienced by many mothers laboring at laundry work, whether in factories, workshops, or their own homes, could and did have deleterious consequences for themselves and their offspring. However, to focus on a mother's paid work as the primary villain behind infant sickness and mortality often meant overlooking the need for structural improvement in the mother's workplace, underestimating the environmental conditions that made many working-class homes poor nurseries, and failing to appreciate the poverty (and its causes) that necessitated a woman's work. Any meaningful appreciation of women's unemployment was clouded by a perspective that viewed married women's work as undesirable.

The paradoxical nature of some of the support for laundry workers was part of a broader pattern of social values. From the beginning of the twentieth century and in particular during and after the First World War, the importance of motherhood and child-rearing gained prominence in public debate and social policy. In contrast with the Malthusian edicts of earlier years, people, especially if white and Anglo-Saxon, were seen to be a nation's strength; as long as population was equated with power, the rearing of the next generation of workers and soldiers would be a top priority. The connection between imperialism and motherhood has been ably documented elsewhere; what is significant in the present discussion is the pressure this ideology—and it was an ideology shared to varying degrees by all classes—placed on mothers who had to seek paid employment.[81] The education of mothers was seen as the linchpin of maternal and child welfare policies; infant mortality and morbidity was blamed on "maternal not medical ignorance."[82] Failures were attributed to mothers, not to the lim-

ited access of the poor to health care, fresh and plentiful food, good housing, and pure air. The onus of guilt was added to the other burdens of the
laundress with young children.

Middle-class social feminists questioned, lobbied, investigated, proselytized, and organized; their actions did much to bring factory inspectors,
industrial legislation, minimum wages, and unions into the laundry. Their
contribution to the welfare of laundresses was substantial, but their failure
to question women's role in the home meant that it was also limited. In
their concern with the deleterious "effects on home life and child life" of
the employment of mothers, "they forget," the *Woman Worker* observed,
"that a woman cannot legally insist on her husband providing her with the
needs of life for herself and her children. She can take no step to enforce
this until she leaves him . . . or until he leaves her."[83] Sisterly help, then,
was a valuable aid to self-help in smoothing the industrial advancement of
laundresses, but that same help also impeded their pursuit of a better life.
In the final analysis, empathy without shared experiences and common
social perspectives is inevitably limited.

CHAPTER 5

Mechanization and Social Change

On 11 February, 1881, Josiah Chater, a prominent Cambridge entrepreneur with interests in the affairs of a number of companies, made the following entry in his diary: "Had a pipe with Ginn the solicitor; he told me about a new project of a Laundry Company he had in view to which I am to be secretary if it comes off. He has the offer of an estate of 4 acres, with buildings on it, at Cherryhinton, opposite the Waterworks, and he has a capital man in view as a manager."[1] Slightly over a month later, Chater, in his capacity as secretary of the newly incorporated Cambridge Steam Laundry Company, had arranged for the printing of an advertising prospectus, obtained a set of books for the venture, and assisted in the allotting of about £1,300 in company shares for public sale. Chater's decision to include a steam laundry among his business interests was soundly conceived: he was investing in a relatively new kind of industrial enterprise, but one that was well enough developed to allay the fears of timorous speculators. A novice in the laundry industry in the 1880s needed to have few qualms about the availability of efficient, tested machinery, experienced managerial staff and employees, or reliable advice regarding the most desirable premises and plant layout.

Most important, investment in a steam laundry seemed likely to yield a good return. The Cambridge Steam Laundry Company's prospectus for potential shareholders very likely contained an endorsement as glowing as that published by another fledgling concern, the Crouch Hill Sanitary Laundry Limited: "The profitable character of well-conducted Steam

Laundries is well known, and careful enquiry into the returns of these undertakings shows that as the work extends the proportion of profit is increased. . . . It should be borne in mind by intending investors that they will not only have the advantage of their washing being efficiently done, but also that the cost will be materially reduced by the handsome dividend anticipated upon the Shares held in the Company."[2] The brochure supported its claims for the financial success of mechanized laundries with a listing of laundry companies whose returns in the previous year had ranged from 7 percent to 15 percent. These statistics, while naturally enough omitting any reference to less than successful firms, did reflect fairly accurately the range of financial return that might be expected in an efficiently managed, well-sited factory laundry. The dividends of firms reported in laundry trade journals generally ranged between 4 percent and 10 percent (15 percent was exceptional); these rates of return were sustained until the beginning of the First World War, when shortages of raw materials (such as imported fats for soapmaking) and labor, and the impressment of horses and vans for the war effort, caused temporary disruption in the industry's modernization.[3]

When Josiah Chater and his colleagues began the Cambridge Steam Laundry Company, mechanized laundries were already well established, even though they did not yet dominate the industry. A few laundries, most of them specializing in the cleansing of flat work for institutions, firms, and restaurants, had installed machinery in the late 1850s and 1860s, and by the later years of the nineteenth century, mechanized laundries formed a significant component of service sector growth. In the 1860s, laundry firms began to appear on the London Stock Exchange, and in 1879, the first syndicated laundry firm, the London and Provincial Steam Laundry Co. Ltd., offered its stocks to the investing public.[4] By the time the Cambridge laundry got underway, power laundries were so common and so generally successful that Josiah Chater was able to sign a laundering contract before his firm began operation. He arranged with the Warden of Cavendish College to have the new firm launder all the college's household linen (at seven shillings per 1,000 articles) as well as personal items for college residents (the latter at one shilling a dozen).[5] Indeed, although neither Chater nor the Warden could have been aware of it, hand laundry work had already reached its peak in 1881 and would thereafter lose ground to mechanized processes. Up to that year, the growth in the number of laundrywomen recorded by the census had roughly kept pace with the growth in the size of the population. After that the rate of growth in the numbers in this occupation declined until 1901 and fell in absolute numbers thereafter.[6] Of the laundry workers who remained more and more were employed in laundries using powered equipment.

Between the 1860s and the First World War, the laundry industry maintained a wide variety of working methods ranging from washing done for profit in one's home with scanty equipment to highly mechanized factories where "a single shirt will pass through seven or eight machines in the process of ironing alone."[7] In some factory firms, such as the King's Cross Laundry in London, as many as 1,000 people might be employed (including staff in receiving offices) and up to 40,000 shirts and collars laundered every week. Despite the existence of these industrial giants, handwork persisted, both on its own and as a part of the work of mechanized laundries. Nonetheless, it was evident by the turn of the century to those who were knowledgeable that the machine would determine the future tone and organization of the industry. "The engine wins," noted Lucy Deane, a Factory Inspector in 1900, "and it seems clear that before long the whole industry will become one of organized factory-labour with some survivals of the other system."[8] H. Llewellyn Smith documented the change that had taken place in London's laundry industry by 1930: "The gradual substitution of hand laundries by power laundries was already taking place in 1896, and the substitution advanced rapidly in the early years of the present century. In 1902 the percentage of power laundries in London was 29. By 1912 it had increased to 46. In 1930 it is estimated to have been 70."[9]

Industrialization of the laundry industry altered the investment options of entrepreneurs and improved the prospects of firms, such as Manlove Alliott, W. Summerscales, I. Braithwaite, and Thomas Bradford, which specialized in manufacturing laundry machinery, and, simultaneously, it altered a traditional occupation forever. Lucy Deane, reflecting on the industry from her perspective as the workers' advocate, recognized mechanization as social change:

"To take in washing" has for so long appeared to be an occupation mainly reserved as a resource for the woman bereft of her "breadwinner," or deprived by circumstances of other means of livelihood, that many people still look on "laundry work" from this point of view. It is perhaps difficult to realise that the radical change which has everywhere transformed industrial conditions has already affected this occupation also, and that for good or evil the washerwoman is passing under the influences which have so profoundly modified the circumstances of her sister of the spinning-wheel and the sewing needle. When the first washing machine and ironing roller were applied to this occupation, alteration in the conditions became as much a foregone conclusion as it did in the case of textile or clothing manufactures, when the spinning frame, the power loom, or the sewing machine appeared.[10]

Under the headline "Passing of the Hand Laundry," the *Morning Post* noted in 1914 that "between the years 1907 and 1912 the number of people employed in commercial factory laundries increased from 86,000 to 102,000, an increase of 19.2 per cent in five years. The number of people employed in laundries where only handwork is done decreased . . . during the same five years . . . about 20 per cent."[11] Observers perceived unusual drama in this example of industrialization because it substantially altered a traditional domestic task and, in so doing, to a large extent removed from many households an almost universally despised job, thereby transforming family work and habits, as well as recasting the nature and organization of one of the most common of all women's occupations.

The Background to Mechanization

Industrial change does not take place in a vacuum. It occurs within a specific economic, social, political, and technological context. In the laundry industry, mechanization and industrial expansion depended not only on forces that were industry-specific but also on those that underlay the development of the service sector as a whole. Laundry growth was stimulated by some of the same conditions that gave rise to the dramatic development of department stores, restaurants, and holiday camps at the seaside. Among the general stimulants to the service sector of the economy were urbanization, the growth and increasing prosperity of the middle classes, rising living standards across the whole population from the 1880s, improved transportation, and the growth in women's employment outside the home. In addition, urban pollution also increased the laundry's business: it soiled clothes and linens quickly and added to the unpleasantness of doing the wash at home because soot rendered the drying of laundry out of doors impractical. Taken together these factors meant that incentives for the development of large factory-style laundries did not occur until the second half of the nineteenth century when the social and economic conditions prevailing in "the workshop of the world" created the demand for them.

Mechanization of the laundry trade occurred in three stages: an early period of haphazard development lasting until the mid-1890s; an era of accelerated expansion that "took off" when legislative regulation of hours and conditions in the industry eliminated (or significantly diminished) competition from "sweated" workshops; and a time of consolidation following the First World War and continuing through the 1920s when the industry amalgamated into larger units supported by numerous receiving offices and motorized delivery vans. During the initial period, industrial development was largely restricted to firms with a specialized flatwork market. The work done by these laundries could benefit most dramatically from the range and quality of machinery then available, machinery that was as yet little suited to varied or delicate items. Thereafter, machinery was adopted by laundries with a varied, general family trade. Even very small launderers installed machinery, which was purchased second-hand or bought on time, or they attached small engines to existing manual appliances in order to speed the turnover of work. In the twentieth century, these small concerns lost ground to mammoth factory laundries with the capital to invest in a broad range of specialized machinery and a sophisticated collection and delivery network. In 1930, London was served by eighty-two establishments with more than 100 employees, two of them employing more than 1,000. Cottage laundries with only two or three hands remained but were "largely the resort of the married woman who wishes to work for only two or three days a week."[12]

Laundry work is a soap and water trade. Its performance is virtually impossible without these key commodities; consequently, the industry's development was profoundly influenced by their availability. Individual laundresses and some small handwork laundries could be successful without benefit of piped water; indeed, Headington Quarry laundresses cleansed the garments of Oxford dons in the water of their village stream well into the twentieth century. But such laundry enterprises were exceptional. Carrying laundry to the stream or transporting water from the standpipe at the end of the street was impractical for all but the smallest laundries. A few large factory laundries, such as the Spring Garden Steam Laundry in Newcastle upon Tyne and the huge King's Cross and Spiers and Ponds laundries in London,[13] were able to draw upon their own wells for a continuous supply of water, but the majority of laundries had to rely on waterworks to supply most or all of their needs. In the laundry trade, progress and piped water went hand in hand. In North Kensington, small laundries proliferated early in the nineteenth century, in part because local well water was abundant and soft, but when these enterprises began to grow in size and number in response to a burgeoning middle-class market, their dependence on piped water grew. In 1857, the Grand Junction Waterworks serving the Kensington "laundryland" erected additional works on Campden Hill with a reservoir capacity of 10 million gallons to meet the needs of the area's major industry as well as those of its households.[14] This pattern of development repeated itself across the country.

The history of the drainage and water supply of English towns in the nineteenth century is complex, and from the perspective of this study, it is important to note that until water supplies were abundant, regular citizens could not spare much water for the frequent washing of clothes. Water or, more accurately, its lack became a public health issue in the middle of the nineteenth century when a variety of studies (for which cholera in particular and alarming urban mortality rates in general were the catalyst) focused attention on the quantity and quality of urban water supplies, drainage, and sewage disposal. Edwin Chadwick's pioneering study of 1842, *Report on the Sanitary Condition of the Labouring Population of Great Britain,* which drew upon and synthesized the findings of a small army of local medical officers and other sanitary investigators, paved the way for the investigation by a royal commission of *The State of Large Towns and Populous Districts* (1845), the passing of the Public Health Act (1848), and the establishment of the London Metropolitan Board of Works (1855) and similar bodies across the country.[15] In the decades following the publication of Chadwick's findings, state intervention gradually replaced laissez-faire approaches to the provision of basic services, with the result that by the turn of the century most English towns enjoyed a continuous and good quality water supply.[16]

The process of achieving an adequate water supply was slow and tedious. The delay in supplying this basic amenity was one factor that inhibited the industrialization of the laundry trade. Some industries had the option of locating near a plentiful supply of water even though it was at a distance from the market for their products. Laundries did not. They had to be situated near their markets, and this made them unusually dependent on the public provision of continuous water supplies. A few firms boasted that they had regular customers as far away as the continent or even West Africa,[17] but the industry's bread and butter was earned much closer to home, within the radius of a handcart or horse-drawn (later motorized) delivery vans. The laundry with an ample and continuous supply of fresh water enjoyed an obvious advantage. The best facilitated laundries assiduously trumpeted their competitive advantage; unstinting use of water was among the boasts of many an advertising circular. "In the course of the washing process," boasted the proprietors of the Spring Garden Laundry in Newcastle, "the goods pass through no less than seven distinct courses of fresh spring water, thoroughly eradicating every lingering impurity, and rendering them at the end beyond suspicion on the grounds of wholesomeness and purity."[18]

When contemplating cleanliness in general and laundering in particular, most people automatically associate soap with water. Soap and water are indeed the essential raw materials of the modern laundry, but this connection, as discussed in chapter 1, is of relatively recent date. Only in the seventeenth and eighteenth centuries did soap begin to supplant lye as the primary cleansing substance for laundering; even then its extensive use was class-defined. "So far as England is concerned," observed a writer in the *Laundry Record* in 1911, "it may be said that our forefathers did not make that intimate acquaintance of the detergent which is now a necessity of everyday life until nearly the middle of the eighteenth century. Even then owing to the high price of soap its use was more honoured in the breach than in the observance."[19] That famous chronicler of seventeenth-century taste, Samuel Pepys, regarded soap as a luxury suitable as a gift for a lady of quality. He recorded in his diary: "In the morning I fell to my lute till 9 o'clock then to my lord's lodging, and set out a barrel of soap to be carried to Mrs. Ann [Lady Ann Montagu]."[20]

The fortunes of the modern commercial laundry are intimately connected with those of the soap industry. Maturation of the latter industry was slowed in turn by the policies of the British government. The growth of the soap industry suffered from two externally imposed constraints: monopoly and taxation. In May 1638, Charles I granted an exclusive charter for the manufacture of soap to a group of London soapers and soapmakers, a measure that temporarily restricted the growth of commercial soapmaking. Secondly, the government levied an excise duty on soap made in the United Kingdom which varied from one pence to three pence per pound. The tax was in effect from 1712 to 1853. A measure of the severity of the tax is the fact that when the levy stood at three pence, it was equal to the value of the product itself. The revenue produced by the tax yielded almost one million pounds in 1835 (when the duty was levied at one and a half pence, and, in 1852, the last year the tax was levied, the government garnered £1,126,046 from this source.[21] Monopoly and particularly taxation combined to inhibit the development of a soap industry of sizable dimensions. Both could be evaded; that they frequently were is supported by evidence of widespread smuggling and of increasing domestic use of soap before the lifting of the excise tax. John Houghton, an eighteenth-century writer, found that respectable households were using annually "about as many pounds of Soap as there be heads in the family" when they washed all their clothes at home. He pointed out, however, that respectable households were greatly outnumbered by poor ones where the "use of bucking and hogs-dung" still predominated.[22] Relatively well-to-do families might meet their needs with a combination of costly "legal" soap, its black-market equivalent, and home-produced products, but until the tax was gone, soap was neither cheap enough nor produced in sufficiently large or reliable quantities to support the development of a large-scale industrialized laundry industry.

It would be inaccurate to suggest that the slow growth of soap production was entirely the consequence of governmental action. Technical questions also played a role. Soap is formed as a result of a chemical reaction between a fat and an alkali, and until the nature of this process was well understood and methods developed for taking commercial advantage of this knowledge, industrial innovation would inevitably be limited. Historians of the industry, however, are in general agreement that essential technical breakthroughs, such as the discovery of an inexpensive way of producing alkali (soda) from common salt, had taken place well before the repeal of the excise tax on soap.[23] Despite these critical discoveries, contemporary soapmakers nonetheless complained that the actions of excise officers to prevent evasion of the unwelcome tax, which included much filling in of forms, weighing of raw materials, submission of "specimens," and other bureaucratic annoyances, "were a continual source of grievance to soapmakers, who insisted that they were utterly impractical and a hindrance to technical improvement."[24] Once the duty was repealed, the soap industry, many historians believe, "advanced by leaps and bounds." The laundry industry provides indirect evidence of this process. By the end of the century, it was possible to find a laundry so large that it employed 350 hands; soapmakers were equal to the task of keeping its storeroom supplied with its "normal stock of some ten tons or so of soap and six tons of starch."[25]

In common with other industries, the laundry industry, for its development, relied on the availability of a technology capable of sustaining its growth as well as on an ample and regular supply of raw materials. To the soap, water, starches, and blues specific to the laundry must be added the broader paraphernalia of industrial growth: motive power (steam, then gas and electricity), machinery, and transportation. More important than all of these advances, however, was the demand that made them necessary. The growth of women's employment outside the home, of the middle classes, of cities, and of services with substantial laundering needs (such as railways, restaurants, and steamships), all helped to push the laundry trade into becoming a large-scale modern industry. Even more significant than these general demand forces, and more obvious, was the impetus to growth provided by the proliferation of readily washable clothing and linens. Cotton was the catalyst. It caused a dramatic increase in the volume of items that needed washing. Domestically produced cotton cloth revolutionized the way people lived. Underwear became both more voluminous and more commonly worn; sheets and nightwear, once largely restricted to those who could afford linen, became more widely used, while towels, table linens, and a veritable avalanche of chintz bed hangings and chair and sofa coverings adorned Victorian homes. Cotton cloth, because it was both relatively inexpensive and readily washed, made frequent changes of clothing standard for all but the poorest in society. Readily laundered cottons, whether heavy duck, muslin, or gauze, influenced fashion and helped to establish "whites" as de rigueur on the tennis court and the cricket pitch as well as in the nursery. Without cotton some of the extravagances of Victorian dress would have been impractical. In the 1850s, full skirts were supported by as many as six or seven petticoats (the majority made of cotton although linen and flannel were also used); corsets were fitted with calico covers and worn with cotton or linen chemises; printed cotton dresses were worn in all levels of society; and cotton collars, caps, cuffs, and kerchiefs adorned less readily cleaned fabrics while cotton aprons and pinafores protected them. Fashions changed over the century—for example, the wearing of knickers and shirtwaists grew more common—but the use of washable fabrics became a permanent presence in everyday life.[26]

Cotton further stimulated the demand for the services of commercial launderers by influencing the way in which laundering was done. Homespun garments of linen, wool, or fustian were coarse enough to withstand washing methods that emphasized pounding, beating, and soaking in strong solutions; cotton cloth, especially when finely woven, could not be subjected to such rough usage with impunity. Soap and water was a much better laundering method for cotton fabric. Washing with soap, unlike other laundry methods, required hot water. The necessity of heating water made washing at home more difficult and disruptive, thereby providing further encouragement for delegating the task to a paid professional. Even those households fortunate enough to have piped water supplies did not enjoy the luxury of hot water on tap, so water had to be heated especially for laundering—in a copper, in vessels over the kitchen fire or stove, or, later, in a gas boiler. (As late as 1942, a Heating of Dwellings Inquiry found that three-quarters of the 5,000 working-class families surveyed had to heat specially the water they needed for laundering.)[27] Cotton, then, was both instrumental in creating the demand that stimulated the growth of commercial laundries and, indirectly, in sustaining that demand.

Another factor that sustained the laundry industry was the exceptionally slow rate at which private households came to adopt labor-saving laundry equipment, especially the domestic washing machine. While the passage of the Electric (Lighting) Act of 1882 stimulated the emergence of electricity companies and the promotion of electricity for vacuum cleaning, clothes washing, and the cooling of food as well as for lighting, the high cost of electricity hampered its widespread adoption. It was not until 1911, when metal filament lamps had been perfected, that electricity became competitive with gas, and even then domestic use of electricity was confined to the wealthy. At the end of the First World War, only half a million houses, or about 6 percent of the total, were wired for electricity, a percentage that doubled by 1921.[28] The price of electricity fell in the following twenty-five years as supplies became more extensive, but its harnessing for clothes washing still lagged well behind other countries, notably the United States and Germany. As late as 1948 only 4 percent of British households owned a washing machine (in contrast to 52 percent of U.S. households in 1941), although 86 percent had electric irons.[29] Washing machines driven by hand power were available, but they remained curiosities since without motor power most were not a noticeable improvement on the washing dolly and hand-turned mangle.

The underdevelopment of home appliances, then, contributed to the sustained vitality of commercial laundering. The domestic washing machine would not become widely marketed until it could be supplied with a source of power and connected to a reliable source of hot and cold water. In the meantime, steam power, which was impractical outside commercial laundries and large institutions, was harnessed to operate washing machines, hydro extractors, and ironing equipment; to heat the necessary quantities of hot water; and to warm the air for drying closets. The possibilities created by steam power also encouraged the development of firms that specialized in the manufacture of laundry machinery and created the profession of laundry engineer. The commercial laundry industry in Great Britain enjoyed a marketing advantage that was not shared by countries which more rapidly adopted domestic electricity. Commercial laundries in Britain remained strong well into the third and fourth decades of the twentieth century. In 1930, one observer of the laundry industry in London noted:

> There has been for many years past a steady and continuous expansion in the trade. The gradual substitution of machine for handwork, a greater degree of subdivision of processes, and improvements in internal organization have all resulted in an increase in the productivity of the industry over and above that represented by the increase in the number of workers employed. The development in machinery has been one of the greatest factors in this expansion. . . . Today the eight roll calender has a capacity of 300-400 sheets an hour, and it is stated that it will deal with smaller articles to the number of about 2,500 in an hour. A washing machine in common use before the War could deal with 120 lb. weight in about 1 1/2 hours. Certain modern washers will cope with 650 lb. weight in 1 1/4—1 1/2 hours, and there is a still later machine with a reputed capacity of 1,000 lb. in the same time.[30]

In 1948, a survey revealed that 60 percent of London's households continued to give work to the professional launderer or laundress; the nationwide percentage was said to be 41.5.[31]

Life and Labor in the Factory Laundry

Mechanization inevitably brought about significant changes in the way laundry work was performed, the nature of the labor force engaged, and the employment prospects open to those employees. Generalizations about the industry are, however, very difficult to make as May Smith, a researcher for the Medical Research Council, discovered when she undertook a study of laundries in 1922. Encountering a bewildering plethora of premises, proprietors, machinery, and personnel, she commented:

> Only one generalization seems to be warranted with regard to the laundry trade as a whole, namely that if a factory calls itself a laundry, then its main occupation is washing soiled linen and clothes. Nothing else can be taken for granted. The building may vary from a modern specially designed laundry with the latest machinery, ventilation appliances, rest and mess rooms, to a converted house, shop, or stable, where all reconstruction has to be modified by the exigencies of the original building and where there is little or no room for expansion or modern requirements; between these two extremes there is every grade of adequate or inadequate building. Proprietors and managers, like the buildings, represent practically every social class and type of education and ability, and while we cannot say quite as much with regard to the

workers, still in many laundries there exist side by side the relics of the old washerwoman of a previous generation with the latest product of high class factory girl. Turning to plant, the same diversity prevails; on the one hand is the firm anxiously distrustful of the effects of machinery on clothes and wishful to do as much of every process by hand as is compatible with its conditions, while on the other hand is the firm that eagerly tries every new appliance and scraps any machine that can be superceded by a better.[32]

This assessment, made well over half a century after the first laundries mechanized, attests to the unevenness of the introduction of steam-powered technology and to the persistence of handwork both within and in competition with mechanized firms. As Raphael Samuel has pointed out, a similar pattern of combined hand power and steam technology was commonplace in many sectors of the English economy in the mid-nineteenth century.[33] The laundry trade's great diversity does not negate the value of exploring the ways in which mechanization altered the nature of laundry employment; rather, it simply indicates the limitations of any such analysis. The remarks that follow, then, are most directly applicable to purpose-built or substantially renovated commercial factory laundries employing twenty-five or more workers. (In London, the average number of employees in power laundries was thirty-three in 1904 and thirty-eight in 1912 as compared with eight and seven respectively for hand laundries.)[34] As a corollary the analysis is also most applicable to London, which not only accounted for 35 percent of all laundry employment in Great Britain but also held the largest concentration of highly sophisticated factory laundries.[35]

The impact of industrialization on laundry labor echoed in many ways that of the earlier Industrial Revolution. Laundry workers, despite their almost legendary independence, became subject to factory discipline; they had to conform, to be punctual, to work relatively regular hours, and to adapt themselves to the rhythms of the machines they tended. This new orderly working environment was both a byproduct of the introduction of technology and a consequence of the enactment of legislation that defined within broad parameters the hours and conditions of work. Specialization of work, or the division of labor, was more unambiguously the outcome of mechanization. An elementary degree of job specialization, comprising washers, ironers, and sometimes finery ironers, as well as collection and delivery employees, existed in large hand laundries, but it was only in large mechanized factory laundries that the division of labor attained its most minute refinements. Factory organization involved a specialization and subdivision of labor processes; the generalist washerwoman was supplanted by workers with narrowly demarcated jobs—workers whose sole responsibility was, for example, to iron shirt bosoms, or to sort and mark soiled laundry. Growth in the size of units of production created a further range of jobs as store front receiving offices or depots were set up (especially in areas where full-time domestic servants were uncommon) to funnel work to and from large laundries. By 1930, it was estimated that the number of receiving offices in London roughly equaled the total number of laundries of all sizes and descriptions; in them were performed some of the tasks that would have been carried out in a self-contained establishment. Receiving offices, supplemented by laundry vanmen, made collection areas with a radius of five miles commonplace and rendered possible a catchment area, in the case of one laundry, of over two hundred square miles.[36]

The division of labor that took place in mechanized laundries is best described, perhaps, by following the progress of the family wash through the laundry. When articles were sent to be laundered, most customers could choose from three kinds of laundry service involving varying costs and degrees of "finish." The first and least costly was the "bag-wash" service (also sometimes called the bobwash or wet wash). This type of laundering, designed to cater to working-class needs, was limited to washing and partial drying; items were returned to the customer damp and ready for ironing. The "bag wash" derived its name from the practice of sending items for cleaning in a washable bag labeled with the customer's name or mark. Prices were originally set according to the size of the bag (frequently one shilling, six pence to two shillings, six pence in the 1920s). Launderers soon complained about the astronomical number of articles some householders could cram into one small bag and began levying charges by weight, usually to a maximum of twenty-eight pounds. Another trade objection came from ironers who feared that the service would deprive them of work, at least if it was used to any significant extent by nonworking-class clientele. On the other hand, young working women with little discretionary time and inadequate facilities were strong supporters of the affordable service.[37]

More conventional were the "semi-finished" and "fully finished" services. "Semifinished" laundry was machine-ironed or, where appropriate, simply folded; it was virtually never starched and charges were levied per dozen articles, although sometimes weight or a combination of number and weight calculations were used. Common prices in the 1920s were two shillings to two shillings, six pence a dozen, four pence per pound, or three pence per pound plus a half pence per article.[38] Gentlemen's shirts, other complicated and highly starched items, and fabrics like silk and flannel that required special handling were consigned to the category of fully finished work. A price was assigned to each item in the customer's bundle for fully finished work according to the time and difficulty involved in laundering it to the customer's specifications. Any launderable article could form part of the fully furnished service. Price lists show much variation and considerable detail: the Faversham Steam Laundry, for example, charged nine pence to launder cricketing trousers, and from four pence for boys' surplices and from six pence for men's surplices.[39] Price diversity, however, frequently resolved itself into remarkable uniformity in any given area. "It is interesting to note," commented one investigator, "that in spite of the free market which exists, there is some tendency for prices to be adjusted to the paying capacity of the area from which the custom is mostly derived; and that the smaller and less well-equipped laundries . . . appear often to be driven to cut prices in order to retain custom."[40] So consistent was regional price uniformity among power laundries that a subcommittee of the Commons Standing Committee on Trusts was appointed in 1920 to investigate price fixing in laundries. The committee, while finding no evidence of a combine, did find that the National Federation of Launderers tried to "influence" prices in this, the most extensive of the trade's services.[41]

Inside those laundries fitted with the latest labor saving machinery, performing a wide range of cleaning, and serving a large clientele, "the division of labour is at least as marked a feature as it is in the majority of non-textile factories."[42] Specialization of labor began before the laundry came into contact with mechanized processes. First, the laundry had to be collected. Collection was done by employees, mostly male, who picked up laundry from customers' homes, or through receiving offices to which customers delivered their bundles of wash. Both the vanman and the receiving office clerk had a good deal of responsibility since both had the duty of collecting payments, advertising the laundry's services, and dealing with customer complaints. Literacy, diplomacy, enthusiasm, and a good head for figures were crucial for these employees, and proprietors of modern factory laundries recognized that "a good vanman may secure new customers, while a bad one may lose existing customers."[43]

Once the goods reached the laundry, they were passed into the hands of the sorters. These workers examined each article, attached the customer's individual mark, marked any stains or tears for special treatment (or to protect the establishment from blame), and sorted it according to color, size, fabric, and desired finish. Each category of soiled linen was placed in a separate bin ready for dispatch to the washhouse; in the largest and most sophisticated establishments, there might be as many as forty different classifications of laundry. Sorting required great accuracy and speed and was normally combined with packing, during which the completed laundry was checked against customers' lists and packed and labeled for delivery. Sorting and packing attracted the mostly highly educated of laundry workers (outside supervisory and managerial ranks), for, despite the unpleasantness of having to handle other people's dirty clothes, "it is also quite skilled work; for upon it depends not only the accurate bookkeeping of the business, but also the proper treatment of woollen, as contrasted with cotton goods, of children's muslin pinafores, as against sheets and counterpanes, and so on. The sorters usually do the packing also, and a quick memory and neat figures are needed in order that everyone may have their own clothes returned, and may receive them in good condition."[44] In all large laundries packing and sorting took place in rooms separated from the main working sections of the firm, a circumstance that, in conjunction with the expertise and education required by the work, distanced these employees from their fellow workers. Social distance was increased by the practice, common at the turn of the century, of referring to these workers as "Miss," while other laundry employees were addressed by their first names, and sometimes as well by the provision of separate mess rooms for packers and sorters. Packers and sorters, invariably women and girls, had most in common with the staff of receiving offices, who, indeed, sometimes performed a portion of the same work because some laundries had the marking of linen done by receiving office staff while the sorters marked only those items collected by the vanmen.

The sorted laundry was conveyed (down a chute, by conveyor belt, or in wheeled trolleys) to the washhouse where further subdivisions of labor could be found. Washing was the only part of the actual laundering process in which men and boys were employed. The only male-dominated laundries were Chinese hand laundries that, in contrast to parts of North America, constituted an insignificant portion of the industry. Men were engaged to operate large washing machines whose capacity of several hundred pounds (machines with a capacity of 650 pounds a load were available by 1930), and whose use for washing of weighty individual items such as bedspreads, blankets, and sheets, made loading and unloading them a very heavy task. In small-to-medium-sized firms, washmen might combine their washhouse tasks with maintenance of the laundry's machinery or with collection and delivery. The largest establishments hired washroom foremen with engineering qualifications to keep the sophisticated technology in good repair and to provide advice to management on the acquisition of new equipment. Across the laundry industry, men never accounted for more than 5 percent of the employees, but in London's large factory laundries, the proportion was considerably higher.

The great bulk of articles laundered, including all of the bag wash and the majority of the contents of the other services, were washed in large rotary or cage-style washing machines, the original prototype for which was invented by one Henry Sidgier in 1782.[45] The standard rotary washer consisted of a watertight metal container within which was a perforated inner cage containing the clothes; the machine was mounted horizontally in contrast to the modern domestic washing machine. In the years following Sidgier's invention a wide range of other laundering equipment was brought on the market, much of it mimicking the beating action of the traditional wash dolly; however, by the end of the nineteenth century, it was estimated that 90 percent of the machines in commercial use were based on the rotary principle, whose operation was described by one writer in the following manner:

> As the cage revolves the clothes are brought into contact with the water and cleansing materials in the container, and by means of ingenious contrivances in the machine the linen is subjected to constant rubbing and is lifted in and out of the soapy water. During the process the cylinder is alternately filled with steam and changes of hot water, after which, without the cylinder being opened, the clothes are rinsed by successive changes of clean cold water. "Blueing" is usually done at this stage by adding liquid blue to the "rinse" water. The starching of certain kinds of article is also done in the washer. The time taken to wash an individual load ranges from an hour upwards.[46]

Some of these machines spun the water out of the clothes after the final rinse, but in the majority of laundries, they were supplemented by hydro-extractors, machines adapted from use in bleaching and dyeworks, which extracted water by powerful centrifugal force. In some laundries, women were put in charge of "hydros," but it was more common to employ men for this work.[47]

Washhouses with a dozen or more washing machines were not uncommon; occasionally thirty or more would be installed.[48] Not all the machines were of the rotary type and not all were large. Smaller machines were used to wash colored items or to clean fabrics that could not withstand the rougher treatment of the large machines. In 1933, the Oakthorpe Laundry advised its customers that it had just acquired a new machine for articles susceptible to shrinkage or to becoming misshapen. Its advertising brochure proclaimed:

> The washing of flannels and woollens require special treatment and for that purpose a new machine "Karntshrink" has been introduced. This machine is fitted with four pairs of power wringers and seven pairs of submerged rollers. The garments pass through a soft soapy liquor by means of endless bands and are gently squeezed through the various rubber rollers. . . . The garments then pass along through a rinsing trough which is fitted with a paddle and eventually leave the machine ready for drying and airing. This new process eliminates all danger of woollen shrinking.[49]

In most laundries, female employees washed special-care items by hand or used small specialized machines. Individual workers might devote themselves exclusively to the washing of silk, woollens, and other delicate items; rates of pay usually reflected the greater expertise and care required to process these materials. Virtually all laundries performing the full range of laundry work, including even those with the most varied and sophisticated of equipment, engaged some employees, often washerwomen with long years of experience, to do specialized hand washing. The other washroom task performed for the most part by women was starching. Starching was a highly skilled operation, only perfected after considerable experience. The starch solution had to be of the correct quality and consistency for the articles to be treated; it had to be applied to the appropriate portion of the garment; and, most important, it had to penetrate the fabric evenly. Some laundries advocated the use of hot water starch solutions, others used cold preparations; the enhanced dissolving properties of hot water probably made the former method more successful. Both hand and mechanized processes were used in starching. The simplest method involved rinsing household linens such as tablecloths and napkins in a starch solution while still in the washing machine. Other items such as detachable collars were prepared in a starch machine, a revolving tub in which every article was rinsed by the operator until the required result was obtained, while shirts, frilled garments, and other items requiring heavy starching were normally treated by hand.

Finally, between the washhouse and the ironing room a portion of the wash was dried—either on outdoor lines, by being suspended in a drying chamber, or, after 1907, by being tumble dried. The work entailed in putting clothes in highly heated chambers were extremely taxing, and as far as possible efforts were made to diminish the need for such labor by using conveyor belts and pulley systems. Open-air drying was highly valued by some customers, so highly mechanized laundries that were located in the suburbs often retained outdoor drying grounds, and in some cases, installed lines for laundry on the roofs of their premises.[50] In most laundries, drying was regarded simply as a continuation of the work of washhouse staff and not as a separate occupation.

At the center of every laundry were its ironing rooms. Here a bewildering array of machines might be installed, including calenders, collar and cuff ironers, shirt-bosom polishers, skirt ironers, curling machines (to give the desired curl to collars), gophering machines (to give the wave to frills), electric or gas-heated irons of various shapes, as well as traditional stove-heated irons, each with a specialist employee to use it. Not all mechanized laundries had the full range of ironing machinery, but the calender machine or Decouden (named after its French inventor) was universal. Calenders came in several different models but all essentially operated on a common principle—that of feeding articles between a series of steam or gas-heated padded rollers or between rollers and a heated bed. Laundered items emerged from the calender dried, ironed and, in some cases, given a certain gloss. These machines were used for the ironing of all flat work including bed and table linen. Of all the modern laundry's technological arsenal, the calender most enabled the factory establishment to outpace the productivity of the hand laundry. The best flatwork ironers ran at speeds of twenty-five feet per minute in the 1890s and of forty to fifty feet per minute by the 1920s.[51] According to one time and motion study, experienced workwomen could at the latter speed iron an average of 310 sheets per hour on a standard calender.[52]

This heavy work was performed exclusively by women, new recruits usually being drawn from girls fourteen to eighteen years of age. Calender work was team work; three or four pairs of workers were employed at each machine. Damp, clean laundry from the washhouse was shaken out ready for smoothing by one set of workers; the next pair of workers fed the machine, each taking one end of a sheet or other large article and straightening it to avoid creases as it passed through the calender; and an additional set of workers stood at the other end of the calender to remove the finished linen. Sometimes this process had to be repeated a second time to ensure dryness, heighten gloss, or remove any remaining creases. Completed articles were passed on to a final set of workers who folded the laundry preparatory to packing and who in the process performed a quality control function by looking for defects in the work.

Calendering was strenuous: it was done standing and involved constant lifting of heavy damp laundry, working at or near hot and steamy machinery, and, unless great attention was paid to adjusting the machines and other conditions to the individual worker, much muscular effort and unnecessary fatigue. For example, when the "feeding table" of a calender was set too high (a common enough occurrence when employees were teenage girls who might not have attained full adult height), getting the job done was made more difficult and productivity decreased. Similarly, ill-maintained machines could exacerbate the strains of working life by requiring more effort to operate or by subjecting the operator to irritating noise or vibrations. The folding of calendered work was free of the direct tyranny of the machine but it too could become onerous through lack of planning. At its best, folding laundry was "a graceful action and demand[ed] no cramped movements" and could be performed with a rhythmic movement determined by the workers themselves. This natural rhythm was hard to achieve, however, when workers were of significantly different heights or had widely varying arm lengths. Poor arrangement of the calendering room could also result in unnecessary wastage of energy. One investigator found that when a woman folding sheets had to take two or three steps to collect the next sheet to be folded she ended up walking an extra twenty miles a week. A slight rearrangement of tables eliminated this superfluous exercise.[53]

Another form of smoothing that was found in some calendering rooms in the twentieth century was the press, which closely resembled that used in modern tailoring and dry-cleaning establishments. Large surfaces were ironed on this machine by pressing the garment between a lower bed and a lid pulled down by the operator, which were locked together by means of a treadle. Overalls, aprons, surplices, chefs' coats, and the like were handled by this machine. It was unpopular with workers, which may account for the fact that it was not found as extensively as other laundry machinery. Workers complained of vibrations and other mechanical defects, but perhaps the greatest cause of the machine's unpopularity was that its operation was socially isolating. Where labor is relatively undemanding intellectually, its social dimensions tend to define its attractiveness. One investigator discovered:

> Calender work . . . is generally popular; . . . it is possible to be fairly sociable on calender work. The hand ironers, too, generally form a definite group,

though the work is individual. But the girl working a press is rather isolated; many laundries possess only one press, which is frequently placed rather far from the other workers. One worker told me that she disliked the press because she had far too much chance to think about herself, whereas on hand ironing the work itself demanded more attention, and also she could talk occasionally to others.[55]

Ironing of articles that were not suitable for calendering was carried out by other workers by hand or by means of a range of appliances operated either by hand or automatically. Laundries might have either powered or manual goffering irons, for example, and would probably only invest in the mechanized version if intricate garments formed a significant portion of their trade. These smaller machines were usually situated apart from the calendering department, either in a separate room or in the hand ironing department, depending on the size of the laundry. Of these small machines, those designed for preparing detached collars were the most numerous since collars were the most significant and exacting of any general laundry's highly starched work. In a laundry's collar department, collars were steamed, polished, molded, and curled; special machines being used for each process. Analogous machinery was employed to stiffen and polish the fronts of gentlemen's dress shirts. In the hand laundry, the polishing of collars, cuffs, and shirt fronts required more "elbow grease" than any other ironing task; in the factory laundry, working conditions were much different. In 1922, May Smith, an investigator for the Medical Research Council, wrote of collar ironing: "This work is always done by women and does not involve any heavy muscular work; in fact it is, from the muscular point of view, the lightest work in a laundry."[56]

Processing of collars entailed a series of procedures. First, the damp collars were "pulled out" in preparation for steaming then placed on the steamer or blocker, which partially dried them and caused the starch to set in the correct shape. Next the collars were moved to another machine that completed the drying process and polished the collars to a high luster. Finally, collars were curled to the right degree and their edges smoothed. This last device required fairly frequent alteration or replacement to keep pace with changes in fashion. Collars were aired to permit evaporation of any remaining moisture before being transferred to the packers. The process was complex; from two to six machines and from one to six women might be employed in the finishing of each collar. Nonetheless, mechanized collar preparation was highly productive. At the Laundry Exhibition in London in 1907, Margaret MacDonald discovered a "collar steamer

and press (steam heated), whose output 'is at least 600 collars per hour,' "
while a factory inspector reported in the same year news of a new Troy
collar machine that was capable of ironing a reputed 3,000 collars an
hour.[57] From the workers' perspective, collar work was among the best jobs
to hold. The work was relatively light and fairly sociable, and it was found
by many laundry workers to be much more interesting than calender work.
"As a rule," observed one writer, "a collar machinist prefers her work to
any other laundry work."[58]

As far as possible machinery was used to iron linen, and in the largest
factories machines were employed to press skirts, nightdresses, handker-
chiefs, and the sleeves and bodies of shirts. Nonetheless, many of these
items required hand finishing; and fine dresses, silk lingerie, and articles of
particular value were ironed entirely by hand. In one Brighton laundry in
about 1920, 40 of the 140 employees were "skilled hand ironers."[59] Many
laundries offered "hand finishing" or all handwork ironing at premium
prices, for, as one successful employer reported,

> People will pay if their clothes are well ironed and delicate things are not
> spoiled. The trade to seek is the most delicate and difficult; that is where the
> profits come in, and people pay 1/- and 1/6 to have silk and lace nightdresses
> properly washed and ironed. But it needs great skill. You really want a girl
> who enjoys delicate work. Most things can be done by machine; but some
> hand washing is needed; shirts and all delicate things and 'finery' are better
> done by hand. The best work and the best profits are to those who have learnt
> to combine machine and hand work.[60]

The talented hand ironer did not lose her job to the machine because her
work was superior to machine work, and, crucially, because her work continued to yield her employer a high rate of profit. Thus, the laundry industry provides evidence to support the observation that "in many cases hand
labour retained favour against machinery because of better performance."[61] Married women with long years of experience held sway in the
ironing room of the factory laundry as they did in the traditional hand
laundry. The difference was that their work was now often eased by the use
of gas-heated irons or electrically heated irons which were cleaner and
lighter than stove-heated flatirons. (The use of electrically heated irons was
largely confined to the carriage trade laundry.)[62] Skilled ironers, then, were
not displaced by mechanization, but those with less talent, and in particular older women who no longer had the speed to match the performance of
the very young women in the calender room, undoubtedly did lose out. It
is perhaps not entirely coincidental that in the first decade during which

labor-saving devices reduced the number of women employed in laundries, the number of charwomen recorded by the census rose. Between 1901 and 1911 the number of women employed in laundries declined by 14.8 percent while the number of charwomen increased by 12.7 percent.[63]

Two more categories of workers complemented the staff of the modern power laundry: clerical and managerial staff. The first group of employees was retained by medium to large laundries; elsewhere the firm's books and accounts were kept by the proprietor or manager. A large clientele necessitated precision in identifying laundry, reconciling items with the customer's list, calculating bills, and managing the ordering of supplies from soap and starch to wicker laundry hampers and shirt wrappings embossed with the firm's logo. A large labor force required management and guidance. Sizeable establishments usually employed a superintendent for each functional area as well as forewomen (foremen in some washhouses) for each department and a manager to take charge of day-to-day operations. The number of these workers was few, but their attitudes and demeanor were critical determinants of the mood and productivity of any workplace. The right manager could motivate her subordinates while others might be disliked for favoritism (real or perceived) in assigning work, for patronizing attitudes, or, most vital, for identifying too heartily with management in industrial disputes.

Thus, in the laundry industry, while the needs of an altered workplace were met by an altered work force, some characteristics of the trade and its employees remained relatively unchanged in even the most sophisticated firm. The profile of the laundry labor force increasingly resembled that of other factory labor. Its workers were younger than in the traditional hand laundry, many were single, and a small percentage were men. In common with other industries, the adoption of machinery was accompanied by an increase in young and relatively unskilled workers. Lucy Deane, a factory inspector, observed that in mechanized laundries at the turn of the century, "girls of fourteen or sixteen years can tend machines, the operations of which, if accomplished by hand, could only be undertaken by older or more skilled workers. Where only one girl under eighteen years was employed eight or nine years ago, now dozens are to be found as machine tenders."[64] Thirty years later, young girls between fourteen and eighteen years of age were still the major source of new recruits to the laundry industry.

Traditionally, older married women had been attracted to the laundry trade because it drew on skills they already had, because its conditions were flexible, because it could be combined readily with other work both paid and unpaid, and because it could be pursued over a lifetime. These attractions largely remained and were augmented in the mechanized laundry by improved hours and conditions of work.[65] But what was there to attract the adolescent girl to a kind of labor that suffered from a reputation as a sweated trade and that even in the best-run establishments was undeniably heavy work? Certainly parents of prospective employees were not always pleased at the choice of laundry work as an occupation. One parent was less than reticent when she expressed her views to a group of investigators: "Put a girl in the laundry trade! Might as well put her in the workhouse at once, I wouldn't put a cat in it! It's them steam laundries have all the trade and they do their work by machinery and children. . . . There ought to be a law to forbid these laundries."[66] One outcome of this attitude was that employers sometimes reported difficulty in obtaining an adequate supply of labor. Analyzing the reasons underlying shortages, H. Llewellyn Smith observed: "The damp and steamy atmosphere of the washing departments, the heat of the ironing room and the changes in temperature to which workers in a laundry are subjected are circumstances which militate in the minds of many girls against employment in laundry work. The evil tradition of its early days still no doubt clings to the trade, and there appears to be even now to be a prejudice against being engaged in 'washing other people's dirty clothes.' "[67]

But there was another side to the picture. Work in a factory laundry offered far more personal freedom than domestic service, one of the few alternatives open to an unskilled working-class girl, particularly in areas like West London that held few possibilities for employment in industry. Also it was infinitely more attractive than employment as a maid, generally the best service post to which an untrained adolescent could aspire. Laundry work could also be more lucrative than serving in a shop or waiting on tables and could be continued as an occupation over a working lifetime. The fact that there was no need to purchase a uniform, as was often required of the beginning servant, shop girl, or waitress, was a further attraction for a girl from a poor family. And for a fortunate few, especially if they were literate and accurate enough to obtain work as sorters and packers, the laundry trade could offer prospects for advancement.

Naturally enough, it was rare for employees to attain senior managerial positions; investigators from the WIC found that of the close to 150 laundries they visited, the manageresses of only two fair-sized firms had risen from the ranks themselves. One of these women had benefited from parents who were able to pay £5 "for her to learn the trade right through;"

she had begun as an ordinary worker but proved to have special aptitude. The investigators were told at many establishments that a capable girl could easily rise to be forewoman, usually with the stipulation that the employee must be in the sorting and packing department to get this chance. Alternately, a woman might move from the packing room to be placed in charge of one of the receiving offices of a large laundry, with the increased independence and authority that the position entailed.[68] Other sources suggest that fine ironers also could sometimes parlay their skills into supervisory positions, particularly if the job involved to any marked degree the training of new employees.[69] In addition, the woman who was especially proficient in all branches of the work and who had gained some managerial experience could consider setting up a laundry on her own.

There were other attractions to laundry work which were of a less tangible sort. The atmosphere to be found in many mechanized laundries was such that "any initial prejudice . . . is quickly overcome once the girls can be got to try the work, and employers and workers are unanimous that if a girl stays a month in a laundry she is there for her working life."[70] Many observers commented upon the domestic or homelike aura that pervaded many laundries. Machinery and legislation did not entirely eradicate sweating or mean-spirited employers or eliminate all the distasteful aspects involved in processing other peoples' dirty linen, but there was nonetheless some truth in the perception of the laundry as a homey workplace. The domestic atmosphere derived in part from the fact that in some establishments laundry work was indeed a family trade: two generations frequently were employed in the same laundry and occasionally "grandmothers, mothers and daughters were all found working together."[71] Middle-class women, drawn to supervisory work in laundries in part because of the opportunity it provided to give "a guiding kindly hand" to rough untrained young girls, added to the maternalistic environment.[72] In fact, ladies were periodically urged to take up laundry management partly in order to "instil into her fellow workers habits of purity and refinement."[73] Approached directly, "improving" measures might have had little appeal, but, clothed in the guise of social clubs, annual outings, and glee clubs, they made many a laundry an appealing environment in which to work.

The domestic atmosphere of the typical laundry workplace also arose from the structural circumstances of the work itself. The wide variety of processes involved in laundry work provided considerable scope for individuality, and in establishments where the management encouraged job rotation, the opportunity to sustain interest in the work through lateral as well as vertical movement of employees. Indeed, a certain amount of informal job rotation was made necessary in most laundries by the unpredictable nature of general household laundry work; accurate forecasting of the mix of flatwork, shirts and collars, and fancy work in any given week's laundry was virtually impossible. As a result, most workers would have had the opportunity to broaden their experience by having to help out with work on machines other than those they usually used. While they looked like factories, mechanized laundries could not be run like manufacturing industries. In the laundry, the discipline of the machine was mitigated by the irregularities of domestic realities. Even the most talented laundry manager could not anticipate with accuracy fluctuations in the volume of work, the timing of its arrival at the laundry, or the number of items that would require extra washing or long soaking. The result was a persistence of part of the old pattern of alternating idleness and rushed work. This inevitable unraveling of rigid working patterns was attractive to many workers.

Progressive employers often took a lively interest in the welfare of their employees and the improvements in the quality of working life they engineered meant that "taking the trade as a whole there is a very good relationship between the proprietor and the worker."[71] So positive was the relationship that two social researchers specializing in detailed industrial time and movement studies concluded that among industrial employees laundry workers were "the happiest they . . . met in the course of their investigations."[75] Norman Burns, the young and energetic manager of the Rochester, Chatham and District Laundry Ltd., was typical of proponents of the welfare-oriented managerial style. It was reported in a trade journal in 1906 that Burns was "working steadily towards the amelioration of the laundry girl's lot, and the result of his efforts can be seen in a marked improvement in the character, class and status of employees."[76] The main vehicle used by Burns was a workers' social club that was provided with a club room by the firm but that was managed and subscribed to by employees. The club staged monthly entertainments, ran a library, and organized indoor games in winter and excursions into the countryside in summer. In addition, special efforts were made to ensure that the working environment was clean, cheerfully painted, and in general conducive to positive working attitudes. The strategy pleased both workers and shareholders since the laundry's turnover more than doubled between 1902 and 1906 and its dividend increased from 2.5 percent to 10 percent, a success due in some measure to a higher quality, better motivated work force.[77]

Burns's approach was by no means unique. Employers were well aware that management practices could do much to dispel what remained of the trade's negative image. Progressive practices could attract a higher quality work force with attendant gains in regularity, productivity, and morale, and they could even serve as a selling point for the laundry's services. In its prospectus, the Oakthorpe Laundry devoted as much space to describing the excellence of employees' working conditions as it did to ironing. At pains to stress that the laundry was not a sweated workplace, the brochure read: "Our wages and conditions are much higher than the minimum under Trade Board legislation and every employee is a member of our Pension Scheme. An annual holiday with full pay is given and sick pay allowances are made to those off work through illness. Every employee is in addition a member of a Trade Union. . . . No effort has been spared in catering for the comfort and welfare of the employees."[78] Incentive schemes such as bonuses for good attendance and prizes for punctuality and annual outings for all employees gradually replaced fines and scrimping on employee amenities in the best-run laundries. The *Laundry Record,* the principal mouthpiece for the laundry industry, actively proselytized for such progressive management practices. It published articles espousing the value of a "social service" attitude on the part of proprietors and managers, and in its series on model laundries, it recorded the attractiveness of their working conditions and the provision of extra amenities alongside data on turnover, profits, and sophisticated machinery.[79]

Josiah Chater and his colleagues at the Cambridge Steam Laundry were among those receptive to this management technique—a blend of emerging management theory and traditional paternalism. In his diary Chater recorded: "On 20 January 1882 there was a Grand Tea Meeting for the employees at the laundry. Lizzy and Junia and I went at six o'clock. . . . Had a little speech, two readings, some songs and duets, then a jolly dance. It was a capital evening."[80] The conditions in well run factory laundries sustained the view that with mechanization came great improvement in the lot of the laundry worker. "Laundry work," wrote May G. Spencer in an article reprinted in the trade union paper *Woman Worker* in 1909, "is a good example of a profession which has emerged from an inferior position to one of great importance. Formerly the conditions of laundry work were exceedingly bad, and we used to think that the worst sort of workers were good enough to clean our clothes. Now under the influence of education conditions are better; the class of workers has improved, and the profession, though still needing a larger band of educated women to raise it, bids fair to be one of the most lucrative a clever girl can take up."[81]

Enlightened management, legislation (including the 1920 order making mess rooms mandatory),[82] efficient organization, and a more highly educated and unionized labor force combined to make working in a laundry a desirable occupation. But such favorable conditions were not universal. Sweated conditions could still be found well into the twentieth century; in 1913, the *Daily Herald* publicized the appalling working conditions of what it termed the "White Linen Serfs." In the laundries investigated by that paper, fines were still very much in evidence, starvation wages were the rule, sanitary infractions were rife, and machinery was used as a pretext for speeding up the work.[83] In Liverpool, similar conditions were recorded.[84] Increased inspection in the wake of press publicity may have improved some conditions, but clearly the transformation of the laundry trade, while dramatic, was by no means complete. Work in a laundry continued to pose risks to health. It involved continual standing and the handling of soiled garments; temperatures were high (up to ninety degrees even in winter), ironing machines posed the risk of accident, and improperly installed or maintained gas-heated irons might emit noxious fumes. "Ironers suffer from headaches and sore eyes," wrote one factory inspector, "which result from constantly bending over the gas-heated irons in general use. The fumes from the tiny gas jets . . . are disagreeably noticeable on entering the room . . . and are of course worst of all just above the iron so heated."[85] Assiduous inspection, educated workers and employers, the employment of engineers to keep machinery in good repair, and specially constructed laundries all helped to reduce these problems. Nonetheless, the health drawbacks of laundry work were sufficient to merit several pages in a 1908 text on occupational diseases and to tarnish the shiny image painted of the mechanized laundry in trade journals.[86]

The superior mechanized laundry not only had well-maintained machinery, it also provided training for its staff or actively sought out employees who had obtained relevant training at a trade school or other similar institutions. However, around the turn of the century, such provisions for training were more the exception than the norm. More than half of the firms inspected by the Women's Industrial Council in 1907 reported that they undertook no training of their employees.[87] The most prevalent practice was simply to put the new employee to work alongside an experienced worker who would informally initiate the new recruit. The relatively unskilled nature of many laundry processes, of which calendering is the chief example, made this haphazard orientation to the industry possible. When Charles Booth investigated the industry in the last decade of the nineteenth century he found training to be uncommon, and where it existed, usually in the hand ironing department, apprenticeship lasted only two to three months. He also found that "masters, with few exceptions, complain of the difficulty in getting skilled hands."[88]

Over the next few years, some of the larger employers moved to rectify the situation by instituting in-house training schemes and by supporting the addition of laundry work to the curricula of trade schools. The huge Spiers and Ponds Laundry in Battersea, for example, instituted a year-long apprenticeship program in its hand ironing department. Here the apprentices were paid at half the ordinary piece-work rates during the first six months of their training, two-thirds of the normal rate in the next three months, and three-quarters the rate in the final period.[89] Analogous courses were found in other laundries, varying in length from three months to a year, and either specializing in skilled hand work or providing more comprehensive learning through the rotation of work assignments. Charges were rarely levied for training below the management level although trainees were sometimes required to work for the first month or two without payment. Where fees or premiums were required, they rarely exceeded one guinea.[90]

Supplementing direct training by employers was institutional training. Philanthropic establishments, as we have seen, frequently featured laundry work prominently in the training given to young inmates, while a variety of other organizations, from the Women's Industrial Council to the Ragged School Union and the Girls' Friendly Society, provided schooling in laundry work and other domestic occupations to enhance the employment prospects of their particular clientele.[91] In the years following compulsory education, board school programs expanded to include classes in domestic economy which, even if they were not designed to prepare girls for work in commercial laundries, did provide the rudiments of knowledge about the laundering process. As early as 1892, a beginning was made at providing technical laundry education when the London School Board and the City of London Guild established laundry classes to be taught using the "apparatus familiar in the district."[92] It is unclear how long this particular educational experiment lasted, but by 1909, the London Council had supplemented it with a laundry trade school that enrolled girls fourteen years of age and over for a two year program, a program that embraced all aspects of the work from hand ironing to chemistry and bookkeeping.[93]

The area of laundry work for which training was most prevalent was preparation of "ladies" for supervisory and managerial positions. This training usually required the payment of a premium and was designed to give the student a familiarity with all aspects of the laundry trade. Such education was usually provided in a working laundry. Laundry work was recommended to educated women who had to support themselves, for "if a woman is good at this work her value increases with age, and there seems to be really no reason why a woman of 55 or 60 should not be equal to continuing her duties as laundry manageress."[94] It is hardly surprising that ex-governesses were among those who gravitated toward an occupation whose training and prospects were described in 1910 as follows:

> Another good opening for an educated woman is in the management of a laundry, for the demand is steady and the salary a good one, varying according to the size and style of the laundry.
> She must have worked as pupil in a large laundry from four to six months, paying a training fee of about £10 10s. or so. Here she must have learned, not only the actual details or sorting, marking, washing, starching, ironing, and packing but the organization of the work. She must have certain conspicuous qualities of her own—tact, firmness, organising ability, good business instinct, much perseverance and coolness under responsibility and worry. If she is really ambitious and flings herself heartily into the work she is practically certain to command good posts and has interesting and lucrative work.[95]

Progressive and thoughtful proprietors, especially those with large and complex establishments, recognized the value of a properly trained staff, especially at the supervisory level. One author insisted that the manager or manageress was the "one person upon whom the success of the laundry depends" and advocated that training should encompass a knowledge of chemistry and of machinery. Commitment to training on the part of the industry was especially evident in 1930 when regional laundry associations joined with the University College of Hull in establishing a two-year diploma course in Industrial Laundry Administration.[96]

Economic Vulnerability

Well-trained staff and knowledgeable and sensitive management employees were, of course, important to a laundry's success. But neither could insulate a firm from the economic fluctuations that made the laundry industry a particularly vulnerable trade. "In one sense it is a parasitic trade and reflects with astonishing accuracy the industrial state of the neighbourhood," mused one investigator.

> To have one's washing done at a laundry is to many people of the nature of a luxury, and hence it is one of the first economies to be practised when neces-

sity so demands; again a strike or lockout in the neighbourhood will markedly reduce the number of workmen's overalls, aprons, etc., sent to the laundry; and even the fine weather affects some laundries, for where there are gardens to houses, clothes can be dried in the garden and so there is less work at such times for the laundry. A launderer's customers are his competitors.[97]

The theme of customer competition was reiterated by the Standing Committee on Trusts that, in 1920, investigated the charge of price fixing in the laundry industry. In exonerating the industry of the charge, the committee concluded that "the laundry proprietor is limited as to prices by the special sensitiveness of the market in which he operates."[98] When prices exceeded a certain limit, the customer simply retained more articles to be washed at home, thereby bringing prices back down again. In other words, it was the externally imposed circumstances of the market that gave to laundry price lists an astonishing uniformity rather than any significant degree of price setting through collusion by laundry owners.

Customer competition, as well as that from institutional laundries, mentioned earlier, did much to shape the modern laundry industry. This competitive vulnerability had a number of significant implications for the organization of the industry. It forced many a small washerwoman out of the industry for "these washerwomen are among the first to suffer in any period of trade depression, for as the first economy in bad times is to do your own washing, the tiny laundry with a very local connection is soon emptied."[99] Overall, in fact, price competition within the industry was so fierce and so damaging that industry leaders generally welcomed trade board minimum wages and trade unions as a better alternative than the unfettered market. In addition, economic vulnerability encouraged the movement toward amalgamation on the part of the largest proprietors in order to achieve economies of scale and provide some insulation against fluctuations in the economy. By 1930, amalgamations of many individual establishments into one conglomerate were occurring frequently in the greater London area (although it was reported that the value of the process had reached its limits by that date).[100]

Finally, the viability of laundries depended, to a considerable extent, upon their ability to adapt to consumer demands attendant upon changes in fashion. Any move away from starched table linens could cause despair, while headlines such as "Fashion Favours Laundry Industry" abounded with the rumors that damask tablecloths were regaining popularity.[101] Volatile clothing fashions could wreak havoc. In the 1860s, the introduction of the cage crinoline dramatically reduced the number of starched petticoats required to support a full skirt. Similarly, a move in men's fashion away

from stiff collars could transform the work of the laundry. "Since the introduction of soft collars," observed one writer, "a laundry specialising in stiff
collars had suffered a reduction in this particular class of articles from
15,000 to 5,000 per week. In another laundry doing general work the
number of collars laundered fell from 64,000 a week to 44,000."[102] Other
changes could largely eliminate laundry custom. A major example is the
change in women's lingerie from starched cotton to silk and synthetics.
The new garments were readily washed out by hand, and despite industry
efforts to "capture the artificial silk market," few such garments ever found
their way into the laundry.[103] The threat posed by changes in both fabric
and fashion inhibited specialization in the laundry industry, just as the
trade's vulnerability to economic fluctuations had encouraged amalgamation and an acceptance of government regulation. Thus, a plethora of
factors—economic, social, technological, and regulatory—helped to bring
about and to shape and to transform the mechanized laundry and the
nature of its work.

By 1930, despite some survivals of traditional methods, the commercial
laundering of clothing and household linens had become a modern industry. Production processes had become mechanized; conditions of work had
come to resemble more closely those of manufacturing industries than
those of the traditional washerwoman; the social and demographic characteristics of the labor force had more in common with a textile factory work
force than with hand laundresses; and ownership was vested in shareholders as well as individual proprietors. Accountants, advertisers, management specialists, time and motion experts, and industrial architects were
all employed by progressive owners. These same laundry owners also organized themselves in order to lobby central and local government, to make
their case known to the public, and to strengthen their bargaining position
in confrontations with organized labor. The laundry labor force underwent
a similar transformation, becoming better educated, more specialized, less
casual, and—even if not unionized—better informed about their rights in
the workplace. Improved wages, enhanced working conditions (both of
which were aided by government regulation), prospects for advancement, a
decline in the stigma that had adhered to the trade: all meant that workers
shared to a degree in the benefits of a modernizing industry—an industry
that was largely transformed, often beneficially so, by those processes of
mechanization that operated so extensively during the two generations
after 1870.

Epilogue

This book has been about the laundry worker and her trade. It has also been about housework, for this is a trade that competes with, or supplements, the work of housewives. It is the relationship between unpaid domestic work and paid professional labor that gives laundry work much of its character. Laundry work and housework are alike widespread and commonplace, predominantly the realm of women, particularly women with families; and, over the past century, both have been profoundly affected by technological change and the burgeoning of the service sector.

As a service sector industry, perhaps the most striking characteristic of the laundry trade was its imperfect and transitory penetration of the domestic laundry market. Throughout the nineteenth century, a great many traditional household tasks, such as the making of beer, bread, or clothing, moved from domestic to market production. Once removed from the domestic environment—and for some tasks the process had begun before the nineteenth century—most of these productive tasks became firmly entrenched in the market economy. In England and in other western countries, the industrial principles of economy of scale and division of labor combined with changes in life-styles, housing, and female employment patterns to ensure that these functions remained in the industrial sphere. To the extent that the brewing of beer, the sewing of garments, or the baking of bread are found in the household today, they are as atavistic, often romanticized recreational activities. Laundry work is an exception to this pattern.

Laundry work is a rare, possibly unique example of a traditional domestic task moving back to the home after its processes had become industrialized. That it moved out of the household, in part or in its entirety, is understandable enough. Laundry work, as we have seen, was the most universally despised of all household tasks. It was extremely arduous; it was disruptive of household routine; its proper performance involved much equipment, numerous processes, and considerable expenditure of time. The loathing for laundering was limited by neither time nor geography; this view was shared by both British and American women and continues today. One modern study of housework found that ironing was the task most disliked by the housewives interviewed: it was despised because it "consists of repetitive actions which tire specific muscles without engaging the attention of the mind or the concentrated energy of the whole body."[1] Given these persistent attitudes, it is all the more intriguing that laundry work returned to the home. Why it happened remains unclear.

A partial answer to the puzzle can be found in the changes that occurred in the commercial laundry industry after the 1920s. In 1930, the English laundry industry was buoyant: its market was growing, its profits increasing, and its prospects seemed unlimited; the laundry industry was, in short, a classic example of the service sector revolution which was transforming the structure of the economy. The laundry trade's most influential journal trumpeted in that year the industry's development and heralded its rosy future; the Minister of Labour, Margaret Bondfield, congratulated the trade on its "amazing progress," lauded its improved working environment, and applauded its contribution to the nation's trade; and a social investigator observed that improvements in the character and working conditions of laundry work since the turn of the century outstripped those of any other industry.[2] The introduction of a greater variety of laundry services, along with favorable external factors such as an increase in the number of families living in flats, a shortage of domestic servants, and a "disinclination on the part of the younger generation, whether of the household or of the staff, to do 'washing' " combined to increase the flow of work to laundries. At the same time, laundry amalgamations and the increased use of machinery were producing economies of scale.[3] Admittedly, changes in fashion had dramatically reduced the number of stiff collars being sent to the laundry, and the introduction of artificial silk lingerie meant that starched underclothing was becoming a thing of the past, but the impact of these changes was not sufficient in 1930 to offset the gains in volume.

Although increased mechanization might have been expected to take its toll in jobs, the laundry worker's lot seemed to be improving. Between 1923 and 1929, according to Board of Trade figures, the number of workers employed in the laundry, dyeing, and cleaning trades increased from 107,280 to 135,030 (excluding laundresses working on their own).[4] At the same time, the increased minimum wage rates established by the Laundry Trade Board in 1919 were substantially sustained through the depression years, yielding, according to one source, higher real wages in the 1930s than at any other time since the war.[5] A forty-eight-hour work week (although individual workdays could be long), lighter work, more pleasant working conditions, and, for most, paid annual holidays had made laundry work between the wars a fairly desirable manual employment, at least for workers in regulated laundries. Government regulation filled part of the gap left by the almost total collapse of laundry unions during the depression.[6]

Prosperity and market dominance continued in the English laundry industry until after the Second World War, with, in contrast to the United States, little indication of increased competition from the householder. The laundry industry formed an important segment of the service sector, but, unlike cinemas and holiday resorts, it was not a luxury in wartime. In a nation at war, especially one with responsibility for billeting hundreds of thousands of foreign troops in addition to its own forces, laundry services were vital. That the industry was crucial to the war effort was acknowledged in 1941 by the appointment of an Inter-Departmental Committee headed by a director of laundry services to coordinate utilization of laundry facilities and by the extension of the Essential Work Order to the trade. Under the order, wages rates were fixed, and workers involved in service work were unable to leave their jobs. For laundry workers, wartime was a boon; wage rates established by the government were higher than those found in any pre-existing trade union agreement, and subsequent negotiations for higher rates resulted in an award by the Industrial Court in February 1944 of the full amount argued for by the unions. In addition, a 1939 order guaranteed a week's paid holidays to all laundry workers, a reform, in the words of one union publication, "deemed visionary" only a few years before.[7] Rationing and shortages of raw materials, as well as the exigencies of the Blitz, virtually guaranteed that domestic appliances, including washing machines, made no inroads during these years.

At the end of the war, it was estimated that the commercial laundries in the United Kingdom numbered between 1,800 and 2,500, with approxi-

mately 127,500 to 190,000 employees.[8] In 1946, the Institute of British
Launderers estimated that the net annual output of the industry was in the
neighborhood of £70 million.[9] An analysis made by the institute in that
year confirmed that a large portion of the industry's business still came
from individual families, an estimated 13 million of which sent about 50
million items to the laundry each week. The institute emphasized as well
that a "vast amount of work is also done for hospitals, hotels, shipping,
industry in general and the armed forces."[10] Despite sustained domestic
demand, the industry's growth was now most pronounced in the commercial sector. The linen hire service led this expansion by providing commercial firms with freshly laundered and repaired linen ranging from sheets,
towels, and table linen to shirts, overalls, and uniforms. This service
proved popular because it enabled industry to respond rapidly to changing
needs and opportunities without having to make a capital investment in
stocks of linen.

On the domestic side of the market, industry experts saw no clouds:
"The habits of the public with regard to laundry services have not shown
any marked tendency to change," they concluded, and little threat was
perceived from the latest laundry innovation, the launderette. Indeed, the
launderette was viewed as a transition step between doing the wash at
home and sending it to a professional laundry. "The Industry," stated the
Institute of British Launderers, "considers that this service takes the laundry out of the home and the next step is probably to the commercial
laundry which offers transport and specialist handling."[11] Others anticipated that the development of economical, fully machine-laundered services would in the future expand the domestic market to include a larger
working-class clientele.[12]

The following decades were to belie this optimism. The trend toward
doing the laundry at home with modern equipment or carrying the family
wash out to the local laundromat became irreversible in Great Britain in
the decades after the war. Conservative British consumers were slower than
their American counterparts in adopting domestic appliances, hindered in
part by the slower expansion of domestic electricity and a lower postwar
living standard, but the affluence of the 1950s and 1960s combined with
social attitudes to change this. Ornate brass or iron trivets for flatirons
were a frequent gift to a housewife in the 1860s; in the 1960s, an automatic
washer was an appropriate choice—a consumer durable the ownership of
which, besides its usefulness, contributed to the family's status.

Economic and social factors added to the attractiveness of the new
domestic technology. If a married woman was not employed in the

marketplace—and in the 1950s middle-class women in particular were encouraged not to do so—there was no obvious opportunity cost in economic terms to doing laundry at home. Indeed, with modern machinery it was feasible to do the wash while at the same time minding the children, tending the soup pot or dusting the parlor. Further, home laundering could appear to be economical, if no value was given to the housewife's labor and the cost of equipment was amortized over a long enough period. As labor costs (aided by minimum wage rates) rose and mass market production lowered washing machine prices, the home laundry appeared ever more appealing. Add to this the widely held belief that garments laundered at home lasted longer and the argument became—in the hands of advertisers at least—irresistible. Finally, in the ideology of the 1950s performing the family wash became a part of "homemaking," an emotional as much as a physical task, a measure of caring.

The moral worth that accrued to the woman who performed all her family's cleansing tasks was much easier to achieve with modern technology. The modern electric washing machine required both less space and less effort than the earlier home laundry with its tubs, boiler, and wringer. Other refinements such as the domestic tumble-dryer, permanent press fabrics, electric and gas-fired water heaters, and synthetic detergents, which only became widespread after the war, further diminished the incentive to send the wash to a commercial laundry. Atomized suburban living, intensive advertising of domestic appliances, liberal hire-purchase terms, and the consumerism that went with it all confirmed the trend toward home laundering. When circumstances or finances did not allow indulgence in conspicuous consumption, there was the self-service launderette to pose competition for the commercial laundry. The launderettes, which had first opened in Britain in the late 1940s, had grown to an estimated 7,500 by the late 1960s and, earlier sanguine predictions to the contrary, seriously challenged the laundry's household clientele.[13]

The revival of laundering at home, however, did not sound the death knell of the laundry industry. The householder has always been the laundry's most volatile customer; the loss of a large segment of that market meant that the industry had to redeploy its resources into a different and essentially more stable market. The domestic laundry bundle became much smaller, but "fortunately," one industry analyst noted in 1970, "the expansion of the tourist trade, the country's rising standard of living which involved greater use of restaurants and hotels than hitherto, and the improved standards of factory and office housekeeping all combined to produce far more industrial laundrywork than previously, representing

contract laundering and linen rental to established . . . firms whose interest in domestic bundle work was rapidly declining."[14] The industry had
adapted to serve both the service sector and the industrial sector, moving
ever farther away from its household origins and from the varied and
complex assortment which made up the average family's wash. Contract
laundering was both less sensitive to slight shifts in economic well-being
and more specialized than household laundering, thus enabling firms to
make plans with the assurance provided by long term contracts and to
achieve economies as a result of gearing its trade to one part of the market
such as work-wear rental or hospital linen.

Inevitably, many laundries with a family trade have closed in the past
twenty years, some of them after fifty or sixty years in business, but still
others have smoothly made accommodations to new conditions.[15] One
example is Wilson's Laundry in Brighton. This laundry, begun in 1850 by
a woman and her daughter working out of their own home without benefit
of piped water, was in 1980 a thriving firm with a staff of 180 that not only
carried on laundering and dry cleaning for both families and institutions
but also ran several launderettes.[16]

One sign that the mid-twentieth century laundry industry was far from
moribund came on 23 February 1960 when thirty-two members of the
laundry and allied industries formally constituted themselves in the City of
London at Chandlers' Hall as the Company of Launderers. Set up to
"foster the craft of laundering," the company's main enterprise over the
next few years was the establishment of a trust to be used to provide
scholarships for studies related to the industry and to dispense charity of a
more general sort. To cement its position, the company adopted a motto—
"Cleanliness is next to Godliness"—a coat of arms, planned a small exhibition for its tenth anniversary, and commissioned a short history of the
trade.[17] On the coat of arms, laundresses stand on either side of the crest
while in the Company of Launderers all the founding members were men.
In its modern industrial guise, the trade is male dominated, though still
largely staffed by women, but where it is performed as unpaid family
labor, women still hold sway, even, it seems, in many of the most liberated
households.[18] In the laundry trade, technology has advanced to computers
and solar water heating. There is even talk of introducing robots and
nuclear power, but many of the social relationships underlying this ancient
craft are little altered.[19]

Doing the wash is an ancient and universal craft. In the pages of this
book, attention has been focused on the English laundress over a period of

one hundred years, and the way in which her trade altered under the impact of technological, social, and market forces. Much of what has been said here is applicable, if with different emphases, to other societies, to other laundry workers. The traditional laundress is gone, her place taken by machines and her work done by an industrialized labor force, or by the individual householder. Yet her image lingers as part of popular and literary culture. Elizabeth Hardwick, in her 1979 novel, *Sleepless Nights,* perceptively captured the feisty independence and toughness of the laundress. She describes one of the last of the traditional laundresses: "Large head, large teeth, large carpet slippers and the large arms that have been wringing, pulling, lifting for a lifetime. All parts of the body hurt in some way even if all are strong. . . . Not much over thirty years old then, but no hint of youth except for the curls which have been formed by pins clamped next to her ears. Reddish curls, large, round, reddish face, and a voice large and reddish." This description is convincing. Even more persuasive is Hardwick's assessment of the laundry worker's attitudes toward her work and her clients: "Finicky patrons mutter about scorchings, but softly, because she is known to be tough and to flare into anger, coming at you with a pugilistic glare in her light, pink eyes. . . . Her lyrical utterance is saved for her work. She admits that she loves wash out on the line. That's where it is lovely and fresh, she insists, her voice rising."[20]

Notes

Abbreviations

NFWW	National Federation of Women Workers
P.P.	Parliamentary Papers
R.C.	Royal Commission
WIC	Women's Industrial Council
WIN	*Women's Industrial News*
WTUL	Women's Trade Union League

Preface

1. Kathleen Woodward, *Jipping Street: Childhood in a London Slum* (London: Harper, 1928), 12. I am indebted to Joy Parr for this reference.

2. There are a few studies that explore the service sector, including: Victor R. Fuchs, *The Service Economy* (New York: Colombia University Press, 1968); James B. Jeffreys, *Retail Trading in Britain, 1850-1950* (Cambridge: Cambridge University Press, 1954); W. Hamish Fraser, *The Coming of the Mass Market, 1850-1914* (London: Macmillan, 1981); G. Anderson, *The Service Occupations of Nineteenth-Century Liverpool* (Salford: University of Salford, Department of Economics, 1981); R. M. Hartwell, "The Service Revolution: The Growth of Services in Modern Economy," in *The Fontana Economic History of Europe*, ed. Carlo Cipolla, 6 vols. (London: Fontana, 1973); vol. 3, *The Industrial Revolution*, 358-96; Peter Mathias, *Retailing Revolution: A History of Multiple Retailing in the Food Trades based on the Allied Supplies Group of Companies* (London: Longmans, 1967).

3. Several recent publications have examined the processes of laundering, but they have almost exclusively considered it as unpaid household work rather than as remunerative employment. Among the more successful recent examples of writing

on the theme of housework are: Caroline Davidson, *A Woman's Work Is Never Done: A History of Housework in the British Isles, 1650-1950* (London: Chatto & Windus, 1982); Ann Oakley, *The Sociology of Housework* (New York: Pantheon, 1974); Susan Strasser, *Never Done: A History of American Housework* (New York: Pantheon, 1982); and Ruth Schwartz Cowan, *More Work for Mother: The Ironies of Household Technology from the Open Hearth to the Microwave* (New York: Basic, 1983).

4. E. J. Hobsbawm, *Labouring Men: Studies in the History of Labour* (London: Weidenfeld & Nicolson, 1964), 317. For discussions of the limitations of some modes of analysis in labor history, see also Patricia Branca, "A New Perspective on Women's Work: A Comparative Typology," *Journal of Social History*, 9 (Winter 1975), 129-53; and Raphael Samuel, "The Workshop of the World: Steam Power and Hand Technology in Mid-Victorian Britain," *History Workshop*, no. 3 (Spring 1977), 6-72.

5. Although a few inventions, such as Seyrig's 1830 patent for a centrifugal extractor, are of an earlier date, significant growth in the use of power machinery did not occur until the later decades of the century. See Ancliffe Prince, *The Craft of Laundering: A History of Fabric Cleaning* (London: Company of Launderers, 1970), 12, 18-20; J. H. Clapham, *An Economic History of Modern Britain*, 3 vols. (Cambridge: Cambridge University Press, 1926-38); vol. 3, *Machines and National Rivalries, 1887-1894, with an Epilogue, 1914-1929* (1938), 184-85; Sidney Tebutt, "Steam Laundry Machinery," in *Proceedings of the Institution of Mechanical Engineers* (London: Institution of Mechanical Engineers, Apr. 1898), 268-307; Thomas Oliver, ed., *Dangerous Trades: The Historical, Social and Legal Aspects of Industrial Occupations as Affecting Health by a Number of Experts* (London: Murray, 1902), especially chap. 47, "Laundry Workers," 663-72.

6. L. Wyatt Papworth and Dorothy M. Zimmern, *The Occupations of Women: According to the Census for England and Wales, 1911* (London: WIC, 1914), table 5, 23.

7. Laundry work whether as a paid employment or household labor receives mention in some studies of women's work although rarely in the context of the family economy. Among the many useful studies of women's work are: Alice Kessler-Harris, *Out to Work: A History of Wage-Earning Women in the United States* (Oxford: Oxford University Press, 1982); Jane Lewis, *Women in England, 1870-1950: Sexual Divisions and Social Change* (Bloomington, Indiana: Indiana University Press, 1984); Elizabeth Roberts, *A Woman's Place: An Oral History of Working Class Women, 1890-1914* (Oxford: Basil Blackwell, 1984); Joan Scott and Louise A. Tilly, "Women's Work and the Family in Nineteenth-Century Europe," in *The Family in History*, ed. Charles Rosenberg (Philadelphia: University of Pennsylvania Press, 1975), 145-78; Joan Scott and Louise A. Tilly, *Women, Work, and Family* (New York: Holt, Rinehart and Winston, 1978); Patricia Branca, *Women in Europe since 1750* (London: Croom Helm, 1978); Sally Alexander, *Women's Work in Nineteenth-Century London: A Study of the Years 1820-50* (London: Journeyman, 1983), originally published in *The Rights and Wrongs of Women*, ed. Juliet Mitchell and Ann Oakley (Harmondsworth: Penguin, 1976); Patricia Hollis, "Working

Women," *History,* 62 *(Oct. 1977), 439-45; Theresa McBride, The Domestic Revolution: The Modernization of Household Service in England and France 1820-1920* (London: Croom Helm, 1976); Theresa McBride, "The Long Road Home: Women's Work and Industrialization," in *Becoming Visible: Women in European History,* ed. Renate Bridenthal and Claudia Koonz (Boston: Houghton Mifflin, 1977), 280-95; Mary Lynn McDougall, "Working-Class Women during the Industrial Revolution," in *Becoming Visible,* ed. Bridenthal and Koonz, 255-79; Neil McKendrick, "Home Demand and Economic Growth: A New View of Women and Children in the Industrial Revolution," in *Historical Perspectives: Studies in English Thought and Society in Honour of J. H. Plumb,* ed. Neil McKendrick (London: Europa, 1974), 152-210; David M. Katzman, *Seven Days a Week: Women and Domestic Service in Industrializing America* (New York: Oxford University Press, 1978).

8. Kessler-Harris, *Out to Work,* 185.

Introduction

1. See, for example, "Four Thousand Years Ago and Now: Laundry Methods of the Past and Possibilities of the Future," *Laundry,* May 1930, 633, 635; Ancliffe Prince, *The Craft of Laundering: A History of Fabric Cleaning* (London: Company of Launderers, 1970), chap. 1; Harry C. Mosley, "Laundry: From Cave Man to Robots," *Dimensions in Health Service* (Toronto: Ontario Hospital Association, Apr. 1983), 17.

2. "Four Thousand Years," *Laundry,* May 1930, 633; "Washing Day in Many Countries," *Laundry Record,* May 1902, 233; "Washerwomen of the World," *Laundry Record,* Aug. 1899, 363; John Crawford Hodgson, ed., *Six North Country Diaries,* (Durham: Surtees Society, 1910), 32, 39; and Caroline Davidson, *A Woman's Work Is Never Done: A History of Housework in the British Isles, 1650-1950* (London: Chatto & Windus, 1982), 139-40.

3. Mary Norvak, *Kitchen Antiques* (New York: Praeger, 1975), 59. See also S. Minwel Tibbott, "Laundering in the Welsh Home," *Folk Life: A Journal of Ethnological Studies,* 19 (1981), 43-44; Davidson, *Woman's Work,* 138-41.

4. Davidson, *Woman's Work,* 141; Tibbott, "Laundering," 44.

5. Norvak, *Kitchen Antiques,* 53-54; Davidson, *Woman's Work,* 142.

6. Prince, *Craft of Laundering,* 7.

7. Christopher Merret, "An Account of Several Observables in Lincolnshire Not Taken Notice of in Camden, or Any Other Author," *Philosophical Transactions of the Royal Society,* 19 (Nov. and Dec. 1696), 349.

8. Anthony S. Wohl, *Endangered Lives: Public Health in Victorian Britain* (London: Dent, 1983), 64.

9. Eunice Lipton, "The Laundress in Late Nineteenth-Century French Culture: Imagery, Ideology, and Edgar Degas," *Art History,* 3,3 (Sept. 1980), 297.

10. P.P., *1861 Census for England and Wales,* 1863 (3221) 53, table 84, 132. Under-reportage resulted from the seasonality of the trade, the fact that it might be just one of a variety of cash-producing activities in which a working-class woman might be engaged, or the pride that might keep some women from listing themselves as other than homemakers. The timing of the census, taken one night at the end of March or the beginning of April, further minimized reportage since this was not one of the peaks of seasonal employment in the laundry trade.

11. Eliza Warren, *How I Managed My House on Two Hundred Pounds a Year* (London: Houlston & Wright, 1865), 12.

12. J. A. Banks, *Prosperity and Parenthood: A Study of Family Planning Among the Victorian Middle Classes* (London: Routledge & Kegan Paul, 1954), 59-63. Banks cites a letter (62) to *The Times,* 25 Jan. 1858, in which the writer details her expenditure: while her income increased by about 54 percent, her expenditure on washing increased by 204 percent.

13. Prince, *Craft of Laundering,* 19.

14. Compiled from P.P., *1891 Census for England and Wales,* 1893-94 (7058) 106, divisional tables, table 6, 9-10.

15. WTUL, *Result of Canvass Amongst Bona Fide Laundresses in Favour of Factory Acts Being Applied to Laundries* (London: Twentieth Century Press, 1891).

16. Fabian Society, *Life in the Laundry,* Tract No. 112 (London: Fabian Society, 1902), 2.

17. Royal Borough of Kensington, *Annual Report of the Medical Officer of Health* (Kensington: Royal Borough of Kensington 1908), 44.

18. Thomas Oliver, *Dangerous Trades: The Historical, Social and Legal Aspects of Industrial Occupations Affecting Health by a Number of Experts* (London: Murray 1902), 664.

19. Prince, *Craft of Laundering,* 18.

20. *Fulham Chronicle,* 23 Nov. 1900, 23 Feb. 1906. Another large concern, incidentally notorious for underpaying its employees, was William Whiteley, Hygienic and Sanitary Laundries, Mornington Park, West Kensington; at the end of the nineteenth century, its premises took up a city block (photograph of Whiteley's Works, c. 1895-1906, Fulham Reference Library).

21. *Liverpool Post,* 1 July 1914; J. H. Treble, "The Seasonal Demand for Adult Labour in Glasgow, 1890-1914," *Social History,* 3,1 (Jan. 1978), app. 1, 60.

22. P.P., *Report of H.M. Inspectors of Factories, as to Hours of Work and Dangerous Machinery in Laundries, and as to Their Sanitary Condition,* 1894 (7418) 21, 8-10. Charitable institution laundries, in addition to private concerns, frequently did laundry for ships, hotels, and restaurants.

23. Banks, *Prosperity and Parenthood,* 96.

24. Calculated from J. S. Neale, "Economic Conditions and Working-Class Movements in the City of Bath," Master's thesis, University of Bristol, 1963, table 7, 14.

25. Raphael Samuel, "Quarry Roughs," in *Village Life and Labour,* ed. Raphael Samuel (London: Routledge & Kegan Paul, 1975), 179-83; Eglantyne Jebb, *Cambridge: A Brief Study in Social Questions* (Cambridge: Macmillan & Bowes, 1906), 43.

Chapter 1: Hand Laundry Work and the Family Economy

1. Lenore Davidoff, "The Employment of Married Women in England, 1850-1950," Master's thesis, London School of Economics, 1956, 216.

2. P.P., *1901 Census for England and Wales,* 1903 (1523) 84, occupational tables, table 3, 222. Overall in 1901, 13 percent of all married women were employed compared with 24 percent in 1851. In 1901, 24 percent of Lancashire cotton operatives were married or widowed (Margaret Hewitt, *Wives and Mothers in Victorian Industry* [London: Rockcliffe, 1958], 17).

3. Unless otherwise indicated, figures for these areas are derived from the census enumerators' books for these localities: P.R.O. MSS Census Enumerators' Books (The Potteries), 1861, RG 9/18; (Kensal New Town), 1861, RG 9/39 and 1871, RG 10/91; (Jennings Buildings), 1861, RG 9/16.

4. Edward Cadbury, M. Cecile Matheson, and George Shann, *Women's Work and Wages: A Phase of Life in an Industrial City* (London: Unwin, 1908), 172.

5. Charles Booth, *Life and Labour of the People of London,* 16 vols. (London: Macmillan, 1902-1903), 2d ser., vol. 8, 264-65.

6. P.P., *R.C. on Labour. The Employment of Women,* 1893-94 (6894) 37, 17 ff.; Booth, *Life and Labour,* 1st ser., vol. 1, 293.

7. Mrs. Bernard (Helen) Bosanquet, ed., *Social Conditions in Provincial Towns* (London: Macmillan, 1912), 63, 112.

8. Raphael Samuel, "Quarry Roughs," in Raphael Samuel, ed., *Village Life and Labour* (London: Routledge & Kegan Paul, 1975), 181.

9. Booth, *Life and Labour,* 1st ser., vol. 1, 246. Overcrowding of these areas as a result of central slum clearances made "the demand for labour so very little that the inhabitants are half starved" (P.P., *R.C. on the Housing of the Working Classes,* 1884-85 (4402) 31, 70-71).

10. P.P., *R.C. on Labour,* 1893-94 (6894) 37, 22-23. See also Mrs. Layton, "Memories of Seventy Years," in *Life as We Have Known It,* ed. Margaret Llewelyn Davies and introd. Anna Davin (London: Virago, 1977), 39-40; Clementina Black, *Married Women's Work: Being the Report of an Enquiry Undertaken by the Women's Industrial Council* (London: Bell, 1915), 16-17; Barbara Kerr, *The Dispossessed: An Aspect of Victorian Social History* (New York: St. Martin's, 1974), 93.

11. Albert Paul, *Poverty-Hardship but Happiness: Those Were the Days, 1903-1917,* 3d ed. (Brighton: Queen Spark, 1981), 9.

12. A. E. Coppard, *It's Me, O, Lord!: An Abstract and Brief Chronicle of Some of the Life with Some of the Opinions of A. E. Coppard* (London: Methuen, 1957), 24. See

also Ted Willis, *Whatever Happened to Tom Mix? The Story of One of My Lives* (London: Cassell, 1970), 8.

13. P.P., *R.C. on the Poor Laws and the Relief of Distress,* 1909 (4850) 42, app. 18, 9.

14. Flora Thompson, *Lark Rise to Candleford* (London: Reprint Society, 1948), 472; S. Minwel Tibbott, "Laundering in the Welsh Home," *Folk Life: A Journal of Ethnological Studies,* 19 (1981), 55; Elizabeth Roberts, *A Woman's Place: An Oral History of Working-Class Women, 1890-1914* (Oxford: Basil Blackwell, 1984), 140. In 1911, one London housewife employed a laundress to come in to do her family's washing. For two shillings, nine pence, her employee performed arduous labor from 8:00 a.m. to 6:30 p.m. (*Daily News,* 11 Oct. 1911).

15. Arthur Sherwell, *Life in West London: A Study and a Contrast* (London: Methuen, 1897), 80-82; Barbara Leigh Hutchins, *Women in Modern Industry* (London: Bell, 1915), 224; *Laundry Record,* 30 Sept. 1893, 144-45; Bosanquet, *Social Conditions,* 24; London School of Economics, Charles Booth MS Collection, B-359, 129 and A-44, vol. 4; Sally Alexander, "Women's Work in Nineteenth-Century London: A Study of the Years 1820-50," in *The Rights and Wrongs of Women,* ed. Juliet Mitchell and Ann Oakley (Harmondsworth: Penguin, 1976), 100. These wages were often reduced by fines and other deductions (Hutchins, *Women in Modern Industry,* app. 9, 291; Margaret Ethel MacDonald, "Report of Enquiry into Conditions of Work in Laundries," *WIN* [June 1907], 637).

16. P.P., *R.C. on Labour,* 1893-94 (6894) 37, 22; Booth, *Life and Labour,* 2d ser., vol. 8, 264-65.

17. George R. Sims, *Off the Track in London* (London: Jarrold, 1911), 6, 41. Booth's observations confirm this view (*Life and Labour,* 1st ser., vol. 1, 246; 3d ser., vol. 5, 90-91, 151-52) as does Sam Shaw's autobiography (*Guttersnipe* [London: Low, Marston, 1946], esp. 46). The nature of communities in London dependent on a variety of casual and itinerant employment has been ably described by Raphael Samuel in "Comers and Goers," *The Victorian City: Images and Realities,* ed. H. J. Dyos and Michael Wolff, 2 vols. (London: Routledge & Kegan Paul, 1973), vol. 1, 123-60.

18. Clementina Black, *Married Women's Work,* 24-25. Roughly 23 percent of her sample came from the North Kensington area. An interesting discussion of the family economy and the middle class assumption that a woman's employment would remove the incentive for her husband to work is contained in Jane Lewis, *Women England, 1870-1950: Sexual Divisions and Social Change* (Bloomington, Indiana: Indiana University Press, 1984), 45-67.

19. Charity Organization Society, *Report of the Committee on Unskilled Labour* (London: Charity Organization Society, 1908), 7. For details on the structure of employment in several slum communities in Notting Hill, see Patricia E. Malcolmson, "Getting a Living in the Slums of Victorian Kensington," *London Journal,* 1,1 (May 1975), 28-55.

20. Enid Porter, *Cambridgeshire Customs and Folklore* (London: Routledge & Kegan Paul, 1969), 262; Black, *Married Women's Work,* 111-12; Davies, *Life as We Have Known It,* 61-62; Henry Mayhew, *London Labour and London Poor* (London: Woodfall, 1851), vol. 3, 307; John Burnett, *Useful Toil: Autobiographies of Working People from the 1820s to the 1920s* (London: Allen Lane, 1974), 285; Lewis, *Women in England,* 57.

21. Bosanquet, *Social Conditions,* 24.

22. *Laundry Record,* 1 May 1894, 22.

23. Booth, *Life and Labour,* 2d ser. vol. 4, app. B.; 17 Samuel, "Comers and Goers," in *Victorian City,* ed. Dyos and Wolff, vol. 1, 135-39; P.P., *R.C. on Labour* 1893-94 (6894) 37, 22. As many as 20,000 workers from other occupations went hop-picking (Isabel Taylor, *A Bibliography of Unemployment and Unemployed* [London: King, 1909], x).

24. Black, *Married Women's Work,* 23.

25. Bosanquet, *Social Conditions,* 112.

26. P.P., *R.C. on Labour,* 1893-94 (6894) 37, 22.

27. Sidney Webb and Arnold Freeman, eds., *Seasonal Trades* (London: London School of Economics, 1911), 46.

28. Evelyn March-Phillips, "The New Factory Bill: As It Affects Women," *Fortnightly Review,* 61 (1894), 740; A. M. Anderson, *Women in the Factory* (London: Murray, 1922), 38.

29. Bosanquet, *Social Conditions,* 24; WIC, *National Conference on the Unemployment of Women Dependent on Their Own Earnings* (London: 1907), 22-23.

30. Paul, *Poverty-Hardship,* 9-16.

31. *Laundry Record,* 1 Apr. 1902, 161.

32. Frederick Rogers, *Labour, Life and Literature: Some Memories of Sixty Years,* introd. David Rubinstein (Brighton: Harvester, 1973), 5.

33. Black, *Married Women's Work,* 112; Davies, *Life as We Have Known It,* 34-35.

34. Davies, *Life as We Have Known It,* 37.

35. P.P., *R.C. on Labour,* 1893-94 (6894) 37, 17, 19, 20. See also London County Council, *Report on the Sanitary Condition and Administration of Kensington* (London: London County Council, 1900, 15); *West London Observer,* 14 May 1881.

36. *Daily News,* 29 Sept. 1911. Employers deplored the irregularity of work and urged customers to spread their laundry more regularly over the week.

37. P.P., *R.C. on Labour,* 1893-94 (6894) 37, 23.

38. London School of Economics, Booth MS Collection, B-262, 175.

39. *Where to Buy at Leamington,* Brochure 1891 (held at Central Divisional Library, Leamington Spa); Roberts, *Woman's Place,* 140.

40. In the early part of the twentieth century, some large steam laundries took on apprentices for training periods as long as nine months; a few laundries required a premium of amounts up to a guinea from their apprentices, but the premium was sometimes refunded at the end of the period if work was satisfactory (Margaret Ethel MacDonald, "Report of Enquiry into Laundries," 633).

41. P.P., *R.C. on Labour,* 1893-94 (6894) 37, 22.

42. George Woodcock, "The Family Bush: A Pre-Autobiographical Exercise," *Queen's Quarterly,* 89,2 (Summer 1982), 377. See also P.P., *Select Committee on Home Work,* 1908 (246) 8, v.

43. Coppard, *It's Me O Lord!,* 40.

44. *Pall Mall Gazette,* as quoted in the *Laundry Record,* 1 June 1894, 47.

45. Alice Mary Bond, "The Old Wooden Mangle," *East Anglian Magazine,* 12 (1952-53), 463-71, 488-96, 549-56, 708-16; and 13 (1953-54), 40-49, passim.

46. Elizabeth Flint, *Hot Bread and Chips* (London: Museum Press, 1963), 32.

47. "Report of the *Lancet* Special Commission on the Spread of Disease through Laundries," *Lancet,* 18 Aug. 1877, 241.

48. For example, "Abuse of Public Washhouses," *Laundry Record,* 1 July 1901, 337; "Misuse of Public Laundries," *Laundry Record,* 1 May 1913, 319; and "Public Washhouses," *Laundry Record,* 1 Oct. 1913, 653.

49. Henry Mayhew, *London Labour and the London Poor* (London: Woodfall, 1851), vol. 3, 307. The tradition of family laundry work was also found among Parisian laundry workers (Joan Scott and Louise A. Tilly, "Women's Work in Nineteenth-Century Europe," *Comparative Studies in History and Society,* 17,1 [Jan. 1975], 46).

50. Ibid.

51. Pauline Hunt, *Gender and Class Consciousness* (New York: Holmes & Meier, 1980), 16-17.

52. As quoted in Samuel, *Village Life,* 183.

53. M. E. Loane, *The Next Street But One* (London: Arnold, 1908), 181-82.

54. Evelyn March-Phillips, "Factory Legislation for Women," *Fortnightly Review,* 63 (May 1895), 735.

55. Trades Union Congress Library (TUCL), Gertrude Tuckwell Collection, Misc. 486 2/3, MS Interview with Mrs. Rose, Canning Town, Laundress; Margaret H. Irwin, *The Conditions of Women's Work in Laundries: Report of an Inquiry Conducted for the Council of the Women's Protective and Provident League of Glasgow* (Glasgow: Women's Protective and Provident League, 1893), 11.

56. Paul, *Poverty-Hardship,* 11-12; transcript of a conversation with Mr. R. Skinner, Fenn Ditton, Cambridge, recorded 2 Nov. 1979.

57. Hunt, *Gender and Class Consciousness,* 16. See also London Child Labour Enquiry as cited in *Laundry Record,* 1 Aug. 1905, 433.

58. Conversation with Mr. R. Skinner with Mrs. Bond, 29 City Road, Cambridge, recorded 15 Oct. 1976. I am indebted to Sallie Purkis, Homerton College, Cambridge, for these references. See also Paul, *Poverty-Hardship,* 11; and Hunt, *Gender and Class Consciousness,* 16.

59. Nettie Adler, "Wage Earning Children in England," in National Union of Women Workers, *Women Workers: Papers Read at the Conference Held at Edinburgh on October 28th, 29th and 30th, 1902* (London: King, 1902), 68.

60. As quoted in Fabian Society, *Life in the Laundry,* 11; Scott Holland and

Gertrude Tuckwell, "Report of the Christian Social Union Committee on Laundries," London, n.d., TUCL, Tuckwell Coll., File No. 14, 3; Lydia M. Mayhew, "Slaves of the Laundry Tub," *Saturday Journal,* 22 Aug. 1908. Children worked for very long hours in steam as well as hand laundries (March-Phillips, "New Factory Bill," 739-40).

61. Bond, "Old Wooden Mangle," 488, 490.

62. Ibid., 491.

63. Louise Jermy, *The Memories of a Working Woman* (Norwick: Goose, 1934), 28-29.

64. As quoted in Samuel, *Village Life,* 180.

65. John Burns, "The Unemployed," *Nineteenth Century,* 32 (Dec. 1892), 848. Here Burns was speaking of unemployed women generally and would have preferred to see an end to work by married women.

66. *Hansard Parliamentary Debates,* 4th ser., 95 (17 June 1901), 653; *Laundry Record,* 1 Mar. 1905, 161.

67. *Laundry Record,* 1 June 1896, 33; Charles Dickens, *Bleak House* (Harmondsworth: Penguin, 1971; originally published in 1853), 262-63.

68. Loane, *Next Street,* 181-82; Roberts, *Woman's Place,* 140.

69. Mayhew, *London Labour,* 463-64.

70. For this information, I am indebted to Mrs. Mills's great-grandson, Charles A. Wilson, Managing Director, Wilson's Laundry, Brighton; *Wilson's of Brighton,* brochure, n.d.; *A Visit to a Modern Family Laundry: Wilson's Arundel Laundry,* brochure, n.d.

71. Loane, *Next Street,* 183.

72. *Wilson's of Brighton,* n.p.

73. James S. Woodforde, *The Diary of a Country Parson: The Reverend James Woodforde,* ed. John Beresford, 5 vols. (Oxford: Oxford University Press, 1926), vol. 5, 198.

74. As quoted in Christina Walkley and Vanda Foster, *Crinolines and Crimping Irons: Victorian Clothes: How They Were Cleaned and Cared For* (London: Owen, 1978), 51. See also William Clift, *The Reminiscences of William Clift of Bramley Born 1828 and Wrote These My Reminiscences* (Basingstoke: Bird, 1908), 71.

75. Thompson, *Lark Rise,* 471.

76. Mrs. Isabella Beeton, *Beeton's Book of Household Management* (London: Cape, reprint, 1974; originally published in 1861), 1008.

77. As quoted in Frances Sheppard, *London, 1808-1870: The Infernal Wen* (Berkeley: University of California Press, 1971), 371. See also Charles Frederick Marmaduke Morris, *The British Workman, Past and Present* (Oxford: Oxford University Press, 1928), 58.

ITrades of Ancient and Modern Times. Copied from Rare Engravings, or 78. John Thomas Smith, *The Cries of London: Exhibiting Several of the Drawn From Life* (London: Nichols, 1839), 81.

79. *Daily News,* 11 Oct. 1911; Thompson, *Lark Rise,* 472; and Walkley and Foster, *Crinolines,* 58.

80. "The Right Day for Washing," *Laundry Record,* 15 May 1891, 44. See also Davidson, *Woman's Work,* 149-50; *The Girl's Own Paper,* 1899, as quoted in Walkley and Foster, *Crinolines,* 57.

81. *Laundry Record,* 30 Sept. 1893, 140.

82. For details of these procedures, see Walkley and Foster, *Crinolines,* passim.

83. Susan Strasser, *Never Done: A History of American Housework* (New York: Pantheon, 1982), 105.

84. Sybil Marshall, *Fenland Chronicle: Recollections of William Henry and Kate Mary Edwards Collected and Edited by Their Daughter* (Cambridge: Cambridge University Press, 1967), 244-45.

85. Ibid., 244. See also Bond, "Old Wooden Mangle," passim; *The Girl's Own Paper,* 1880, as quoted in Walkley and Foster, *Crinolines,* 53.

86. Marshall, *Fenland Chronicle,* 244.

87. For further information concerning the manufacture and sale of laundry soaps, see: A. E. Musson, *Enterprise in Soap and Chemicals: Joseph Crosfield & Sons, Limited, 1815-1965* (Manchester: Manchester University Press, 1965); William H. Simmons, *Soap: Its Composition, Manufacture and Properties,* 3d ed. (London: Pitman, 1933); R. Lucock Wilson, *Soap through the Ages* (London: Unilever, 1952); H. R. Edwards, *Competition and Monopoly in the British Soap Industry* (Oxford: Clarendon, 1962); Charles Wilson, *The History of Unilever: A Study in Economic Growth and Social Change,* 3 vols. (London: Cassell, 1970).

88. Walkley and Foster, *Crinolines,* chap. 10 and apps. 1 and 2, provide interesting detail concerning Victorian cleaning and stain removal agents.

89. As quoted in Musson, *Enterprise in Soap,* 102-103.

90. Mary Bayly, *Ragged Homes and How to Mend Them* (London: Nisbet, 1860), 26-27. See also Malcolmson, "Getting a Living in the Slums," 28-55.

91. Royal Borough of Kensington, *Minutes of the Works Committee,* 25 Aug. 1869, 386 (held at Central Library, Royal Borough of Kensington and Chelsea); London County Council, *Report on the Sanitary Condition and Administration of Kensington* (London: London County Council, 1900), 16; Frank T. Bullen, *Confessions of a Tradesman* (London: Hodder & Stoughton, 1908), 5-7.

92. Marshall, *Fenland Chronicle,* 245. In private households, a washing copper could also be used to brew beer, boil Christmas puddings, and heat water for other purposes.

93. "Washing Machines of Old," *Laundry Record,* 2 May 1910, 267. See also Mary Norvak, *Kitchen Antiques* (New York: Praeger, 1975), 54.

94. Marshall, *Fenland Chronicle,* 243-44.

95. Bleaches and water softeners were often added to the wash water to whiten the linen; soda and borax were most common, but other agents, such as saltpeter and potato, might also be used. See Walkley and Foster, *Crinolines,* 59-60; Beeton, *Household Management,* 1008-13; Caroline Reed Wadhams, *Simple Directions for the Laundress* (London: Longmans, Green, 1917), 16.

96. *Laundry Record,* 30 Sept. 1892, 111.

97. B. A. Cutter and H. C. Town, "Some Recollections of the Domestic

Wringer and Mantle Industry," *Edgar Allen News,* 45, 528 (June 1966) as cited in Davidson, *Woman's Work,* 156; Norvak, *Kitchen Antiques,* 59; Bond, "Old Wooden Mangle," passim; Walkley and Foster, *Crinolines,* 53, 58, 135.

98. Thompson, *Lark Rise,* 472.

99. Mangle cloths were seldom washed as this destroyed the polish that they gave to linen. Brown Holland mangling cloths, supplied by the manufacturer, were considered to be vastly superior to common Irish linen for giving the correct finish.

100. As quoted in Walkley and Foster, *Crinolines,* 134.

101. Ronald Blythe, *The View in Winter: Reflections on Old Age* (Harmondsworth: Penguin, 1980), 117.

102. Holland and Tuckwell, "Report on Laundries," 3, 5.

103. *Kensington News,* 15 Jan. 1876; and Florence M. Gladstone, *Notting Hill in Bygone Days* (London: Unwin, 1924), 205. See also Booth MS Coll., A-43, xciv.81; P.P. *R.C. on Labour,* 1893-94 (6894) 37, 23; Holland and Tuckwell, "Report on Laundries," 10; and *Daily News,* 29 Sept. 1911. Similar problems were encountered by American laundresses ("The Relief of Widows," *Charity Organization Review,* 19 [Jan. 1906], 32).

104. Special Commissioner, "West-End Poverty 1. The Latymer Road District," *Quiver,* (1883), 45.

105. "Municipal Creches: Why They Are Needed in Laundry Centres," *Laundry Record,* 1 Feb. 1906, 81, and 1 Mar. 1906, 145; "Laundries in Acton," *Laundry Record,* 1 Sept. 1908, 489, 491; "Day Nurseries and the Laundry Industry," *Laundry,* 24 Feb. 1912, 90; "Where Women Must Work," *Laundry Record,* 1 Feb. 1908, 75.

106. P.P., *R.C. on Labour,* 1893-94 (6894) 37, 22-23; Black, *Married Women's Work,* 19-20; Lewis, *Women in England,* 56. Children might also be sent to school as early as possible (Alexander Paterson, *Across the Bridges* [London: Arnold, 1911], 35).

107. Black, *Married Women's Work,* 19.

108. *Laundry Record,* 1 Feb. 1906, 81.

109. *Woman Worker,* Mar. 1920, 4; See also Loane, *Next Street,* 175; *Laundry Record,* 30 Sept. 1893, 144.

110. Paterson, *Across the Bridges,* 35.

111. Eliza Warren, *How I Managed My House on Two Hundred Pounds a Year* (London: Houlston & Wright, 1867), 76-77.

112. Mayhew, *London Labour,* vol. 1, 39.

113. Coppard, *It's Me, O Lord!,* 30. See also Woodward, *Jipping Street,* 8, 21.

114. G. A. Simpson, *My Life and Family Reminiscences* (London: n.p., 1888), 33-34. See also Holland and Tuckwell, "Report on Laundries," 9; P.P., *R.C. on Labour,* 1893-94 (6894) 37, 23.

115. Holland and Tuckwell, "Report of Christian Social Union," 2.

116. P.P., *Annual Report of Chief Inspector of Factories and Workshops,* 1907 (3586) 10, 233-34. See also Violet R. Markham, *May Tennant: A Portrait* (London: Falcon,

1949), 54-55; P.P., *Report of the Chief Inspector of Factories and Workshops for the Year 1910. Report of the Principal Lady Inspector,* 1910 (5191) 28, 159; *Daily Herald,* 25 Nov. 1913, 15; Anderson, *Women in the Factory,* 153.

117. P.P., *R.C. on Labour,* 1893-94 (6894) 37, 23; Layton, "Memories," in *Life as We Have Known It,* ed. Davies, 34-35; *Woman Worker,* Mar. 1920, 4; Woodward, *Jipping Street,* 20-22; Holland and Tuckwell, "Report on Laundries," 9-10 and passim; May Tennant, "Infantile Mortality," in Gertrude Tuckwell et al., *Women in Industry from Seven Points of View* (London: Duckworth, 1910), 87-119.

118. Black, *Married Women's Work,* 24.

119. Laura Oren, "The Welfare of Women in Labouring Families: England, 1860-1950," in *Clio's Consciousness Raised: New Perspectives on the History of Women,* ed. Mary Hartman and Lois W. Banner (New York: Harper, 1974), 226-44.

120. Booth MS Coll., A-43, fol. 15; P.P., *R.C. on the Poor Laws,* 1909 (4850) 42, 29. See also Booth MS Coll., A-44, fol. 4; B-325, 5; A-43, xciv.81; Booth, *Life and Labour,* 2d ser., vol. 4, 255-58; 3d ser., vol. 3, 158; *London City Mission,* Aug. 1844, 119, and, May 1871, 86.

121. *Laundry Record,* 1 May 1902, 37.

122. *Second Report of the Bath Union,* 1 Aug. 1836; *Bath and Cheltenham Gazette,* 28 Feb. 1836; P.P., *Report of Inspector,* 1907 (3586) 10, 233-34, and P.P., *Report of Inspector,* 1910 (5191) 28, 159.

123. Bosanquet, *Social Conditions,* 63; Samuel, *Village Life,* 181.

124. *Laundry Record,* 1 May 1894, 22; P.P., *R.C. on Labour,* 1893-94 (6894) 37, 22. See also "A Voice from the Laundries," *Woman Worker,* June 1919, 2.

125. Loane, *Next Street,* 183.

126. Christian Social Union, "Report of Inquiry into the Employment of Women after Childbirth," 1908, 10 (held at TUCL, Tuckwell Coll.); *Woman Worker,* June 1919, 2: P.P., *R.C. on Labour,* 1893-94 (6894) 37, 22: Black, *Married Women's Work,* 23, 112.

127. Black, *Married Women's Work,* 23.

128. P.P., *R.C. on Labour,* 1893-94 (6894) 37, 22.

129. Willis, *Tom Mix,* 22.

130. Woodward, *Jipping Street,* 13.

131. Amy Bulley, "The Employment of Women (The Lady Assistant Commissioner's Report)," *Fortnightly Review,* 55 (Jan. 1894), 46.

132. March-Phillips, "New Factory Bill," 739; *The Pioneer,* 14 June 1834, 407; Booth, *Life and Labour,* 2d ser., vol. 4, 266; P.P., *R.C. on Labour,* 1893-94 (6894) 37, 21; Arthur Sherwell, *Life in West London,* 82; *Laundry Record,* 30 Sept. 1893, 47.

133. Woodward, *Jipping Street,* 13-14.

134. Brian Harrison, *Drink and the Victorians: The Temperance Question in England 1815-1872* (London: Faber, 1971), 47.

135. Booth, *Life and Labour,* 3d ser., vol. 3, 191-92. In this area, various public houses remained open all day Sunday in defiance of the Licensing Laws (*Bayswater Chronicle,* 27 June 1860).

136. P.P., *R.C. on Labour,* 1893-94 (6894) 37, 22.
137. Cited in *The Times,* 21 Apr. 1851, 5.
138. Sims, *Off the Track,* 34-35.
139. Cadbury et al., *Women's Work,* 212.

Chapter 2: Regulating the Trade

1. H. Llewellyn Smith, ed., *The New Survey of London Life and Labour,* 9 vols. (London: King), 1930-35; *London Industries II,* vol. 5 (1933), 371.

2. Asa Briggs, in an influential article, "The Welfare State in Historical Perspective," *Archive Europeenes de Sociologie,* 2 (1961), 222, distinguished between the "social service state" in which minimum standards are set for the poor and the "welfare state" whose aim is optimum standards for the whole population. On this criterion, "social service state" is clearly a more accurate description for Britain before the First World War.

3. Among the many works that bear on the ideas behind social reform and related pressures on politicians are: C. L. Mowat, "The Approach to the Welfare State in Great Britain," *American Historical Review,* 58 (1952-53), 55-63; H. V. Emy, *Liberals, Radicals and Social Politics, 1892-1914* (Cambridge: Cambridge University Press, 1973); A. Marwick, "The Labour Party and the Welfare State in Britain 1900-48," *American Historical Review,* 73 (1967), 380-403; A. M. MacBriar, *Fabian Socialism and English Politics, 1884-1918,* (Cambridge: Cambridge University Press, 1962); E. J. Hobsbawm, *Labouring Men: Studies in the History of Labour,* 2d ed. (London: Weidenfeld & Nicolson, 1968); R. Davidson, "Llewellyn Smith, The Labour Department and Government Growth," in *Studies in the Growth of Nineteenth Century Government,* ed. G. Sutherland (Totowa, N.J.: Rowman & Littlefield, 1972), 227-62.

4. Richard M. Titmuss, "Poverty Versus Inequality," in *Poverty,* ed. J. L. Roach and J. K. Roach (Harmondsworth: Penguin, 1972), 321.

5. Beatrice Webb, *My Apprenticeship* (Harmondsworth: Penguin, 1971), 266. See also T. S. Simey and M. B. Simey, *Charles Booth: Social Scientist* (Oxford: Oxford University Press, 1960), 215; P. Ford, *Social Theory and Social Practice. An Exploration of Experience* (Shannon: Irish University Press, 1968), 49; and Gareth Stedman Jones, *Outcast London: A Study of the Relationship between Classes in Victorian Society* (Oxford: Clarendon, 1971), 54-56. While it was influential in changing some views, Booth's study served to confirm other attitudes, such as the widely held view that there was among the poor a degenerate "residuum" that might "infect" others in times of economic crisis (Stedman Jones, *Outcast London,* 320-21).

6. Davis F. Schloss, "The Reorganization of Our Labour Department," *Journal of the Royal Statistical Society,* 56 (Mar. 1893), 44-45 and P.P., *R.C. on Labour,* 1892 (6708) 34, 3; and *R.C. on Labour. The Employment of Women,* 1893-94 (6894) 37, iii.

7. *WIN,* Jan. 1914, 205.

8. P.P., *R. C. on the Factory and Workshop Act,* 1876 (1443) 19, xcvii, xx; P.P., *Report of the Chief Inspector of Factories and Workshops for 1895,* 1896 (8067) 19, 17; and *Hansard Parliamentary Debates,* 4th ser., 32 (22 Apr. 1895), 1414.

9. *Laundry Record,* 30 Sept. 1893, 145.

10. P.P., *R.C. on the Factory Act,* 1876 (1443) 20, 641.

11. Amy Harrison and Barbara Leigh Hutchins, *A History of Factory Legislation* (London: King, 1911), 188. Henry Fawcett, urging a similar exclusion of women from the 1874 Bill, stated that the determination of acceptable hours and conditions of work "ought to be left to the good sense and increasing intelligence of the people themselves" (ibid., 185).

12. *Hansard Parliamentary Debates,* 4th ser., 32 (22 Apr. 1895), 1413.

13. Ibid. Joseph Chamberlain testified to similar results among Birmingham women whose trades came under the factory acts (ibid., 188, 190).

14. See, for example, Lee Holcombe's fine study *Victorian Ladies at Work: Middle Class Working Women in England and Wales, 1850-1914* (Newton Abbot: David & Charles, 1973). The two volumes edited by Martha Vicinus, *Suffer and Be Still: Women in the Victorian Age* (Bloomington, Ind.: Indiana University Press, 1973) and *A Widening Sphere: Changing Roles of Victorian Women* (Bloomington, Ind.: Indiana University Press, 1977) provide solid insights into the major issues as well as highly useful bibliographies by Barbara Kanner.

15. Harrison and Hutchins, *Factory Legislation,* 184.

16. E. J. Boucherett, *The Fall of Women's Wages in Unskilled Work* (London: Stock, 1889), 11.

17. Inspired by Harriet Martineau (whose article on female industry in the *Edinburgh Review* first drew attention to the problem of redundant women), Boucherett was instrumental in founding this society (E. J. Boucherett and Helen Blackburn, *The Condition of Working Women and the Factory Acts* [London: Stock, 1896], 43; and Holcombe, *Victorian Ladies,* 10-11).

18. Boucherett and Blackburn, *Working Women,* 55-59; and *Laundry Record,* 1 May 1894, 27.

19. Boucherett and Blackburn, *Working Women,* 57. Boucherett did not cite her source which is clearly hyperbolic as the 1891 census recorded only 2,649 women employed in laundry, washing, and bathing services in Glasgow.

20. Ibid., 36. C. B. Stuart Wortley, M.P., shared the suspicion of "the general spirit of trade unionism" that supported the laundry clause (*Hansard Parliamentary Debates,* 4th ser., 32 (22 Apr. 1895), 1404).

21. Quoted in Margaret Hewitt, *Wives and Mothers in Victorian Industry* (London: Rockcliff, 1958), 177-78; and Duncan Crow, *The Victorian Woman* (London: Allen & Unwin, 1971), 320-21.

22. *Hansard Parliamentary Debates,* 4th ser., 32 (22 Apr. 1895), 1405. This line of argument continued until the vote was granted. " 'What right have we to promote

legislation to restrict the wage-earning of married women, without giving them a voice in the matter?' questioned Dr. Mary Murdoch" ("The Wage-Earning of Married Women," in National Union of Women Workers of Great Britain and Ireland, *Women Workers: The Papers Read at the Conference Held in Manchester, October 22nd,-25th, 1907* [London: King, 1907], 79); while E. J. Boucherett stressed the political reality that M.P.s found it harder to resist the demands of enfranchised men launderers than unenfranchised laundresses (Boucherett and Blackburn, *Working Women,* 21).

23. Boucherett and Blackburn, *Working Women,* 65, 64-76. Beatrice Webb complained that feminists' support for sanitary provisions of factory legislation tended to be rather half-hearted (Sidney Webb and Beatrice Webb, *Problems of Modern Industry* [London: Longmans, Green, 1902], 83). Certainly, feminists were not anxious to support such provisions if they thought poor laundresses might have to close down as a result. Agreement with Blackburn's distinctions depended on the exemption of small workshops from legislation.

24. Boucherett and Blackburn, *Working Women,* 67-68.

25. *The Laundry Record,* 30 Nov. 1893, 173-76. The report also supported the view that legislation would mean the displacement of female with male labor.

26. *Laundry Record,* 30 Sept. 1893, 147.

27. Ibid., 148.

28. Freedom of Labour Defence Association, Record of Quarterly Meeting, 7 May 1901, Fawcett Library Coll., Misc. 486, 2.

29. *Hansard Parliamentary Debates,* 4th ser., 32 (22 Apr. 1895), 1486. See also *Laundry Record,* 30 Sept. 1893, 148.

30. Frederick Rogers, *Labour, Life and Literature: Some Memories of Sixty Years,* introd. David Rubinstein (Brighton: Harvester, 1973), 92. The Webbs too saw Paterson as "the real pioneer of modern women's trade unions" (Sidney Webb and Beatrice Webb, *History of Trade Unionism* [London: Longmans, Green, 1921], 336-37). Ada Heather-Bigg was another member of the Women's Protective and Provident League who was a laissez-faire activist in the Women's Employment Defence League.

31. Hutchins and Harrison, *Factory Legislation,* 187-88.

32. *Women's Union Journal,* 31 Jan. 1877.

33. K. A. MacKenzie, *Edith Simcox and George Eliot,* (Oxford: Oxford University Press, 1961), 39-42. See also Norbert Soldon, *Women in British Trade Unions 1874-1976* (London: Gill and Macmillan, 1978), 11-26.

34. Gladys Boone, *The Women's Trade Union Leagues in Great Britain and the United States* (New York: Columbia University Press, 1942), 26 and Soldon, *Women in Unions,* 35-36.

35. Webb and Webb, *Modern Industry,* 91.

36. *Result of Canvass among Bona Fide Laundresses in Favour of Factory Acts being Applied to Laundries* (London: Twentieth Century Press, 1891).

37. Gertrude Tuckwell, "Laundries and the Factory Bill" (letter printed by the WTUL, n.d. c. 1893).

38. Violet R. Markham, *May Tennant: A Portrait* (London: Falcon, 1949), 17-18.

39. *The Times,* 13 June 1891, 15.

40. "A Wail From the Tub, a Reminiscene of Sunday, The 14th of June," *Punch, or the London Charivari,* 27 June 1891, 301; and *The Times,* 15 June 1891, 15.

41. *The Times,* 15 June 1891, 15.

42. Ibid.

43. "The New Tale of a Tub: Or, The Not-At-Home Secretary and the Laundresses," *Punch,* 20 June 1891, 290-91.

44. Emilia F. S. Dilke, "Women and the Royal Commission," *Fortnightly Review,* 50 (Oct. 1891), 536-37. The commission had sent a schedule of questions to secretaries of all trade organizations, but Dilke argued that the meager extent of female unionization and the lack of funds of those that existed made this an inadequate investigatory tool (ibid., 535-36). See also Barbara Leigh Hutchins, *Women in Modern Industry* (London: Bell, 1915), 129; and P.P., *R.C. on Labour,* 1891 (6708) 34, 8249-50.

45. H. Dendy, "The Position of Women in Industry," *National Review,* 23 (Aug. 1894), 806.

46. Beatrice Webb, "The Failure of the Labour Commission," *Nineteenth Century,* 36 (July 1894), 9. Webb criticizes the report in general for its complacency and its overlooking of trade union issues and collectivist approaches, lack of statistical rigor, and the setting up of an insoluble conundrum in their directives to researchers (ibid., passim).

47. P.P., *R.C. on Labour,* 1893-94 (6894) 37, 17-23.

48. Margaret H. Irwin, *The Conditions of Women's Work in Laundries. Report of an Inquiry Conducted for the Council of the Women's Protective and Provident League of Glasgow* (Glasgow: Women's Protective and Provident League, 1893), 3.

49. Royal Borough of Kensington, *Annual Report of the Medical Officer of Health* (London, 1908), 44; Rose E. Squire, *Thirty Years in the Public Service: An Industrial Retrospect* (London: Nisbet, 1927), 19.

50. The *Lancet* as quoted in the *West London Observer,* 12 Feb. 1881. In 1876 the *Lancet* commented that "as compared with productions of the same kind . . . it [Dr. Dudfield's Annual Report] evinces a very thorough and painstaking appreciation of the responsible work attached to such a post" (quoted in *West London Observer,* 11 Nov. 1876). See also T. Orme Dudfield, "Metropolitan Sanitary Administration," *Transactions of the Society of Medical Officers of Health* (London, 1883-84), 1-15; and Patricia E. Malcolmson, "The Potteries of Kensington: A Study of Slum Development in Victorian London," M. Phil. thesis, University of Leicester, 1970, chap. 4, especially 126-31.

51. As quoted in Squire, *Thirty Years,* 20. See also T. Orme Dudfield, "Women's Place in Sanitary Administration," A Paper Read to the Women

Sanitary Inspectors Association, 11 Nov. 1904 (London, 1904), passim. The advocacy of such an influential person as Dudfield helped to overcome the widespread opposition to women working in such an "unladylike" occupation as sanitary inspector. In following years, other local authorities began the systematic inspection of laundries and other women's workshops, usually by female inspectors (e.g., Chelsea Vestry Minutes, 1896-97 [held at Chelsea Public Library], 12, 60, 80, 204).

52. Lucy E. A. Deane joined the factory inspectorate in 1894 and Rose E. Squire in 1896. For further details of their training, see Squire, *Thirty Years,* 20-24.

53. Ibid., 22-23.

54. Ibid., 25-26.

55. P.P., *Laundries. Reports of H.M. Inspectors of Factories, as to Hours of Work, Dangerous Machinery, and Sanitary Condition,* 1894 (7418) 21, 3.

56. Ibid., passim.

57. Boucherett and Blackburn, *Working Women,* 27.

58. P.P., *Laundries,* 1894 (7418) 21, esp. 5, 8, 11. The inspectors noted that a few of the most progressive establishments had voluntarily placed themselves under the Act or had broadly adopted its guidelines.

59. *Laundry Record,* 30 Sept. 1893, 149.

60. Ibid., 30 Nov. 1893, 173.

61. *The Times,* 22 June 1895, 15. Sometimes an employer, while supporting some regulation of weekly hours, preferred that this come about through trade union pressure rather than legislation (see Margaret Bateson, *Professional Women upon their Professions* [London: Cox, 1895], 100-101. I am indebted to Anna Davin for this reference).

62. *Hansard Parliamentary Debates,* 4th ser., 31 (1 Mar. 1895), 175.

63. *The Times,* 6 May 1895, 9; 11 May 1895, 15; 13 May 1895, 11; 22 June 1895, 15; and 24 June 1895, 6; *Laundry Record,* 1 May 1894, 24, 26; and P.P., *Laundries,* 1894 (7418) 21, esp. 5, 7, 9.

64. *Laundry Record,* 1 May 1894, 26-28.

65. As quoted in ibid., 27.

66. Helen Bosanquet, Louise Creighton, and Beatrice Webb, "Law and the Laundry," *Nineteenth Century,* 41 (Feb. 1897), 224.

67. Miss Gray, "What Can Be Done by Legislation to Improve the Condition of Laundries?," *WIN,* Dec. 1900, 206.

68. "Report of the Lancet Special Commission on the Spread of Disease Through Laundries," *Lancet,* 18 Aug. 1877, 240-42. See also *Lancet,* 20 Apr. 1894. The Women's Trade Union League reprinted and circulated this article in defence of their campaign for laundry regulation. See also "Small-pox from the Laundry," *Lancet,* 24 Feb. 1877, 287; *Laundry Record,* 30 Sept. 1893, 146; and *Daily Chronicle* as quoted in *Laundry Record,* 1 May 1894, 28.

69. Bosanquet et al., "Law and the Laundry," 230.

70. *Laundry Record,* 30 Sept. 1893, 140. See also P.P., *Report of Chief Inspector of Factories for 1908. Report of Principal Lady Inspector,* 1909 (4664) 21, 149.

71. *Laundry Record,* 30 Sept. 1893, 140-41 and P.P., *Laundries,* 1894 (7418) 21, esp. 1, 5, 8, 9.

72. *Hansard Parliamentary Debates,* 4th ser., 32 (22 Apr. 1895), 1483.

73. Fabian Society, *Life in the Laundry,* Tract No. 112 (London: Fabian Society, 1902), 14.

74. Hutchins and Harrison, *Factory Legislation,* 194; and Evelyn March-Phillips, "Factory Legislation for Women," *Fortnightly Review,* 63 (1895), 736.

75. *Hansard Parliamentary Debates,* 4th ser., 32 (22 Apr. 1895), 1482. See also Squire, *Thirty Years,* 159.

76. *Hansard Parliamentary Debates,* 4th ser., 32 (22 April 1895), 1455 and P.P., *Laundries,* 1894 (7418) 21, 3.

77. P.P., *List of Religious and Charitable Institutions in Which Laundries Are Carried on, 1902,* 1905 (2500) 72, passim. See also Barbara Kerr, *The Dispossessed: An Aspect of Victorian Social History* (New York: St. Martin's, 1974), 76-77; *Laundry Record,* 30 Sept. 1893, 139; Irwin, *Conditions in Laundries,* 15; Liverpool Magdalen Institution, *51st Annual Report of the Liverpool Magdalen Institution, 8 Mount Vernon Green for the Year 1905* (Liverpool, 1906), 5; Frances Finnegan, *Poverty and Prostitution: A Study of Victorian Prostitutes in York* (Cambridge: Cambridge University Press, 1979), 177-78; and Liverpool Female Penitentiary, *Introductory Report of the Society for the Establishment of a Magdalen Asylum in Liverpool, Instituted October 25, 1809; with the Particulars of a Plan Successfully Adopted in the London Female Penitentiary and a Few Extracts from Late Reports of Similar Institutions* (Liverpool, 1809), Bye Law No. 7, 40 (held by the Liverpool Record Office).

78. Margaret Ethel MacDonald, "Report on Enquiry into Conditions of Work in Laundries," *WIN,* June 1907, 635.

79. P.P., *Report of the Chief Inspector of Factories and Workshops for the Year 1905. Report of Principal Lady Inspector,* 1906 (3036) 15, 259.

80. Earl of Lytton for Industrial Law Committee, *Laundries, II: Institution Laundries and Exempted Smaller Laundries* (London: n.d.), 1 and Fabian Society, *Life in the Laundry,* 9.

Chapter 3: Amelioration, Administration, and Public Policy

1. Sidney Webb and Beatrice Webb, *Problems of Modern Industry* (London: Longmans, Green, 1902), 85.

2. *Factory and Workshop Act,* 1895 (58 & 59 Vict. Ch. 37), Sec. 22.

3. P.P., *Report of Inspector of Factories and Workshops for 1895,* 1896 (8067) 19, 17-18.

4. Ibid., p. 18.

5. Evelyn March-Phillips, "Factory Legislation for Women," *Fortnightly Review,* 63 (1895), 733.

6. Rose E. Squire, *Thirty Years in the Public Service: An Industrial Retrospect* (London: Nisbet, 1927), 25.

7. P.P. *Report of the Chief Inspector of Factories and Workshops for the Year 1896. Report of Principal Lady Inspector,* 1897 (8561) 17, 67. With ffeeble step in progress but it was also in laundries that she the advantage of hindsight, Squire was later able to see this enactment as the encountered the longest hours of all the industries she inspected (Squire, *Thirty Years,* 65-66, 71).

8. Charles Booth, *Life and Labour of the People of London,* 16 vols. (London: Macmillan, 1902-1903), 3d ser., vol. 8, 262-63.

9. P.P., *Report of Inspector,* 1897 (8561) 17, 58.

10. Adelaide M. Anderson, *Women in the Factory: An Administrative Adventure, 1893-1921* (London: Murray, 1922), 33 and P.P. *Report of Inspector,* 1897 (8561) 17, 42-43.

11. P.P., *Report of Inspector,* 1897 (8561) 17, 42.

12. For example, *Review of Newcastle and Tyne and District,* (Newcastle, 1896), 64-66, 83; *A Visit to a Modern Family Laundry: Wilson's Arundel Laundry,* brochure, n.p.; *Spennell's Almanack and Directory* (Leamington, 1892), 155; *Kelly's Kensington, Notting Hill, Brompton and Knightsbridge Directory for 1913* (London, 1913), 118a; *Tyneside Industries* (Newcastle, 1889), 158, 1895, 108; *Newcastle Chamber of Commerce Journal, Exhibition Year Supplement,* 1929, 74, 210-11; and *Thomason's Directory of Hounslow* (London, 1913), 58.

13. P.P., *Report of Inspector,* 1897 (8561) 17, 42. During the act's first year 1,069 factory laundries and 5,026 workshop laundries were registered (ibid.).

14. Helen Bosanquet, Louise Creighton, and Beatrice Webb, "Law and Laundry," *Nineteenth Century,* 41 (Feb. 1897), 224; and Sidney Webb and Beatrice Webb, *Industrial Democracy* (London: Longmans, 1902), 365.

15. Scott Holland and Gertrude Tuckwell, "Report of the Christian Social Union Committee on Laundries," London, n.d., Trades Union Congress Library (TUCL), Gertrude Tuckwell Collection, File No. 14, 1.

16. P.P., *Report of the Chief Inspector of Factories and Workshops for the Year 1902. Report of Principal Lady Inspector,* 1903 (1610) 12, 174.

17. Edward Cadbury and George Shann, *Sweating* (London: Headley, 1907) 5; and Miss Gray, "What Can Be Done by Legislation To Improve the Conditions of Laundries?," *WIN,* Dec. 1900, 206.

18. Bosanquet et al., "Law and the Laundry," 227; and Fabian society, *Life in the Laundry,* Tract No. 112 (London: Fabian Society, 1902), 6-7.

19. P.P., *Report of the Chief Inspector of Factories and Workshops for 1899. Annual Report on the Work of H. M. Women Inspectors of Factories,* 1900 (223) 11, 268.

20. P.P., *R.C. on Labour. The Employment of Women,* 1893-94 (6894) 37, 23.

21. P.P., *Report of the Chief Inspector of Factories and Workshops for 1904. Annual Report of Principal Lady Inspector,* 1905 (2569) 10, 268.

22. Margaret Ethel MacDonald, "Report of Enquiry into Conditions of Work in Laundries," *WIN,* June 1907, 641-42; and P.P., *Report of Inspector,* 1900 (223) 11, 269.

23. P.P., *Report of Inspector,* 1900 (223) 11, 268-70; and *Report of Inspector,* 1905 (2569) 10, 269.

24. Anderson, *Women in the Factory,* 33. See also P.P., *Report of Inspector,* 1905 (2569) 10, 268; and Gray, "What Can Be Done?," 207.

25. P.P., *Report of Inspector,* 1905 (2569) 10, 252; P.P., *Report of the Chief Inspector of Factories and Workshops for the Year 1911. Report of Principal Lady Inspector,* 1912-13 (6289) 25, 152; and Anderson, *Women in the Factory,* 33.

26. Bosanquet et al., "Law and the Laundry," 228.

27. P.P., *Report of Inspector,* 1900 (223) 11, 266-69; P.P., *Report of the Chief Inspector of Factories and Workshops for the Year 1900. Report of Principal Lady Inspector,* 1901 (668) 10, 387; and P.P., *Report of the Chief Inspector of Factories and Workshops for the Year 1906. Report of Principal Lady Inspector,* 1907 (3586) 10, 224.

28. Margaret Ethel Macdonald, "Report of Enquiry into Laundries," 641. See also Squire, *Thirty Years,* 71.

29. P.P., *Report of Inspector,* 1900 (223) 11, 268 and *Report of Inspector,* 1907 (3586) 10, 224. The most illegal overtime was worked by packers and sorters who had to deal with the work at both the beginning and end of the laundry process.

30. P.P., *Report of Inspector,* 1900 (223) 11, 269; Miss England, "What Can Be Done To Improve the Condition of Workers in Laundries by Moral Influence?" in National Union of Women's Workers, *Women Workers: Papers Read at the Conference Held at Brighton, October 23rd-26th, 1900* (London: King, 1900), 198; and Holland and Tuckwell, "Report on Laundries," 1-2.

31. H. Llewellyn Smith, The *New Survey of London Life and Labour,* 9 vols. (London: King, 1930-35); *London Industries II,* vol. 5, 371.

32. Holland and Tuckwell, "Report on Laundries," 4. See also Booth, *Life and Labour,* vol. 8, 263.

33. Bosanquet et al., "Law and the Laundry," 229. See also P.P., *Report of Inspector,* 1903 (1610) 12, 174.

34. P.P., *Report of Inspector,* 1903 (1610) 12, 173-74 and Squire, *Thirty Years,* 23.

35. P.P., *Report of Inspector,* 1901 (668) 10, 387; *Report of Inspector,* 1905 (2569) 10, 268; and Squire, *Thirty Years,* 37.

36. P.P., *Report of Inspector,* 1900 (223) 11, 266-68.

37. P.P., *Report of Inspector,* 1903 (1610) 11, 174.

38. WIC, *Annual Report,* 1904-1905, 19-20. See also Fabian Society, *Life in the Laundry,* 11-15; and Gray, "What Can Be Done?," 207.

39. Katherine Graves Busbey, *The Women's Trade Union Movement in Great Britain* (Washington, D.C.: Bulletin of the Bureau of Labor No. 83, 1909), 53. That

laundry work was not classified as a "dangerous trade," subject to stringent rules, indicated to the WTUL a special need of outside help in monitoring the trade's conditions. See also "Industrial Law Committee," *Daily Citizen,* 21 Aug. 1913; and "Women's Work in the Coming Winter: Notes on Some of the Chief Programmes," *Daily News,* 11 Oct. 1911.

40. Violet R. Markham, *May Tennant: A Portrait* (London: Falcon, 1949), 18; and Anderson, *Women in the Factory,* 180.

41. P.P., *Report of Chief Inspector of Factories and Workshops for the Year 1893,* 1894 (7368) 21, 27. Although there was often in such institutions a scarcity of work, spells of intensive working could occur when a large restaurant or hotel order was received (ibid.).

42. Ibid., 5 and P.P., *Report of Inspector,* 1902 (1112) 12, 155. Since inmates were unpaid, legislation did not completely end this source of complaint and it was argued instead that charities often gained a further advantage from special rates for supplies such as soap (Liverpool Post, 1 July 1914).

43. Liverpool Magdalen Institution, *51st Annual Report,* 1905, n.p.; *Liverpool Post,* 1 July 1914; and P.P., *List of Religious and Charitable Institutions in Which Laundries Are Carried On, 1902,* 1905 (2500) 72, 8, 11. Although Adelaide Anderson reported that the number of inmates working in laundries never exceeded 9,417 during her tenure of office [to 1921], a concentration of such workers in one area competing for a particular market was perceived as a clear threat by commercial launderers (Anderson, *Women in the Factory,* 180).

44. *Hansard, Parliamentary Debates,* 4th ser., 95 (11 June 1901), 114.

45. Ibid., 119-20, 127, 133-41; and 17 June 1901, 644, 654-58, 675.

46. Ibid., 17 June 1901, 657; and 13 Aug. 1901, 686.

47. *Hansard Parliamentary Debates,* 4th ser., 95 (13 Aug. 1901), 651, 652-91.

48. Ibid., 13 Aug. 1901, 689-90.

49. P.P., *Report of Inspector,* 1903 (1610) 12, 147.

50. Evidence for the preceding paragraph is drawn from P.P., *Report of Inspector,* 1902 (1112) 12, 152; P.P., *Report of Inspector,* 1903 (1610) 12, 147 and apps. A, B, and C, 198-206; and Anderson, *Women in the Factory,* 182-89. Sympathetic bodies added publicity and their own findings to the officials' work (for example, Fabian Society, *Life in the Laundry,* 9-10; Earl of Lytton for Industrial Law Committee, *Laundries, Part II: Institution Laundries and Exempted Smaller Laundries* [London: n.p. n.d, held at TUCL, Tuckwell Coll.] 1-3; and Lucy C. F. Cavendish, "Law and the Laundry: Part 2, Laundries in Religious Houses," *Nineteenth Century,* 41 [Feb. 1897], 232-35).

51. P.P., *List of Laundries,* 1905 (2500) 72, 5.

52. P.P., *Report of the Chief Inspector of Factories and Workshops for the Year 1907. Report of Principal Lady Inspector,* 1908 (4166) 12, 144-46 and app. 1, 203-208; P.P., *Report of the Chief Inspector of Factories and Workshops for the Year 1905,* 1906 (3036) 15, 256; P.P., *Report of Inspector,* 1910 (5191) 28, 149; and Squire, *Thirty Years,* 159-60.

53. Lytton, *Laundries: II,* 1-2.

54. Frances Finnegan, *Poverty and Prostitution: A Study of Victorian Prostitutes in York* (Cambridge: Cambridge University Press, 1979), 177-78. By 1878 the receipts for washing were £217.14.4, a substantial contribution to expenses of £386.0.0 (ibid., 178 fn). See also P.P., *Report of Inspector,* 1906 (3036) 15, 257; P.P., *Report of Inspector,* 1908 (4166) 12, 146; P.P., *Report of Inspector,* 1905 (2569) 10, 269; Fabian Society, *Life in the Laundry,* 10; and Anderson, *Women in the Factory,* 184. This work was especially heavy since it was power assisted in only a minority of cases (P.P., *Report of Inspector,* 1909 [4664] 21, 122).

55. Anderson, *Women in the Factory,* 185; and P.P., *Report of Inspector,* 1909 (4664) 21, 130.

56. Squire, *Thirty Years,* 161-62; P.P., *Report of Inspector,* 1908 (4166) 21, 204; P.P., *Report of Inspector,* 1909 (4664) 21, 123; and P.P., *Report of Inspector,* 1910 (5191) 27, 152.

57. Quoted by Factory Inspector in P.P., *Report of Inspector,* 1906 (3036) 15, 257.

58. Fabian Society, *Life in the Laundry,* 10; and Lytton, *Laundries, Pt. II,* 2.

59. *The Times,* 2 May 1907, 16.

60. *Hansard Parliamentary Debates,* 4th ser. 175 (4 June 1907), 431.

61. P.P., *Report of Inspector,* 1910 (5191) 27, 150.

62. P.P., *Report of the Chief Inspector of Factories and Workshops for the Year 1910. Report of Principal Lady Inspector,* 1911 (5693) 12, 131-32; P.P., *Report of Inspector,* 1910 (5191) 27, 152; P.P., *Report of Inspector,* 1912-13 (6239) 25, 153-54; and Anderson, *Life in the Factory,* 187-89.

63. See A. M. Crowther, "The Later Years of the Workhouse, 1890-1929," in *The Origins of British Social Policy,* ed. Pat Thane (London: Croom Helm, 1978), 36-55.

64. As quoted in Thomas Oliver, *Dangerous Trades: The Historical Social and Legal Aspects of Industrial Occupations as Affecting Health by a Number of Experts* (London: Murray, 1902), 664-65.

65. Dressmakers and milliners also received intensive inspection in the West London District. Like the laundry trade, these were seasonal, hard to regulate trades. Administratively, the inspector's specialization enabled her to build up liaison with local authorities to maximize the effectiveness of sanitary inspectors and to evolve more efficient techniques of recording data (P.P., *Report of Inspector,* 1901 [668] 10, 349-51; P.P., *Report of Inspector,* 1907 [3586], 10, 185; P.P., *Report of Inspector,* 1905 [2569] 10, 250; and P.P., *Report of Inspector,* 1912-13 [6239], 25, 127; and for examples of the work of local governments with regard to laundry conditions, see Acton Urban District council, *Minutes,* 1903-1904, 297; *Minutes,* 1904-1905, 528, 1103; *Minutes,* 1905-1906, 221; *Minutes,* 1907, 721; *Minutes,* 1908, 411; *Annual Report of the Chelsea Medical Officer of Health,* 1904, 23, 25-26; 1905, 41; and 1910, 35-41 (held at Chelsea Public Library); and WIC, *London Borough Councils and the Welfare of Women Workers* (London: WIC, 1903), 2.

66. P.P., *Report of Inspector,* 1905 (2569) 10, calculated from table 7.B, 24.

67. Calculated from Anderson, *Women in the Factory,* 143. See also the series of

reports on laundry accidents in the annual reports of the chief inspectors of factories and workshops (for example, P.P., *Report of Inspector,* 1905 [2569] 10, 247-53; and P.P., *Report of Inspector,* 1904 [2139] 10, 208).

68. P.P., *Report of Inspector,* 1902 (1112) 12, 171.

69. Ibid., 170.

70. P.P., *Report of Inspector,* 1911 (5693) 12, 119-20; *The Times,* 7 Apr. 1910, 21; and P.P., *Memorandum on Fencing of Machinery and Prevention of Accidents in Laundries,* 1911, Form No. 414, TUCL. Fines of up to 100 pounds could be levied against occupiers failing to fence machinery. The measure seemed especially imperative in 1911 when the combination of a coronation year and an "exceptionally long hot summer" combined to increase both the pressure of work in laundries and the number of inexperienced workers engaged (P.P., *Report of Inspector,* 1912-13 [6239] 25, 139-41).

71. P.P., *Report of Inspector,* 1900 (223) 11, 266; P.P., *Report of Inspector,* 1904 (2139) 10, 209-12; P.P., *Report of Inspector,* 1905 (2569) 10, 247-48; and P.P., *Report of Inspector,* 1907 (3586) 10, 184, 202. Poor Law laundries were regulated by local government board inspectors who availed themselves of the expertise of the Home Office inspectors (P.P., *Report of Inspector,* 1907 [3586] 10, 184; P.P., *Report of Inspector,* 1911 [5693] 12, 110).

72. P.P., *Report of Inspector,* 1905 (2569) 10, 250. See also P.P., *Report of the Chief Inspector of Factories and Workshops for the Year 1903. Report of Principal Lady Inspector,* 1904 (2139) 10, 209.

73. P.P., *Report of Inspector,* 1902 (1112) 12, 170.

74. P.P., *Report of Inspector,* 1904 (2139) 10, 210.

75. P.P., *Report of Inspector,* 1905 (2569) 10, 252.

76. P.P., *Report of Inspector,* 1904 (2139) 10, 210; P.P., *Report of Inspector* 1907 (3586) 10, 206. In Leeds reliance on young workers showed up in the statistics of severe injury: in one year 38.7 percent of accidents happened to girls under eighteen; all of them worked unguarded machines (P.P., *Report of Inspector,* 1904 [2139] 10, 209).

77. P.P., *Report of Inspector,* 1902 (1112) 12, 169; P.P., *Report of Inspector,* 1904 (2139) 10, 211; 1905 (2569) 10, 250; Barbara Leigh Hutchins, *Women in Modern Industry* (London: Bell, 1915), 289; and Cadbury and Shann, *Sweating,* 16fn.

78. P.P., *Report of Inspector,* 1904 (2139) 10, calculated from table B, 238; P.P., *Report of Inspector,* 1903 (1610) 12, 186; and P.P., *Report of Inspector,* 1907 (3586) 10, 205-206.

79. As cited in P.P., *Report of Inspector,* 1903 (1610) 12, 168-69.

80. Margaret Ethel MacDonald, "Report of Enquiry into Laundries," 639. See also Kathleen Woodward, *Jipping Street: Childhood in a London Slum* (London: Harper, 1928), 93; Harry Gordon Maule and May Smith, *Industrial Psychology and the Laundry Trade* (London: Pitman, 1947), iv-v; P.P., *Report of Inspector,* 1902 (1112) 12, 178-79; and Oliver, *Dangerous Trades,* 667-71. The material for the laundry

trade in Oliver's work was written by Lucy E. A. Deane, Inspector for the West London District.

81. P.P., *Report of Inspector,* 1903 (1610) 12, 168, 172; P.P., *Report of Inspector,* 1910 (5191) 17, 130; Anderson, *Women in the Factory,* 127; and Oliver, *Dangerous Trades,* 668-71. Heat was another persistent problem (for example, P.P., *Report of Inspector,* 1897 [8561] 17, 42, 65; P.P., *Report of Inspector,* 1904 [2139] 10, 154-55, 205, 207; P.P., *Report of Inspector,* 1907 [3586] 10, 199; and P.P., *Report of Inspector,* 1908 [4166] 12, 158-59).

82. Oliver, *Dangerous Trades,* 671.

83. P.P., *Report of Inspector,* 1905 (2569) 10, 252.

84. *Hansard Parliamentary Debates,* 4th ser., 174 (7 May 1907), 736-48; 175 (4 June 1907) 421-34; 175 (13 June 1907), 1543-52; 179 (6 Aug. 1907), 1922-28; 181 (21 Aug. 1907), 914-22; (24 Aug. 1907), 1517-27; *The Times,* 15 May 1907, 6; and British Association, *Report on Women's Labour* (London: n.p., 1903), 35.

85. *Factory and Workshop Act,* 1907 (7 Edw. 7, Ch. 39); and Secretary of State, No. 1010, 26 Dec. 1907.

86. P.P., *Report of Inspector,* 1911 (5693) 22, 124.

87. Margaret Ethel MacDonald, "Confusion for Laundry Workers," *WIN,* June 1908, 28; Black, "Legislative Proposals," 203; and P.P., *Report of Inspector,* 1909 (4664) 21, 127. See also *WIN,* Sept. 1908, 50-51.

88. *The Times* 25 Mar. 1908, 9. Mr. MacDonald had acted with the support of the Legal Committee of the Women's Industrial Council (Margaret Ethel MacDonald, "Confusion," 28).

89. P.P., *Report of Inspector,* 1910 (5191) 28, 123, 135-38. Cleanliness was a persistent problem in some of the small laundries as these were the poorest and least well facilitated workplaces (*ibid.,* 128).

90. P.P., *Report of Inspector,* 1911 (5693) 12, 27, 120. A lack of supervision of the youngest workers (14 year olds) was believed by one inspector to be the major remaining source of accidents (1910 [5191] 28, 137). The year after the First World War saw further improvement in safety, partly attributable to technological improvement and the replacement of older machinery (P.P., *Report of the Chief Inspector of Factories and Workshops for 1919,* 1920 [941] 16, 25-26).

91. P.P., *Report of Inspector,* 1912-13 (6239) 25, 152; P.P., *Report of Inspector,* 1910 (5191) 28, 131, 149-50; and P.P., *Report of Inspector,* 1911 (5693) 12, 32. Short-lived seasonal overwork was also a problem in London, where simultaneous pressure in laundries and on dressmakers and milliners made thorough investigation and enforcement difficult (P.P., *Report of Inspector,* 1910 [5191] 28, 126-27).

92. P.P., *Report of Inspector,* 1911 (5693) 12, 131. It was poverty which created this overwork (P.P., *Report of Inspector,* 1910 [5191] 28, 149).

93. P.P., *Report of Inspector,* 1909 (4664) 21, 127; and P.P., *Report of Inspector,* 1910 (5191) 127.

94. Dorothy Sells, *British Wages Boards: A Study in Industrial Democracy*

(Washington, D.C.: Brookings, 1939), 15-17; Davidson, "Llewellyn Smith and the Labour Department," 250; J. Ramsay MacDonald, "Sweating and Wages Boards," *Nineteenth Century,* 64 (November 1908), 748-62; and Constance Smith, "The Minimum Wage," in Gertrude Tuckwell et al., *Women in Industry From Seven Points of View* (London: Duckworth, 1911), 25-69. For a discussion of the campaign to establish a minimum wage for sweated trades, see also James A. Schmiechen, *Sweated Industries and Sweated Labor: The London Clothing Trades, 1860-1914* (Urbana, Ill.: University of Illinois Press, 1984), 161-79.

95. J. Ramsay MacDonald, "Sweating," 757 and passim. MacDonald would have preferred a system of licencing of home workers to improve conditions and discourage casual employers (*ibid.,* 762).

96. P.P., *Report of the Select Committee on Home Work,* 1907 (290) 6, passim; P.P., *Report of the Lords Committee on the Sweating System,* 1890 (169) 17, passim; Women's Industrial Council, *Home Industries of Women in London. Report of an Inquiry by the Investigation Committee of the Women's Industrial Council* (London: WIC, 1908), passim; Clementina Black, *Sweated Industry and the Minimum Wage* (London: Duckworth, 1907), passim; Margaret H. Irwin, *The Problem of Home Work* (Glasgow: Davidson, 1903), passim; Gertrude Tuckwell, "The Regulation of Women's Work" in Tuckwell et al., *Women in Industry,* 1-23; and Cadbury and Shann, *Sweating,* passim.

97. Definition of the *Select Committee on Home Work* as cited in Sells, *British Wages Boards,* 19.

98. For example, *Daily News,* 29 Sept. 1911.

99. *The Times,* 14 Apr. 1913, 10; William Kent, *John Burns: Labour's Lost Leader* (London: Williams & Norgate, 1950), 38; *Daily Citizen,* 14 Apr. 1913; Busbey, *Women's Trade Union Movement,* 52-53; and *Laundry Institution and Engineer,* 6 July 1912, 367.

100. *Standard,* 20 Mar. 1913. A mass meeting of workers at Queen's Hall, London passed a unanimous resolution demanding extension of Trade Boards to a number of trades including the laundry industry (Mary Agnes Hamilton, *Mary Macarthur. A Biographical Sketch* [London: Parsons, 1925], 122).

101. Acton Urban District Council, *Minutes* (held in the Local History Collection, Central Library, London Borough of Ealing), 1913, 15 July, 351; 21 July, 371-73; 28 July, 393-95; 11 Aug., 396-99; 19 Aug., 426; 16 Sept., 444; 7 Oct. 470-71; 21 Oct. 506-507; *The Times,* 12 Aug. 1913, 10; *Middlesex County Times,* 16 Aug. 1913; and *Gazette,* 25 July, 15 Aug. and 10 Oct. 1913.

102. *Star,* 3 July 1913; *Common Cause,* 10 Oct. 1913; *Leicester Post,* 9 July 1913; *The Times,* 12 Mar. 1914, 10; 19 June 1914, 5; 23 June 1914, 3; *Standard,* 30 July 1914; *Newcastle Chronicle,* 20 June 1914; *Reynold's Newspaper,* 3 May 1914; *Manchester Guardian,* 27 Apr. 1914; and *Daily Chronicle,* 28 Apr., 2 Mar. 1914.

103. *New Statesman,* 10 Oct. 1914. Much of the board's wages testimony was based on the 1906 wages inquiry supplemented by figures collected by Miss Collet in 1912 from four London labor exchanges (*ibid.*).

104. Dorothy Sells, *British Trade Boards System* (London: King, 1923), 7, 88-89 and Sells, *British Wages Boards,* 165. See also *Hansard Parliamentary Debates,* 5th ser., 112 (26 Feb. 1919), 1730-31; 107 (24 June 1918), 714-15; *The Times,* 18 Feb. 1919, 10, 17 May 1919, 7; *John Bull,* 31 May 1919; and *Woman Worker,* May 1919, 10.

105. P.P. Report of the War Cabinet Committee, *Women in Industry,* 1919 (135), 6-7; and *Daily News,* 23 Jan. 1919.

106. P.P., Trade Board Acts, 1909 and 1918, *Laundry Trade (Great Britain) General Minimum Time Rates and Overtime Rates for Certain Classes of Male Workers,* Statutory Rules and Orders (S.R. & O.), 1922 (W [11]), 2.

107. Sells, *British Trade Boards,* 92; and HMSO, Trade Boards Acts 1909 and 1918, *Laundry Trade (Great Britain). Minimum Rates for Female Workers,* S.R. & O., 1921, No. 1896 (W [10]), passim.

108. *Woman Worker,* Aug. 1919, 3. Overtime was payable at time and a quarter rising to time and a half after two hours on Saturday and double time for any Sunday work.

109. Sells, *British Wages Boards,* 296; and Llewellyn Smith, *New Survey,* vol. 5, 374.

110. *Woman Worker,* June 1920, 1; Dec. 1920, 2; Sells, *British Trade Boards System,* 93; and *The Times,* 27 Mar. 1920, 11.

Chapter 4: Self-Help, Sisterly Help, and Industrial Action

1. Historians have largely neglected the noninstitutional ways in which workers modified or exerted control over the labor process. A major exception is Richard Price's excellent study of the building industry *Masters, Unions and Men: Work Control in Building and the Rise of Labour, 1830-1914* (Cambridge: Cambridge University Press, 1981), an innovative addition to the study of labor history that stresses the importance of the work group as the nexus of industrial relations within this sector of the economy. Another important study is: Patrick Joyce, *Work, Society and Politics: The Culture of the Factory in Later Victorian England* (Brighton: Harvester, 1980); the author moves behind the superstructure of industrialization and unionization to explore the work culture underpinning labor relations. See also J. Foster, *Class Struggle and the Industrial Revolution,* (London: Methuen, 1974).

2. Several recent studies have devoted attention to women's trade unionism and to the role of middle-class women in organizing and encouraging them. See Norbert Soldon, *Women in British Trade Unions, 1874-1976* (London: Gill and Macmillan, 1978), passim; Barbara Drake, *Women in Trade Unions* (London: Labour Research Department, Trade Union Series, No. 6, 1921), passim; and Sheila Lewenhak, *Women and Trade Unions: An Outline History of Women in the British Trade Union Movement* (New York: St. Martin's 1977), passim. Lewenhak's study is particularly valuable for its outline of women's unionization before the formation of the Women's Protective and Provident League (later the WTUL). An essay that

articulates one aspect of interclass tensions is: Robin Miller Jacoby, "Feminism and Class Consciousness in the British and American Women's Trade Union League, 1890-1925," in *Liberating Women's History: Theoretical and Critical Essays,* ed. Bernice A. Carroll (Urbana, Ill.: University of Illinois Press, 1976), 137-60. Lee Holcombe's *Victorian Ladies at Work: Middle Class Working Women in England and Wales 1850-1914* (Newton Abbott: David & Charles, 1973) contains discussion of trade unionism among middle-class service sector workers such as shop assistants and clerical workers. See also contemporary accounts of trade unionism by activists, for example, Mary R. Macarthur, "Trade Unionism," in Gertrude Tuckwell et al., *Women in Industry From Seven Points of View* (London: Duckworth, 1910), 61-83; Emilia F. S. Dilke, "Trades Unionism Among Women," Part 1, *Fortnightly Review,* 55 (May 1891), 741-46; Florence Routledge, "Trade Unionism Among Women," Part 2, *Fortnightly Review,* 55 (May 1891), 746-50; and biographical accounts such as Mary Agnes Hamilton, *Mary Macarthur: A Biographical Sketch* (London: Parsons, 1925), passim; and Violet R. Markham, *May Tennant. A Portrait* (London: Falcon, 1949), passim.

3. P.P., *R.C. on Labour. The Employment of Women,* 1893-94 (6894) 37, 22. See also P.P., *R.C. on Factory Act,* 1876 (1443) 30, 205. In chapter 2 discussion included some indication of the independence, assertiveness, and resourcefulness of the "free-lance" laundress working in her own home, the homes of employers, or the public washhouse, but our concern here is with larger units of laundry employment.

4. Margaret Ethel MacDonald, "Report of Enquiry into Conditions of Work in Laundries," *WIN,* June 1907, 367.

5. M. Mostyn Bird noted a similar range of personalities among laundresses in *Woman at Work: A Study of the Different Ways of Earning a Living Open to Women* (London: Chapman & Hall, 1911), 24.

6. *Laundry Record,* 1 May 1894, 23.

7. Frank T. Bullen, *Confessions of a Tradesman* (London: Hodder & Stoughton, 1908), 31. I am indebted to Anna Davin for this reference.

8. P.P., *Report of Inspector,* 1908 (4166) 12, 149. Herbert Nield, M.P. for Ealing, confirmed laundresses' readiness (at least in his constituency) to express displeasure over the circumstances of their work (*Star,* 3 July 1913).

9. Bird, *Woman at Work,* 124.

10. Thomas Oliver, *Dangerous Trades: The Historical, Social and Legal Aspects of Industrial Occupations as Affecting Health by a Number of Experts* (London: Murray, 1902), 672.

11. Ibid., 671; and P.P., *R.C. on Labour,* 1893-94 (6894) 37, 17.

12. *The Times,* 11 May 1895, 15.

13. P.P., *Report on Laundries,* 1894 (7418) 21, 21, 24; and Margaret H. Irwin, *The Conditions of Women's Work in Laundries. Report of an Inquiry Conducted for the Council of the Women's Provident and Protective League of Glasgow* (Glasgow: Women's Provident and Protective League, 1893), 5, 11-14.

14. P.P., *Laundries,* 1894 (7418) 21, 21; P.P., *R.C. on Labour,* 1893-94 (6894) 37, 17-19; and P.P., *R.C. on Factory Act,* 1876 (1443) 30, 204-205.

15. P.P., *R.C. on Labour,* 1893-94 (6894) 37, 19.

16. Ibid.

17. Ibid., 23; and P.P., *Report of Inspector,* 1907 (3586) 10, 234.

18. Special Commissioner, "West End Poverty, I: The Latymer Road District," *Quiver* (1883), 44-46 (I am indebted to Anna Davin for this reference.); and P.P., *R.C. on Labour,* 1893-94 (6894) 37, 23.

19. Barbara Leigh Hutchins, *Women in Modern Industry* (London: Bell, 1915), app. no. 9, 291; *Star,* 23 Sept. 1913; and *Daily Herald,* 26 Sept. 1913, 4. In some laundries, further charges were made for the use of messrooms, stoppage of machinery, and the cost of heating irons, or deductions were made if an item had to be re-ironed (*Liverpool Review:* 25 Oct. 1890, *Star,* 23 Sept. 1913; and *Daily Herald,* 26 Sept. 1913).

20. For example, *Daily News,* 29 Sept. 1911.

21. P.P., *Report of Inspector,* 1907 (3586) 10, 224-25.

22. P.P., *R.C. on Labour,* 1893-94 (6894) 37, 18. Another witness testified that the better the worker, the harder it was to motivate her to work regularly (ibid., 19).

23. P.P., *R.C. on Labour,* 1893-94 (6894) 37, 22; and P.P., *Report of Inspector,* 1894 (7368) 21, 11-12.

24. P.P., *R.C. on Factory Act,* 1876 (1443) 30, 205. Proprietors of the smallest laundries, fearful of losing any of their small clientele, frequently worked very late, often overnight, along with members of their immediate families in order to finish the work for a lady's dinner party or travel requirements.

25. Ibid.

26. Ibid., 204.

27. Ibid.

28. *The Times,* 15 June 1891, 15; William Hamling, *A Short History of the Liverpool Trades Council, 1848-1948* (Liverpool: Liverpool University Press, 1948), 25; Liverpool Trades Council, *Minutes,* Oct. 1890 (held at Liverpool Record Office); and *Liverpool Review,* 25 Oct. 1890. Other women's unions, of course, represented part of the thrust of Trades Council and TUC encouragement for organization of laundry workers.

29. *Pioneer,* 14 June 1834; Taylor, "The Men Are as Bad," 18; and Harold Goldman, *Emma Paterson* (London: Lawrence & Wishart, 1974), 17.

30. *The London Trades Council 1860-1950* (London: Lawrence & Wishart, 1950), 42; and Macarthur, "Trade Unionism," 64. This study is not the place for a general overview of both male support of and hostility to women's unionism. For more on this issue see Lewenhak, *Women and Trade Unions,* passim; and Soldon, *Women in Trade Unions,* passim.

31. *Middlesex County Times,* 7 Oct. 1911; *Liverpool Post,* 11 July 1914; *Fulham*

Chronicle, 17 Nov. 1911; *Woman Worker,* Nov. 1917, 6 and *Daily Herald,* 28 Mar. 1914.

32. *Yorkshire Gazette,* 30 Aug., 27 Sept., 4 Oct. 1913.

33. *Fulham Chronicle,* 17 Nov. 1911. For the text of the agreement reached between York Laundry Proprietors and the NFWW, see NFWW, *Seventh Annual Report* (Manchester: National Labour Press, 1914), 47-48.

34. *Woman Worker,* Aug.-Sept. 1920, 14.

35. *Eastern Morning News,* 7 July 1920; and *Woman Worker,* Aug.-Sept. 1920, 14.

36. *Eastern Morning News,* 8, 10 July 1910; and *Woman Worker,* Aug.-Sept. 1920, 14.

37. *Woman Worker,* Aug.-Sept. 1920, 14; *Eastern Morning News,* 1 July 1920; and *Weekly News,* 14 Aug. 1920.

38. *Woman Worker,* Aug.-Sept. 1920, 14.

39. *Weekly News,* 14 Aug. 1920; and *The Times,* 13 Aug. 1920, 5.

40. *Pioneer,* 14 June 1834, 407; *Leamington Spa Courier,* 30 Sept. 1893, 4, 7 Oct. 1893, 4; *Nuneation Chronicle* as quoted in *Laundry Record,* 30 Sept. 1893, 139; *Daily Citizen,* 6 June 1913; and *Woman Worker,* Dec. 1916, 7. The WTUL received reports of several strikes by unorganized workers in the North and West of England (*Women's Trade Union Review,* 1 July 1891, 4).

41. Leamington Spa Laundry Company (advertisement), *Spennell's Almanack and Annual Directory,* 1892 (held in Central Division Library, Leamington Spa), 155.

42. *Leamington Spa Courier,* 7 Oct. 1893, 4. See also Sidney Tebbutt, "Steam Laundry Machinery," in *Proceedings of the Institution of Mechanical Engineers* (London, Apr. 1898), 268-307. Much of the strikers' hostility was directed against Miss Monteith, manageress of the laundry, but the surviving evidence does not make clear the nature of their complaints.

43. As quoted in Leslie Woodcock Tentler, *Wage-Earning Women: Industrial Work and Family Life in the United States, 1900-1930* (Oxford: Oxford University Press, 1979), 79.

44. *Women's Union Journal,* 31 Jan. 1877, 22; and 15 June 1877, 38. Other unions were formed over the next fifteen years at Kensal Green, Wandsworth, Putney, Notting Hill, and Croydon; and throughout the metropolitan area in the wake of the 1891 Hyde Park demonstration (*Women's Union Journal,* Apr. 1882, 15 Feb., 15 Nov., and 16 Dec. 1889, 15 May 1890; and *Women's Trade Union Review,* Apr. 1891, 14-15; and July 1891, 4).

45. For shop assistants see Robert R. Dolling, *Ten Years in a Portsmouth Slum* (London: Swan Sonnenschein, 1896), 131-32; *The Times,* 4, 12 Feb. 1909, 12 Apr. 1909; Holcombe, *Victorian Ladies at Work,* chap. 5; Margaret Bondfield, *A Life's Work* (London: Hutchinson, 1948); Joseph Hallsworth and Rhys J. Davies, *The Working Life of Shop Assistants: A Study of Conditions of Labour in the Distributive Trades* (Manchester: National Labour Press, 1910); *Woman Worker,* 5 May 1908, 30; 12 May 1908, 10; 19 May 1908, 88; 14 Aug. 1908, 295; 6 Jan. 1909, 21; 20 Jan.

1909, 54; 27 Jan. 1909, 77; and 3 Feb. 1909, 101; and *Women Folk,* 23 March 1910, 825. For domestic workers and bedmakers, see *Woman Worker,* Apr. 1918, 5; June 1918, 6; July 1918, 12; Feb. 1919, 5; Aug. 1919, 9-10; Oct. 1920, 8; Nov. 1920, 10; Apr. 1921, 14; May 1921, 4; and Boone, *Women's Trade Union Leagues,* 32. For waitresses, see *Woman Worker,* 5 June 1908, 7; 28 Aug. 1908, 333; 5 May 1909, 413; Aug. 1918, 6: Feb. 1920, 8; Aug.-Sept. 1920, 15; Oct. 1920, 14; and Dec. 1920, 14.

46. Drake, *Women in Trade Unions,* 46; P.P., *R.C. on Labour,* 1892 (6795) 36, 886-87; *Women's Trade Union Review,* Apr. 1891, 14-15, 1 July 1891, 4.

47. P.P., *R.C. on Labour,* 1893-94 (6894) 37, 23.

48. Charles Booth, *Life and Labour of the People of London,* 16 vols. (London: Macmillan, 1902-1903), 2d ser., vol. 8, 267.

49. D. Reid, letter to Lady Dilke, 22 Dec. 1902 (Gertrude Tuckwell Coll., TUCL).

50. See, for example, *Daily Herald,* 26 Aug. 1913; 10, 15, 20, 26 September 1913; and 25 Nov. 1913; *Daily Citizen,* 12 July 1913; 16 Sept. 1913; *The Times,* 12 Aug. 1913, 10; *Middlesex County Times,* 16 Aug. 1913; and *Gazette,* 15 Aug. 1913; 10 Oct. 1913.

51. For a more complete account of the provisions of the National Health Insurance Act and its implications for women's unions, see Soldon, *Women in Trade Unions,* 68-69.

52. NFWW, *Seventh Annual Report,* 1914, 26-27 and 32-33, NFWW, *Eighth Annual Report,* 1915, 34; *Daily Citizen,* 6 June 1913; 15 July 1913; *Reynold's Newspaper,* 21 Sept. 1913; *Yorkshire Gazette,* 30 Aug. 1913; 27 Sept. 1913; 4 Oct. 1913; *Liverpool Post,* 11 July 1914; 1 Aug. 1914; and *Sheffield Daily Telegraph,* 11 March 1914; 25 May 1914. While most of these negotiations covered only female workers, in Liverpool van drivers, enginemen, and delivery boys were part of the same union as the women (*Liverpool Post,* 11 July 1914).

53. *Daily Herald,* 24 Mar. 1914. See also *Daily Herald,* 26 Aug. 1913; 10, 15, 20, 26 Sept. 1913; 24 June 1914; 25 Nov. 1914. The *Daily Herald*'s cause was taken up by the *Daily Citizen,* which reported on "Laundry Slaves in Croyden" (for example, *Daily Citizen,* 25 Sept. 1913; 3 Oct. 1913).

54. West London Observer, 7 Oct. 1911; *Middlesex County Times,* 7 Oct. 1911; *Daily News,* 3, 29 Sept. 1911; 2 Oct. 1911; 16 Sept. 1913; *Daily Citizen,* 18 Aug. 1913; *Woman Worker,* May 1916, 11; and NFWW, *Sixth Annual Report,* 1913, 4. During the same period, Cardiff laundry workers organized and achieved increased wages, paid overtime, and an end to fines (*March Western Mail,* 2 Oct. 1911; and *Daily News,* 30 Sept. 1911).

55. *Woman Worker,* Dec. 1916, 12; Mar. 1917, 17; June 1917, 10; Feb. 1918, 16; May 1918, 3; June 1918, 3; Oct. 1918, 14; June 1919, 8; Aug. 1919, 3; and *Sheffield Daily Telegraph,* 29 Jan. 1915. These settlements occurred at public as well as private laundries (for example, *Woman Worker,* Dec. 1918, 5).

56. *Woman Worker,* May 1918, 3-4; June 1918, 3; and Aug. 1918, 6.

57. *Weekly Dispatch,* 10 June 1917.

58. *Woman Worker,* Dec. 1920, 5.

59. Ibid.

60. *Woman Worker,* June 1919, 3.

61. Hamilton, *Mary Macarthur,* 179-80; Lewenhak, *Women and Trade Unions,* 166; and Drake, *Woman in Trade Unions,* 104-105.

62. *Woman Worker,* June 1919, 2. See also, ibid., May 1918, 8; and WTUL, *Minutes,* 19 May 1918; 11 July 1918; 10 Apr. 1919; and 8 May 1919.

63. Black, "Position of Women in Unskilled Work," 18.

64. See, for example, *Woman Worker,* Dec. 1918, 12; Feb. 1919, 11; Sept. 1919, 3; Oct. 1919, 2, 8, 9; Nov. 1919, 4; Feb. 1920, 11; Mar. 1920, 11; and WTUL, *Minutes,* 11 Dec. 1918 and 11 July 1919.

65. *Amalgamated Union of Co-operative Employees Journal,* 28 Jan. 1919. See also *The Times,* 5 Mar. 1919, 12; *Eastern Morning News,* 3 July 1920; and *Laundry Record,* 1 Mar. 1919, 135.

66. Sells, *British Wages Boards,* 310, 312.

67. WTUL, *Committee Minutes,* 11 July 1918 (held at TUCL).

68. *Woman Worker,* June 1920, 1.

69. Ibid., Mar. 1920, 4.

70. Ibid., Apr. 1920, 11 and *Liverpool Post,* 28 Apr. 1920.

71. *The Times,* 12 June 1920, 13 and *Woman Worker,* May 1920, 8; July 1920, 3, 10, 11.

72. *Woman Worker,* Oct. 1920, 9. For other agreements see *Woman Worker,* July 1920, 2; Oct. 1920, 5; Nov. 1920, 8; Jan. 1921, 5; Feb. 1921, 12; Mar. 1921, 12; and May 1921, 11.

73. Ibid., Dec. 1920, 2. One positive benefit was the Laundry Welfare Order, 1920, which made mess rooms and protective clothing mandatory (*The Times,* 20 May 1920, 11; and *Woman Worker,* July 1920, 9).

74. *Daily Herald,* 26 Sept. 1913; P.P., *Report of Inspector,* 1911 (5693), 12, 16; *Daily Citizen,* 6 June 1913; 3 Oct. 1913; *Woman Worker,* July 1917, 10; Oct. 1918, 11; Mar. 1920, 8; and *Westminster & Pimlico News,* 9 Feb. 1912.

75. See, for example, WIC, "What Has Already Been Done," *WIN,* Sept. 1905, 1-2.

76. Ester Longhurst, "How Can I Earn a Living? Work for Educated Women," *Woman Worker,* 26 Jan. 1910, 662.

77. In a rare exception, members of the Birmingham section of the National Laundry Workers Union in 1919 demanded equal pay for equal work but otherwise accepted that men should earn double the minimum female wage (*Laundry Record,* 1 Mar. 1919, 135). More usual was the stance of the Women's Industrial Council which, when consulted about industrial training programs and unemployment schemes, consistently suggested the needletrades, domestic training, laundry work, and other traditional women's trades such as artificial flowermaking.

78. See, for example, Mrs. J. R. MacDonald and Mrs. Player, *Wage-Earning Mothers* (pamphlet), (London: Women's Labour League, 1911); Markham, *Tennant*, 53; and Mrs. Mary Murdoch, "The Wage-Earning of Married Women," 74-80.

79. MacDonald and Player, *Wage-Earning Mothers*, 5; and Loane, *From Their Point of View*, 131. See also Christian Social Union, *Employment after Childbirth; Ragged School Union Magazine*, Feb. 1892, 32; Mary Bayly, *Mended Homes and What Repaired Them* (London: Nisbet, 1861), 57, 65-66; *WIN*, Oct. 1909, 6; and Isabel Taylor, *A Bibliography of Unemployment and the Unemployed* (London: King, 1909), xiii.

80. P.P., *Report of Inspector*, 1910 (5191) 28, 159.

81. See for example, Anna Davin, "Imperialism and Motherhood," *History Workshop* (Spring 1978), 9-65.

82. Ibid., 55.

83. *Woman Worker*, 14 Aug. 1908, 277.

Chapter 5: Mechanization and Social Change

1. Enid Porter, *Victorian Cambridge: Josiah Chater's Diaries, 1844-1884* (London: Phillimore, 1975), 180.

2. Crouch Hill Sanitary Laundry, Limited, "Prospectus" (c. 1890; held by Haringay Public Libraries), n.p.

3. Trade journals such as the *Laundry Record* and the *Laundry* regularly summarized the annual reports of corporated laundry firms. See, for example, *Laundry Record*, 1 Apr. 1896, 10-12; and "Laundry Share Quotations," *Laundry*, 2 Mar. 1912, 96.

4. Ancliffe Prince, *The Craft of Laundering: A History of Fabric Cleaning* (London: Company of Launderers, 1970), 18; Harry A. Lay, "Evolution of the Laundry," *Laundry Record*, 1 Dec. 1911, 687. In the United States, the first power laundries began about 1850 to meet the needs of those who had followed the lure of gold to California (F. de Armond, *The Laundry Industry* [New York: Harper, 1950], 7-8).

5. Porter, *Victorian Cambridge*, 181.

6. J. H. Clapham, *An Economic History of Modern Britain*, 3 vols. (Cambridge: Cambridge University Press, 1926-38), vol. 3, *Machines and National Rivalries, 1887-1894, with an epilogue 1914-1929* (1938), 184.

7. Lucy E. A. Deane, "Laundry Workers," in *Dangerous Trades: The Historical Social and Legal Aspects of Industrial Occupations as Affecting Health by a Number of Experts*, ed. Thomas Oliver (London: Murray, 1902), 665.

8. Ibid., and "King's Cross Laundry," *Laundry Record*, 2 Jan. 1905, 21.

9. H. Llewellyn Smith, ed., *The New Survey of London Life and Labour*, 9 vols. (London: King, 1930-35); vol. 5, *London Industries II*, 373.

10. Deane, "Laundry Workers," 665.

11. "Passing of the Hand Laundry," *Morning Post,* 23 June 1914.

12. Llewellyn Smith, *New Survey,* vol. 5, 355, 338.

13. *Review of Newcastle-on-Tyne and District* (Newcastle: Advertising brochure, 1896), 64-66; and *Laundry Record,* 2 Jan. 1905, 21, 1 July 1905, 385. In Sunderland, the pure and abundant water that established the town as a brewing center from the eighteenth century made large laundries possible in the nineteenth and twentieth centuries (*Newcastle and Gateshead Chamber of Commerce Journal, Exhibition Year Supplement* [Newcastle, 1919], 211).

14. *Illustrated London News,* 3 Oct. 1857, 341.

15. Edwin Chadwick, *Report on the Sanitary Condition of the Labouring Population of Great Britain 1842,* ed M. W. Flinn (Edinburgh: Edinburgh University Press, 1965). See also James P. Kay, *The Moral and Physical Condition of the Working Classes* (Manchester, 1832); P.P., *Health of Towns Commission, Report of the Commissioners for Reporting into the State of Large Towns and Populous Districts,* 1840 (384) 11; P.P., *Report of the Lords Select Committee on the Supply of Water to the Metropolis,* 1840 (354) 22; T. F. Reddaway, "London in the Nineteenth Century: The Fight for a Water Supply," *Nineteenth Century and After,* 148 (1950), 118-30; Royston Lambert, *Sir John Simon 1816-1904 and English Sanitary Administration* (London: MacGibbon & Kee, 1963); and Caroline Davidson, *A Woman's Work Is Never Done: A History of Housework in the British Isles, 1650-1950* (London: Chatto & Windus, 1982), chap. 1.

16. Stefan Muthesius, *The English Terraced House* (New Haven: Yale University Press, 1982), 55-56.

17. *Laundry Record,* 1 July 1905, 381.

18. *Review of Newcastle and District,* 64; *Newcastle Journal supplement,* 211; *Where to Buy at Leamington,* 51; *Wilson's Arundel Laundry,* n.p.; and *Yorkshire Gazette,* 12 Mar. 1885.

19. Lay, "Evolution of the Laundry," 681. See also, Prince, *Craft of Laundering,* 8.

20. Lay, "Evolution of the Laundry," 681.

21. "Soap," *Encyclopaedia Britannica,* 11th ed., vol. 25, 299; Lay, "Evolution of the Laundry," 681; William H. Simmons, *Soap: Its Composition, Manufacture and Properties,* 3d ed. (London: Pitman, 1933), 1-2; and A. E. Musson, *Enterprise in Soap and Chemicals; Joseph Crosfield & Sons Limited, 1815-1865* (Manchester: Manchester University Press, 1965), 26.

22. John Houghton, *Husbandry and Trade improv'd,* ed. Richard Bradley, 2d ed. (London: Woodman & Lyon, 1728), vol. 1, 348-54 as quoted in Davidson, *Woman's Work,* 145. See also Musson, *Enterprise in Soap and Chemicals,* 27.

23. In 1790, Nicholas Leblanc developed the process of producing soda from common salt, thereby diminishing the trade's reliance on ashes and seaweed (barbilla) as an alkali source. By 1814, the process was in use in St. Helen's, Lancashire (Davidson, *Woman's Work,* 144). See, for example, Musson, *Enterprise in Soap and Chemicals;* Simmons, *Soap;* and Charles Wilson, *The History of Unilever: A Study in Economic Growth and Change,* 3 vols. (London: Cassell, 1970).

24. Musson, *Enterprise in Soap and Chemicals,* 27.

25. *Laundry Record,* 1 July 1905, 377.

26. See, for example, Christina Walkley and Vanda Foster, *Crinolines and Crimping Irons: Victorian Clothes: How They were Cleaned and Cared For* (London: Owen, 1978); C. W. Cunnington and P. Cunnington, *Handbook of English Costume in the 19th Century* (London: Faber, 1959); Anne Buck, *Victorian Costume and Costume Accessories* (London: Jenkins, 1961); Janet Arnold, *Patterns of Fashion (c. 1660-1860)* (London: Wace, 1964); and idem, *Patterns of Fashion (c. 1860-1940)* (London: Wace, 1966).

27. P.P. The Heating and Ventilation (Reconstruction) Committee of the Building Research Board of the Department of Scientific and Industrial Research, *Heating and Ventilation of Buildings,* Post War Buildings Series No. 19, 1945, 133.

28. Leslie Hannah, *Electricity before Nationalization: A Study of the Development of the Electricity Supply Industry in Britain to 1948* (Baltimore: Johns Hopkins University Press, 1979), 186 and T.A.B. Corley, *Domestic Electric Appliances* (London: Cape, 1966) 19.

29. Corley, *Domestic Electric Appliances,* 19; Geoffrey Brown, *Patterns of British Life: A Study of Certain Aspects of the British People at Home, at Work, and at Play, and a Compilation of Some Relevant Statistics* (London: Hulton Research, 1950), 103; Hannah, *Electricity,* 159, 187; and "Prices, and the Cost and Standard of Living," *Monthly Labor Review,* 61 (Dec. 1945), 1220-21 as quoted in Ruth Schwartz Cowan, *More Work for Mother: The Ironies of Household Technology from the Open Hearth to the Microwave* (New York: Basic, 1983), 94.

30. Llewelyn Smith, *New Survey,* vol. 5, 376-77.

31. W.F.F. Kelsey and David Ginsberg, *The Social Survey, Consumer Expenditures Series. Expenditures of Laundries, Dyeing, and Cleaning, Mending and Alterations and Shoe Repairing Services* (London: Central Office of Information, Aug. 1949).

32. May Smith, *Reports of the Industrial Fatigue Research Board, No. 22: Some Studies in the Laundry Trade,* Laundry Series No. 1 (London: Medical Research Council, HMSO, 1922), 1.

33. Raphael Samuel, "The Workshop of the World: Steam Power and Hand Technology in Mid-Victorian Britain," *History Workshop,* no. 3 (Spring 1977), 6-72.

34. Llewellyn Smith, *New Survey,* vol. 5, 373.

35. Ibid., table 6, 387; 350.

36. Ibid., 347. See also Chelsea Medical Officer of Health, *Annual Report for 1904,* 25; and P.P., *Report of Inspector,* 1910 (5191) 28, 153.

37. *Woman Worker,* May 1921, 11; and June 1921, 14; Llewellyn Smith, *New Survey,* vol. 5, 348. Controversy surrounding the bagwash became particularly heated when the Fulham Borough Council tried to introduce a bagwash scheme to be operated through municipal washhouses. Local laundry owners obtained an injunction against the municipality which effectively ended the experiment (*Woman Worker,* May 1921, 11).

38. Llewellyn Smith, *New Survey,* vol. 5, 349.

39. *Faversham Sanitary Steam Laundry Co., Ltd.*, Advertising Brochure (c. 1910, held at the Kent County Record Office, n.p.). For further examples of laundry prices see: *Laundry Record*, passim; "Yorkshire Laundries, Ltd: New and Revised Price List," *Yorkshire Gazette*, 11 Mar. 1905; Walkley and Foster, *Crinolines*, 57; *The Times*, 20 Mar. 1920, 13.

40. Llewellyn Smith, *New Survey*, vol. 5, 350.

41. *The Times*, 20 Mar. 1920, 13; 17 Aug. 1920, 7; and P.P., *Standing Committee on Trusts to Inquire into Combines of Launderers and the Effect, if any, upon Prices*, 1920 (903), 1-5. Evidence of informal price fixing is obvious from a perusal of trade journals and was not restricted to fully finished laundry service. See, for example, "Bobwash," *Laundry Record*, 1 Nov. 1912, 629.

42. Deane, "Laundry Workers," 665.

43. Llewellyn Smith, *New Survey*, vol. 5, 350. See also *Laundry Record*, 14 Mar. 1891, 10-11.

44. Margaret Ethel MacDonald, "Report of Enquiry into Conditions of Work in Laundries," *WIN*, June 1907, 632. See also Smith, *Studies in the Laundry Trade*, 3; Booth, *Life and Labour*, 2d ser., vol. 8, 257-58; *Laundry Record*, 1 Feb. 1897, 24; 1 July 1905, 377.

45. "The First Patent Washing Machine," *Laundry Record*, 1 Dec. 1903, 651; Lay, "Evolution of the Laundry," 685; Prince, *Craft of Laundering*, 11.

46. Llewellyn Smith, *New Survey*, vol. 5, 351; Tebbutt, "Steam Laundry Machinery," 272-73; and Lay, "Evolution of the Laundry," 685.

47. Smith, *Studies in the Laundry Trade*, 3; Deane, "Laundry Workers," 665-66; Sidney Tebbutt, "Steam Laundry Machinery," in *Proceedings of the Institution of Mechanical Engineers* (London: Institution of Mechanical Engineers, Apr. 1898), 279-80; Prince, *Craft of Laundering*, 12; Llewellyn Smith, *New Survey*, vol. 5, 351-52.

48. See, for example, *Laundry Record*, 1 Oct. 1892, 119; 1 Jan. 1905, 25; 1 Apr. 1905, 213; 1 July 1905, 379; 1 May 1918, 209; *Wilson's Arundel Laundry*, brochure, n.p.; *Oakthorpe Laundry*, Advertising Brochure (1933), n.p.; *Laundry*, 23 Mar. 1912, 153. Fuller information regarding the details of laundry machinery can be obtained from trade journals such as the *Laundry Record*, from catalogues of laundry machinery (e.g. Fred Townsend and Co., *Modern Laundry Machinery* [Acton, London; n.d.], held at the Gunnerbury Park Museum); from Tebbutt, "Steam Laundry Machinery;" and from Prince, *Craft of Laundering*.

49. *Oakthorpe Laundry*, brochure, n.p.

50. See, for example, advertisements for Bazley's Laundry, Starch Green, and the Mayfield Laundry, Finsbury Park (*Kelly's Kensington, Notting Hill, Brompton & Knightsbridge Directory* [1888], 465; and [1913] 118a); *Faversham Steam Laundry*, brochure, n.p.; Springfield Laundry, Leamington (*Where to Buy at Leamington*, 49); Leamington Spa Steam Laundry Co., Leamington (*Spennell's Almanack and Annual Directory for 1900*, 52).

51. Tebbutt, "Steam Laundry Machinery," 287; and Leslie Woodcock Tentler,

Wage-Earning Women: Industrial Work and Family Life in the United States 1900-1920 (Oxford: Oxford University Press, 1979), 31.

52. H. G. Maule, "Time and Movement Study in Laundry Work" *The Human Factor*, 10 (1913), 351. I am indebted to Richard Price for this reference.

53. Smith, *Studies in the Laundry Trade*, 15.

54. Maule, "Study in Laundry Work," 359.

55. Smith, *Studies in the Laundry Trade*, 52-53.

56. Ibid., 3.

57. Margaret Ethel MacDonald, "Report of Enquiry into Laundries," 630; and P.P., *Report of Inspector*, 1907 (3586) 10, 190.

58. Smith, *Studies in the Laundry Trade*, 10.

59. *Wilson's Arundel Laundry*, brochure, n.p. See also *Oakthorpe Laundry*, brochure; *Faversham Steam Laundry*, brochure; and descriptions of working laundries in the trade journals such as the *Laundry* and the *Laundry Record*.

60. As quoted in Margaret Ethel MacDonald, "Report of Enquiry into Laundries," 630-31.

61. Samuel, "Workshop of the World," 56.

62. Llewellyn Smith, *New Survey*, vol. 5, 354; *Laundry Record*, 30 Mar. 1893, 1 May 1894; P.P., *Report of Inspector*, 1912-13 (6239) 25, 135.

63. Barbara Leigh Hutchins, *Women in Modern Industry* (London: Bell, 1915), 86.

64. Deane, "Laundry Workers," 667.

65. See, for example, Annie Besant, "Women Workers of London: The Washer-woman" as reprinted in the *Laundry Record*, 15 Apr. 1891, 22-24.

66. Margaret Ethel MacDonald, "Report of Enquiry into Laundries," 630. This commentator, with connections in the hand-work portion of the trade, was less than impartial but nonetheless expressed more widely held prejudices.

67. Llewellyn Smith, *New Survey*, vol. 5, 363. See also *Laundry Record*, 1 Jan. 1913, 17; P.P., *Report of Inspector*, 1911 (5693) 22, 113.

68. Margaret Ethel MacDonald, "Report of Enquiry into Laundries," 635-36.

69. *Laundry Record*, 1 Sept. 1908, 489; and 1 Feb. 1911, 87.

70. Llewellyn Smith, *New Survey*, vol. 5, 363.

71. Ibid.

72. *Woman Worker*, 26 Jan. 1910, 662.

73. For example, La Lessive, "A Wail from the Wash-tub, addressed to Ladies," *Work and Leisure*, 1882, 158-60.

74. Smith, *Studies in the Laundry Trade*, 1.

75. Maule, "Study in Laundry Work," 359.

76. *Laundry Record*, 1 May 1906, 265.

77. Ibid., 265, 267.

78. *Oakthorpe Laundry*, brochure, n. p. The Oakthorpe Laundry was operated as part of the enterprises of the Cooperative Society.

79. See, for example, *Laundry Record,* 1 Jan. 1905, 25; 1 Mar. 1905, 164-67; 1 July 1905, 385; "The Laundry Girl," *Laundry Record,* 1 Nov. 1905, 657, 659; and Dec. 1905, 683, 685; Mar. 1908, 143; "On the Proper Treatment of Employees," *Laundry Record,* 1 June 1909, 343; "Profit Sharing in Laundries: One Solution of the Labour Problem," *Laundry Record,* 1 Feb. 1914, 101, 103; Llewellyn Smith, *New Survey,* vol. 5, 356.

80. Porter, *Victorian Cambridge,* 181.

81. *Woman Worker,* 17 Mar. 1909, 224. See also "Attractions of Laundry Work," *Laundry Record,* 1 Feb. 1911, 87; "Skilled Trades for Girls," *Laundry Record,* 1 Sept. 1908, 489.

82. *Factory and Workshop Welfare Order,* 1920, No. 654.

83. *Daily Herald,* 26 Aug. 1913, 3; 15 Sept. 1913, 5; 18 Sept. 1913, 4; 20 Sept. 1913, 4; 26 Sept. 1913, 5; and 27 May 1914, 7. See also *Daily News,* 30 Sept. 1911, 11 Oct. 1911; P.P., *Report of Inspector,* 1907 (3586) 10, 224; Sheila Lewenhak, *Women and Trade Unions: An Outline History of Women in the British Trade Union Movement* (New York: St. Martin's, 1977), 211.

84. *Liverpool Echo,* 12 May 1914, 14 May 1914, 1 July 1914; *Liverpool Post,* 15 May 1914.

85. Deane, "Laundry Workers," 670. See also P.P., *Report of Inspector,* 1896 (8067) 19, 20; P.P., *Report of Inspector,* 1912-13 (6239) 25, 135; P.P., *Report of Inspector,* 1920 (941) 16, 10; Margaret H. Irwin, *The Conditions of Work in Laundries. Report of an Enquiry Conducted for the Council of the Women's Protective and Provident League of Glasgow* (Glasgow: Women's Protective and Provident League, 1893), 5-6; *Laundry Record,* 30 Mar. 1893, 2; Fabian Society, *Life in the Laundry,* Tract No. 112 (London: Fabian Society, 1902), 2; Hutchins, *Women in Modern Industry,* 289.

86. Thomas Oliver, *Diseases of Occupation: From the Legislative, Social and Medical Points of View* (London: Methuen, 1908), 386-92; *Laundry Record,* 1 Aug. 1911, 443; P.P., *Report of Inspector,* 1901 (1112) 12, 178; 1907 (3586) 10, 189; and 1910 (5191) 28, 128.

87. Margaret Ethel MacDonald, "Report of Enquiry into Laundries," 633.

88. Booth, *Life and Labour,* 2d ser., vol. 8, 265.

89. *Laundry Record,* 1 Mar. 1907, 167.

90. Margaret Ethel MacDonald, "Report of Enquiry into Laundries," 633; Llewellyn Smith, *New Survey,* vol. 5, 363-65; *Woman Worker,* 26 May 1909, 503-504; Aug. 1909, 119.

91. *Ragged School Union Magazine,* May 1859, 97-98; *Laundry Record,* 30 July 1892, 69; 31 Oct. 1892, 118; 30 Mar. 1893, 12; WIC, *Annual Report, 1904-1905,* 10-12. See also WIC, *Technical Education for Women and Girls at Home and Abroad* (London: WIC, 1905), 47, 56. This work also provides information about comparable training offered in other countries such as France, Belgium, Germany, and Italy.

92. *Laundry Record,* 23 Mar. 1892, 14.

93. P.P., *Report of Inspector,* 1910 (5191) 18, 124; Clapham, *Economic History,* vol. 3, 184.

94. Ester Longhurst, "How Can I Earn a Living," *Woman Worker,* 26 Jan. 1910, 662.

95. M. Mostyn Bird, *Woman at Work: A Study of the Different Ways of Earning a Living Open to Women* (London: Chapman & Hall, 1911), 122-23. See also *Standard* 30 June 1914; *Laundry Record,* 30 June 1893, 62 and 1 Oct. 1896, 99-100; Margaret Bateson, *Professional Women Upon Their Professions* (London: Cox, 1895), 101; Margaret Ethel MacDonald, "Report of Enquiry into Laundries," 633-35.

96. *Laundry Record,* 1 May 1930, 628. Beresford Ingram, Chief Inspector of Technology for the London County Council, expressed the opinion that "the initiative for the training classes in the laundry industry had come from the trade itself" (*Laundry Record,* 1 June 1930, 768).

97. Smith, *Studies in the Laundry Trade,* 1-2.

98. *The Times,* 17 Aug. 1920, 7.

99. Edward Cadbury, M. Cecile Matheson, George Shann, *Women's Work and Wages: A Phase of Life in an Industrial City* (London: Unwin, 1908), 172.

100. Llewellyn Smith, *New Survey,* vol. 5, 383, 367; P.P., *Report of Inspector,* 1908 (4166) 12, 148-49; P.P., *Report of Inspector,* 1911 (5693) 12, 112; *Laundry Record,* 1 Feb. 1901, 71; *Daily News,* 3 Sept. 1911 and 30 Sept. 1911.

101. See, for example, *Laundry Record,* 1 Dec. 1930, 1353.

102. Llewellyn Smith, *New Survey,* vol. 5, 378.

103. *Laundry Record,* 30 Sept. 1930, 1053.

Epilogue

1. Ann Oakley, *The Sociology of Housework* (New York: Pantheon, 1974), 50.

2. *Laundry Record,* 1 Jan. 1930, 35; 1 Apr. 1930, 507, 525; H. Lewellyn Smith, ed., *The New Survey of London Life and Labour,* 9 vols. (London: King, 1930-35); *London Industries II,* vol. 5 (1933), 371.

3. Llewellyn Smith, *New Survey,* vol. 5, 378.

4. *Laundry Record,* 1 Jan. 1930, 35. These figures are lower than those for the census (125,038 in 1921) because they include only insured workers, not employers and those working on their own.

5. A. W. Burrows, "The Story of Laundry Workers' Wages" (Reprinted from "New Dawn" [n.p., c. 1944]), n.p.

6. Dorothy Sells, *British Wages Boards. A Study in Industrial Democracy* (Washington, D.C.: Brookings, 1939), 312; and Sheila Lewenhak, *Women and Trade Unions: An Outline History of Women in the British Trade Union Movement* (New York: St. Martin's, 1977), 211.

7. Burrows, "Laundry Wages," n.p.

8. Ibid.; and Institute of British Launderers Limited, "A Review of the Laundry Industry" (London, 1946) (a copy at Gunnersbury Park Museum), 1.

9. British Launderers, "Review," 1.

10. Ibid., 2.

11. Ibid.

12. Burrows, "Laundry Wages," n.p.

13. Ancliffe Prince, *The Craft of Laundering: A History of Fabric Cleaning* (London: Company of Launderers, 1970), 20.

14. Ibid. David F. Thomas and Brenda J. Sowen, *The Walton Lodge Sanitary Laundry: The Story of an Enterprise* (London: Greater London Archaeological Society, 1976), 3.

15. For example, *Gazette and Post,* 30 Sept. 1960; 7 Oct. 1960; and *Acton Gazette,* 19 Aug. 1976 (clippings held at Gunnersbury Park Museum).

16. *Wilson's of Brighton,* n.p.

17. Prince, *Craft of Laundering,* chap. 5.

18. Ann Oakley, *Taking It Like a Woman* (London: Cape, 1984), 153.

19. Harry C. Moseley, "Laundry: From Cave Man to Robots," *Dimensions in Health Service,* Apr. 1983, 17.

20. Elizabeth Hardwick, *Sleepless Nights* (New York: Vintage, 1980), 135-36.

Bibliographical Essay

The research for this book is based on a wide range of materials, including newspapers, memoirs, local histories, and parliamentary papers, as well as modern analyses. Doing social history is very much like a treasure hunt: it yields nuggets of unexpected data in unexpected places. This book is no exception. The detailed map to the story of laundresses and their work is found in the notes. In addition, most chapters contain references to works that establish a context for discussion. This essay does not attempt to replicate these citations in full. Instead, it is intended to provide a guide to some of the general approaches that can be used by the reader who wishes to explore this subject in greater depth.

Laundry work was so ubiquitous that scattered reference to it can be found in any number of studies, including such local histories as Flora Thompson, *Lark Rise to Candleford* (London: Reprint Society, 1948); Florence Gladstone, *Notting Hill in Bygone Days* (London: Unwin, 1924); Ted Willis, *Whatever Happened to Tom Mix? The Story of One of My Lives* (London: Cassell, 1970); Enid Porter, *Victorian Cambridge: Josiah Chater's Diaries, 1844-1884* (London: Phillimore, 1975); and Margaret Llewelyn Davies, ed., *Life as We Have Known It,* introd. Anna Davin (London: Virago, 1977); and works of journalism and social reportage—for example, Edward Cadbury, M. Cecile Matheson, and George Shann, *Women's Work and Wages: A Phase of Life in an Industrial City* (London: Unwin, 1908); John Hollingshead, *Ragged London in 1861* (London: Smith, Elder, 1861); Arthur Sherwell, *Life in West London: A Study and a Contrast* (London: Methuen, 1897); George R. Sims, *Off the Track in London* (London: Jarrold, 1911); Mary Bayly, *Ragged Homes and How to Mend Them* (London: Nisbet, 1860). London local histories are particularly useful because of the concentration of laundry work in the metropolis. Unfortunately, mention of laundry work in these sources rarely extends beyond a few lines or a page or two. More promising are works written by the relatives of laundry workers, usually sons and daughters who spent some of their youth helping with the work. Among the memoirs and autobiographies in which laundry labor plays a prominent part are: Alice Mary Bond, "The Old Wooden Mangle," *East Anglian Magazine,* 12 (1952-53), 463-71, 488-96, 549-56, 613-20, 708-16; and 13 (1953-54), 40-49; A. E. Coppard, *It's Me, O Lord!: An Abstract & Brief Chronicle of Some of the Life with Some of the Opinions of A. E. Coppard* (London: Methuen, 1957); Albert Paul, *Poverty-Hardship but Happiness: Those Were the Days, 1903-1917,* 3d ed. (Brighton: Queen Spark, 1957); and Kathleen Woodward, *Jipping Street: Childhood in a London Slum* (London: Harper, 1928).

Fuller, if less personal, accounts of the working conditions and family circumstances of laundry workers are to be found in the reports of contemporaries who based their findings on a combination of personal observation, interviews, and analyses of medical, economic, and statistical materials. Prominent among these observers were social activists and reformers, including Fabians and members of trade union organizations and the Women's Industrial Council (WIC). These works include: Clementina Black, *Married Women's Work: Being the Report of an Enquiry Undertaken by the Women's Industrial Council* (London: Bell, 1915); Fabian Society, *Life in the Laundry,* Tract No. 112 (London: Fabian Society, 1902); Margaret H. Irwin, *The Conditions of Women's Work in Laundries: Report of an Inquiry Conducted for the Council of Women's Protective and Provident League of Glasgow* (Glasgow: Women's Protective and Provident League, 1893); Scott Holland and Gertrude Tuckwell, "Report of the Christian Social Union Committee on Laundries," London, n.d., Trades Union Congress Library, Gertrude Tuckwell Collection, File No. 14; and Gertrude Tuckwell et al., *Women in Industry From Seven Points of View* (London: Duckworth, 1910).

Newspapers and periodicals associated with reform causes, as well as related annual reports and conference proceedings, contain material on laundry workers or their concerns as workers, mothers, and citizens. Such journals include: *Women's Industrial News (WIN)* (1895-1908) and its successor *Woman Worker* (1908-21); *Women's Trade Union Review* (1891-1919); *Fortnightly Review; Nineteenth Century Review;* as well as such daily or weekly newspapers as the *West London Observer, Daily News, Daily Herald, Punch,* and *The Times.* The latter primarily contain reports of laundry workers at times when demonstrations, official reports or parliamentary debates made the subject newsworthy, although some journals examined laundry work as part of their investigative journalism (e.g., *Daily Herald,* 26 Aug.; 10, 15, and 26 Sept.; and 26 Nov. 1913). The clipping collections of local libraries and county record offices can also yield information about laundry work. The richest collections I discovered were in the Gertrude Tuckwell Collection at the Trades Union Congress Library; the local history collection of the Royal Borough of Kensington and Chelsea; and the archival materials held by the Gunnersbury Park Museum in West London, and the Cambridgeshire, Essex, and Kent County Record Offices. Detailed references are contained in the chapter notes, but the following constitute a sample of the sort of articles that appear: Emilia F. S. Dilke, "Trade Unionism

among Women—Part 1," *Fortnightly Review*, 55 (May 1891), 741-46; Florence
Routledge, "Trade Unionism among Women—Part 2," ibid., 746-50; Miss
England, "What Can Be Done To Improve the Condition of Workers in Laundries
by Moral Influence?" in National Union of Women Workers, *Women Workers:
Papers Read at the Conference Held at Brighton, October 23rd-26th, 1900* (London: King,
1900); Miss Gray, "What Can Be Done by Legislation To Improve the Conditions
of Laundries," *WIN*, Dec. 1900, 203-208; Helen Bosanquet, Louise Creighton,
and Beatrice Webb, "Law and the Laundry: Part 1, Commercial Laundries,"
Nineteenth Century (Feb. 1897), 224-31; Lucy C. F. Cavendish, "Law and the Laundry: Part 2, Laundries in Religious Houses," ibid., 232-35; Margaret Ethel Mac-
Donald, "Report of Enquiry into Conditions of Work in Laundries," *WIN*, June
1907, 629-42; Margaret Ethel MacDonald, "Confusion for Laundry Workers,"
WIN, June 1908, 27-35; "Our Laundry Workers," *Woman Worker*, 49 (Mar. 1920),
4; "A Voice from the Laundries," *Woman Worker*, 41 (June 1919), 2; "York Launderies: Allegations of Sweating," *Yorkshire Herald Supplement*, 28 June 1913.

The pioneering social investigators of the nineteenth and early twentieth centuries devoted some attention, usually in scattered references, to laundry work.
Their studies also help to establish much of the context in which laundresses and
their work must be examined. These works include: Charles Booth, *Life and Labour
of the People of London*, 16 vols. (London: Macmillan, 1902-1903) and the related
manuscript collection (Charles Booth MS Collection) held at the British Library of
Political and Economic Science, London School of Economics; Edward Cadbury,
M. Cecile Matheson, and George Shann, *Women's Work and Wages: A Phase of Life in
an Industrial City* (London: Unwin, 1908); British Weekly Commissioners, *Toilers in
London; or Inquiries Concerning Female Labour in the Metropolis* (London: Hodder &
Stoughton, 1889); Henry Mayhew, *London Labour and the London Poor*, 4 vols. (Lon-
don: Woodfall, 1861); H. Llewellyn Smith, ed., *The New Survey of London Life and
Labour*, 9 vols. (London: King, 1930-35). All of these works discuss the complex
economic survival strategies of the laboring people.

Other studies can also stimulate ideas about the working-class family economy
of which laundry work was so often a part. See, for example, Raphael Samuel,
"Comers and Goers," in *The Victorian City: Images and Realities,* ed. H. Dyos and
Michael Wolff, 2 vols. (London: Routledge & Kegan Paul, 1973), vol. 1, 123-60;
Jane Lewis, *Women in England 1870-1950: Sexual Divisions and Social Change*
(Bloomington, Ind.: Indiana University Press, 1984), 45-74; Laura Oren, "The
Welfare of Women in Labouring Families: England, 1860-1950," in *Clio's Con-
sciousness Raised: New Perspectives on the History of Women*, ed. Mary Hartman and
Lois W. Banner (New York: Harper, 1974), 226-44; Gareth Stedman Jones, *Outcast
London: A Study of the Relationship between Classes in Victorian Society* (Oxford: Claren-
don, 1971); Patricia E. Malcolmson, "Getting a Living in the Slums of Victorian
Kensington," *London Journal,* 1,1 (May 1975), 28-55; Sidney Webb and Arnold
Freeman, eds. *Seasonal Trades* (London: London School of Economics, 1911). In

addition, more general historical studies such as Standish Meacham's *A Life Apart: The English Working Class, 1890-1914* (Cambridge, Mass.: Harvard University Press, 1977) or personal recollections such as Robert Roberts' *The Classic Slum: Salford Life in the First Quarter of the Century* (Manchester: Manchester University Press, 1973) can provide the reader with the broad context of the societies and communities within which most laundresses lived and worked, even if such books do not deal with the trade directly. Since references to works of this kind are readily found in the bibliographies of many surveys of nineteenth-century English social history, no details are provided here.

Parliamentary Papers provide a particularly rich source of information about working conditions, safety and health, and mechanization in the laundry industry, in part because of the industry's prominence in the late nineteenth- and early twentieth-century debates about factory legislation and women's paid labor. Therefore, a researcher can profit by exploring these papers, the most important of which are: *Royal Commission on Labour. The Employment of Women,* 1893-94 (6894) 37; the *Report of the Chief Inspector of Factories and Workshops. Report of the Principal Lady Inspector,* especially from 1894 through 1913; and *Hansard* during the periods when women's employment and the factory acts were being debated in 1891, 1895, 1901, and 1907. Women factory inspectors were among the keenest and best informed observers of the work of laundresses. For this reason, their official reports are especially valuable. In addition, two of these pioneering inspectors discussed their years of experience in other publications: Lucy E. A. Deane, "Laundry Workers," in *Dangerous Trades: The Historical, Social and Legal Aspects of Industrial Occupations as Affecting Health by a Number of Experts,* ed. Thomas Oliver (London: Murray, 1902), 663-73; and Rose E. Squire, *Thirty Years in the Public Service: An Industrial Retrospect* (London: Nisbet, 1927).

The standard studies on women's work and the factory acts, even though they deal only indirectly with laundry work, are useful to help establish some of the structural differences and similarities between laundry work and other forms of women's employment. Among these works are: Adelaide Anderson, *Women in the Factory: An Administrative Adventure, 1893-1921* (London: Murray, 1922); E. J. Boucherett and Helen Blackburn, *The Condition of Working Women and the Factory Acts* (London: Stock, 1896); Margaret Hewitt, *Wives and Mothers in Victorian Industry* (London: Rockcliff, 1958); Barbara Leigh Hutchins, *Women in Modern Industry* (London: Bell, 1915); Amy Harrison and Barbara Leigh Hutchins, *A History of Factory Legislation* (London: King, 1903); Wanda Neff, *Victorian Working Women 1832-50* (London: Allen & Unwin, 1929); Ivy Pinchbeck, *Working Women and the Industrial Revolution 1750-1850* (London: Routledge, 1930). Similarly, studies of domestic service yield some information about laundry work itself within the broader context of domestic employment: Christina Violet Butler, *Domestic Service: An Enquiry by the Women's Industrial Council* (London: WIC, 1916); Pamela Horn, *The Rise and Fall of the Victorian Servant* (London: Gill and Macmillan, 1975);

Theresa M. McBride, *The Domestic Revolution: The Modernization of Household Service in England and France 1820-1920* (London: Croom Helm, 1976). Other contemporary observers of women's employment were concerned less with working conditions than with employment prospects. Two books that discuss laundry employment, primarily from the perspective of the middle-class woman interested in managerial work, are: Margaret Bateson, *Professional Women upon Their Professions* (London: Cox, 1895); and M. Mostyn Bird, *Woman at Work: A Study of the Different Ways of Earning a Living Open to Women* (London: Chapman & Hall, 1911).

Many modern works deal with women and work, but only a few examine laundry employment. They include: Sally Alexander, *Women's Work in Nineteenth-Century London: A Study of the Years 1820-50* (London: Journeyman, 1983), originally published in *The Rights and Wrongs of Women,* ed. Juliet Mitchell and Ann Oakley (Harmondsworth: Penguin, 1976); Patricia E. Malcolmson, "Laundresses and the Laundry Trade," *Victorian Studies,* 24,4 (Summer 1981), 439-62; Eunice Lipton, "The Laundress in Late Nineteenth-Century French Culture: Imagery, Ideology, and Edgar Degas," *Art History,* 3,3 (Sept. 1980), 295-313; Ancliffe Prince, *The Craft of Laundering: A History of Fabric Cleaning* (London: Company of Launderers, 1970); Raphael Samuel, "Quarry Roughs," in *Village Life and Labour,* ed. Raphael Samuel (London: Routledge & Kegan Paul, 1975); and, for the United States, F. D'Armond, *The Laundry Industry* (New York: Harper, 1950).

Since laundry work was household labor as well as paid employment, much can be learned about the trade, its processes, and conditions of work—when carried out in the home—from studies, both English and American, which are concerned with housework. Among the few works to address household laundering in a British setting are: Caroline Davidson, *A Woman's Work Is Never Done: A History of Housework in the British Isles, 1650-1950* (London: Chatto & Windus, 1982); Christina Walkley and Vanda Foster, *Crinolines and Crimping Irons: Victorian Clothes: How They Were Cleaned and Cared For* (London: Owen, 1978); S. Minwel Tibbott, "Laundering in the Welsh Home," *Folk Life: A Journal of Ethnological Studies,* 19 (1981), 36-57; Ann Oakley, *Woman's Work: The Housewife Past and Present* (New York: Pantheon, 1975); Ann Oakley, *The Sociology of Housework* (New York: Pantheon, 1974); and Elizabeth Roberts, *A Woman's Place: An Oral History of Working Class Women, 1890-1914* (Oxford: Blackwell, 1984).

North American studies of this subject are much more extensive both as paid work and household labor. On housework, see: Ruth Schwartz Cowan, *More Work for Mother: The Ironies of Household Technology from the Open Hearth to the Microwave* (New York: Basic, 1983); Mary Norvak, *Kitchen Antiques* (New York: Praeger, 1975); and Susan Strasser, *Never Done: A History of American Housework* (New York: Pantheon, 1982). Books about women's work include: Janice Acton, Penny Goldsmith, and Bonnie Sheppard, eds., *Women at Work in Ontario, 1850-1930* (Toronto: University of Toronto Press, 1974); Alice Kessler-Harris, *Out to Work: A History of Wage-Earning Women in the United States* (Oxford: Oxford University Press, 1982);

David M. Katzman, *Seven Days a Week: Women and Domestic Service in Industrializing America* (New York: Oxford University Press, 1978); Barbara Mayer Wertheimer, *We Were There: The Story of Working Women in America* (New York: Pantheon, 1977); and Leslie Woodcock Tentler, *Wage-Earning Women: Industrial Work and Family Life in the United States, 1900-1930* (Oxford: Oxford University Press, 1979).

The development of public policies to regulate and control the laundry trade along with efforts to unionize its workers, as well as the spirited opposition to both of these efforts, can be culled from many of the books, periodicals, and official documents already mentioned. In addition, unionization can be examined in general and sometimes for the laundry trade in particular through the materials contained in the archives at the Trade Union Congress Library, studies of the women's trade union movement, and the biographies of and writing of prominent trade union activists. (Details of the very scattered references to laundry unionizing activities are found in the notes to chapter 4.) Works that warrant attention are: Gladys Boone, *The Women's Trade Union Leagues in Great Britain and the United States* (New York: Columbia University Press, 1942); Katherine Graves Busbey, *The Women's Trade Union Movement in Great Britain* (Washington, D.C.: Bulletin of the Bureau of Labor, No. 83, 1909); Barbara Drake, *Women in Trade Unions* (London: Labour Research Department, Trade Union Series No. 6, 1921); Robin Miller Jacoby, "Feminism and Class Consciousness in the British and American Women's Trade Union Leagues, 1890-1925," in *Liberating Women's History: Theoretical and Critical Essays,* ed. Bernice A. Carroll (Urbana, Ill.: University of Illinois Press, 1976), 137-60; Sheila Lewenhak, *Women and Trade Unions: An Outline History of Women in the British Trade Union Movement* (New York: St. Martin's, 1977); Dorothy Sells, *British Wages Boards: A Study in Industrial Democracy* (Washington, D.C.: Brookings, 1939); Norbert Soldon, *Women in British Trade Unions 1874-1976* (London: Gill and Macmillan, 1978); Mary Agnes Hamilton, *Mary Macarthur: A Biographical Sketch* (London: Falcon, 1949); Margaret Ethel MacDonald, *Labour Laws for Women: Their Reason and Results* (London: Independent Labour Party, 1900); J. Ramsay MacDonald, *Margaret Ethel MacDonald* (London: Allen & Unwin, 1924); and Mona Wilson, *Our Industrial Laws: Working Women in Factories, Workshops and Laundries, and How to Help Them* (London: Duckworth, 1899).

Tracing the mechanization and modernization of the laundry industry can be carried out by means of parliamentary papers, local history, newspapers, and the histories of such related industries as soap, electricity, and domestic appliances. However, by far the richest source for this aspect of the industry's development is the trade journal. A number of these were consulted, but the single most important is the *Laundry Record*; it began publication in 1891, and it reported on the trade during the years in which it industrialized, organized, and was placed under government regulation. A major function of such a journal was to inform its readers about technological advances, managerial innovations, trade unions, and government regulation and to provide a focus for the concerns of the people in the trade. The *Laundry Record,* therefore, is an excellent source for employee attitudes and anxieties, including those concerning Chinese laundries that were few in number and rarely found outside of a handful of port cities, as well as for the nature and the timing of technological and organizational change. A few other works bear directly on mechanization of the laundry industry and the impact of those changes on the work force. They include: Harry Gordon Maule and May Smith *Industrial Psychology and the Laundry Trade* (London: Pitman, 1947); Harry Gordon Maule, "Time and Movement Study in Laundry Work," *The Human Factor,* 10 (1936), 351-59; Sidney Tebbutt, "Steam Laundry Machinery," *Proceedings of the Institution of Mechanical Engineers* (London: Institution of Mechanical Engineers, Apr. 1898), 268-307; and May Smith, *Reports of the Industrial Fatigue Research Board, No. 22: Some Studies in the Laundry Trade,* Laundry Series No. 1 (London: Medical Research Council, HMSO, 1922).

Index

Tentler, Leslie Woodcock, 114
Textile manufacturing, compared with
    laundry industry, 128-29, 156
Thames Embankment, 57
Thompson, Flora, 24, 33
The Times, 57, 64
Titmuss, Richard, 46
Trade, Board of, 78, 98
Trade Boards, 96-102, 120-21, 122, 151
Trade, Grand Committee on, 67
Trade unions. *See* Unionization
Trades Union Congress, 55, 109
Training, 18, 152-54
    apprenticeship, 152, 170 n.40
    laundry trade school, 152
    managerial staff and, 153-54
    training fee, 154
    wages for trainees, 153
Transport Workers Federation, 112
Trusts, Standing Committee on, 139, 155
Tuckwell, Gertrude, 56, 61, 97, 98

Unionization, xiv, 70, 109-122. *See also*
    Strikes
    difficulty of, 55
    factory legislation and, 54-58
    labor supply and, 120
    laundry unionization,
        encouragement to, 116-17
        location of, 115
        support of organized labor, 110, 111
        support of women's organizations, 115
        timing of, 114-15, 116
    Trade Boards and, 120
    wage negotiations, 117, 118
    wartime experiences and, 118-120
    women's unions
        difficulty in forming, 114, 118
        impermanence of, 116, 118
        organizing, 118, 119
United States, xiv, 89, 135
Urbanization, 129

Vine, George, 98-99

Wages, 13, 14, 101, 121, 122, 159, 194
    n.77. *See also* Trade boards
    beer as part payment, 13
    payment in kind, 13
    Trade Board rates, 14, 101, 121
Wales, 4, 7
Wandsworth and Clapham Infirmary, 93

Wandsworth Common Deaf and Dumb
    Residential School, 68
War Cabinet Committee on Women in
    Industry, 100
Warehouse Workers Union, 110
Warren, Eliza, 7
Washerwomen. *See* Laundresses
Water heating, 3
Water supply, 20, 130, 131, 134-35
Webb, Beatrice, 58, 70
Welfare state, 45, 176 n.2
Wells, H. G., 97
West Africa, 131
West London District, 89-93, 185 n.65
    conditions in, 92-93
    special inspection district
        accidents in, 89-92
        disease in, 93
        establishment of, 89-90
Westminster, 121
Westmoreland, 111
Whitelegge, Arthur, 73
Widows, laundrywork and, 11, 18, 19,
    27
Willenhall, 118
Willesden, 121-22
Willis, Ted, 41
Wilson's Laundry, 22-23, 162
Wollstonecraft, Mary, 50
Wolverhampton, 118
Woman Worker, 119, 151
Women Ropemaker's Association, 57
Women's employment, xii, 46, 47, 119
    in laundries
        factory legislation and, 48-69, 54-55
        middle-class women and, 49-50, 54
        Royal Commission on Labour and, 58-
            59
Women's Employment Defence League, 51
Women's Industrial Council (WIC), 46, 47,
    56, 61, 64, 81, 123, 148, 152, 153
    factory legislation and, 64
    investigation of women's employment,
        47, 56
    legal committee, 81
    traditionalism of, 123
    women's rights and, 123
Women's Industrial Defence Committee,
    53, 54, 66, 67
Women's Labour League, 98
Women's Protective and Provident League,
    54, 110

THE LIBRARY
ST. MARY'S COLLEGE OF MARYLAND
ST. MARY'S CITY, MARYLAND 20686

DATE DUE
